The Notorious
Bacon Brothers

The Notorious Bacon Brothers

Inside Gang Warfare on Vancouver Streets

Jerry Langton

John Wiley & Sons Canada, Ltd.

Wiley publishes in a variety of print and electronic formats and by print-on-demand. Some material included with standard print versions of this book may not be included in e-books or in print-on-demand. If this book refers to media such as a CD or DVD that is not included in the version you purchased, you may download this material at http://booksupport.wiley.com. For more information about Wiley products, visit www.wiley.com.

National Library of Canada Cataloguing in Publication Data
Langton, Jerry, 1965-
   The notorious Bacon Brothers : inside gang warfare on Vancouver streets /
Jerry Langton.

Includes index.
Issued also in electronic formats.
ISBN 978-1-118-38867-9

   1. Bacon Brothers (Gang).   2. Gangs—British Columbia—Vancouver.   3. Violent crimes—British Columbia—Vancouver.   4. Vancouver (B.C.)—Social conditions. I. Title.

HV6439.C32V3 2012   364.106′60971133   C2012-902325-6

ISBN: 978-1-118-40460-7 (ebk); 978-1-118-40457-7 (ebk); 978-1-118-40459-1 (ebk)

Production Credits
Cover design: Adrian So
Typesetting: Thomson Digital
Cover images: Thinkstock/iStockphoto
Printer: Friesens

Editorial Credits
Executive editor: Don Loney
Managing editor: Alison Maclean
Production editor: Pamela Vokey

John Wiley & Sons Canada, Ltd.
6045 Freemont Blvd.
Mississauga, Ontario
L5R 4J3

Printed in Canada

1 2 3 4 5 FP 17 16 15 14 13

CONTENTS

Map		vii
Key Players		ix
PART I: WELCOME TO LOTUSLAND		**1**
1	**The Surrey Six: October, 2007**	7
2	**The Gangster's Playground: 1907–1998**	19
3	**United Nations: 1997–2001**	53
PART II: THE PATH TO WAR		**73**
4	**Bumps in the Road: 2001–2004**	77
5	**Going Global: 2005–2006**	93
6	**New Friends: 2006–2007**	121
7	**Going Public: 2007–2008**	135

PART III: BREAKING THE BACONS   161

8   Paralysis: 2008–2009   165

9   War: February–May, 2009   177

10   The Year of the Rat: 2009–2010   193

11   The Wolf Pack: 2010–2011   215

12   Bacons' End: 2011–2012   233

Index   249

Bacon Country: The British Columbia Lower Mainland

The Vancouver region has always been different from the rest of Canada, and almost certainly always will be. There are two interconnected reasons for that—geography and history.

The word that best describes Vancouver's geography from a human perspective would be isolated. From the west, the open Pacific, to find it, you would almost have to be looking for it specifically. Nestled behind two huge land masses—Vancouver Island and Washington State's Olympic Peninsula—the site of Vancouver would be easy for explorers from the Pacific to miss, and they often did. From the east, the area is surrounded by tall mountains with only the valley of the Fraser River, which winds more than 850 miles from its source of dripping snow high up in the Rockies to salt water.

Key Players

Principal Lower Mainland Gangs and Their Leaders

- The Indo-Canadian (or the Punjabi) Mafia—Bhupinder "Bindy" Singh Johal
- The Big Circle Boys (originating in China)
- The Hells Angels Motorcycle Club
- Red Scorpions—Quang Vinh "Michael" Le and Eddie Narong
- The United Nations—Clayton Roueche, later Barzan Tilli-Choli and Doug Vanalstine
- The Independent Soldiers

Lesser Lower Mainland Gangs

- The Renegades
- The King Pin Crew
- The Game Tight Soldiers

Special Law Enforcement Agencies

- Integrated Homicide Investigation team (IHIT)
- Combined Forces Special Enforcement Unit (CFSEU)
- U.S. Immigration and Customs Enforcement (ICE)

Part I

Welcome to Lotusland

"You're just going to go buy crack!" the woman screamed. The toddler she was holding looked terrified, but the man she was shouting at only looked bothered, and a bit embarrassed. He wouldn't look directly at her while she begged him to come back home, do the right thing, and reassume his role as father and husband.

This intensely sad little drama took place at the corner of West Georgia and Thurlow in downtown Vancouver a year ago when I was in the city to address a symposium on true accounts in the media. To my surprise, the other people on the busy corner, including a tour group from Japan who were staying in my hotel, did their best to ignore the couple even though the woman was wailing and the man had openly threatened her physically a couple of times. I couldn't ignore them. Years of reporting have effectively forced me to investigate such things. Noticing my attention, the man shot me a glare, and asked "What are you looking at?" before walking quickly away.

The woman, a dazed look on her face, paused for a moment, then walked away dejectedly in another direction. The toddler, who had been silent throughout the exchange, looked back at me as though there was something I could do to help.

It was a far cry from where I had been earlier that day, even though it was physically just a few blocks. Walking through the West Vancouver neighborhoods like Kiltsilano and Arbutus, the handler the university provided me proudly pointed out some of the most expensive real estate in North America. It's very pretty and captures all of the physical beauty the Vancouver area is famous for. The old stone mansions and super-modern condos are impressive. Running, as many do, about $6 million or so, it's hard to imagine who can afford them.

So I asked a couple of real estate agents who told me that they were mainly owned by families in East Asia. One agent laughed and told me she hadn't sold anything to a Canadian in at least ten years. They're investment properties, for the most part, and are often occupied by the family's children who may be going to university or just having an extended childhood.

The almost unlimited supply of foreign investors—and a booming population—has driven Vancouver's real estate prices through the roof. The effect has led to huge numbers of people moving from the city. They settle in what were small towns but have recently become sprawling suburbs and even cities unto themselves.

My handler had another appointment and asked me if I needed a ride back to the hotel. I told her I'd walk. It's a great hotel—comfortable, friendly and well-appointed—and I wouldn't stay anywhere else in Vancouver. My favorite part is the old dog who greets guests in the lobby. I'm pleased every time she remembers me.

On the way there, the atmosphere changed. Downtown Vancouver always struck me as an impersonal place, even more so than Toronto. There are the obvious trappings of commercial success there, but I always get a feeling that there's something a little wrong. A lot of the businesses appealing to young people have an aesthetic that seems to me a bit brutish. I was a little surprised to see a few windows boarded up—a grim reminder of the Stanley Cup riots a few months before my visit. There were lots and lots of modified cars, trucks and motorcycles, more than a few intentionally made to be aggressively and annoyingly loud. There were plenty of panhandlers, some quite insistent, and a number of people who seemed not quite altogether there. Maybe it's because of what I write about, but I tend to blame stimulant drugs like cocaine or methamphetamine every time I see someone acting erratically in public.

After that incident, I came back to my senses. I kept walking until I got to the Downtown Eastside. Widely referred to in the media as the worst neighborhood in Canada, it certainly lives up to its reputation. According to *The Globe and Mail,* the average annual income for the residents of Downtown Eastside is just $14,024—$6,282 if you take away government checks. That's a ridiculously small amount of money to live on in one of the most expensive cities in the world. The result is absolute squalor. Homeless are everywhere, and so are prostitutes. Drug use is commonly seen out in the open. It's like a different country. "We've basically got a Third World country stuck in the middle of downtown Vancouver," said Krishna Pendakur, a professor of economics at Simon Fraser University and co-director of Metropolis British Columbia, an urban think tank. From outward appearances and the lack of hope in the people I spoke with there, I think he's right.

From there I took the SkyTrain—the Vancouver area's rail transit—to Surrey, British Columbia's second-biggest city. It's more familiar; it looks like many Canadian cities that have grown quickly. It's full of newer buildings, strip malls and other hastily constructed amenities. The only thing really striking about Surrey to me was how segregated it was. In one area, all the signs, shops and restaurants catered to Koreans; a few blocks over, all the text was Vietnamese.

Later, I drove down the Fraser Valley to see the towns in which most of the action in this book took place. Towns like Abbotsford and Chilliwack made Surrey look like Ancient Rome. Truly suburban, these towns seem utterly devoid of any structure more than 20 years old. In between developments, there are lush stands of trees, but where the houses are, there are only recently planted saplings, none thicker than my arm.

In the Southern reaches of this region, where there are still some farms, you come to 0 Avenue. It doesn't look like much— just a lonely highway with a few houses and farms on each side. But it's much more than that. It's the border between Canada and the United States. Unlike most international borders, it's absolutely unprotected. Crossing it is no more difficult than looking both ways and walking 30 feet or so.

And that's another ingredient in the strange mixture that has led to the gang wars in British Columbia. America, as it always has, beckons with the siren song of easy money. The kids from places like Abbotsford know that the quickest way for them to be parking a Porsche at a Kitsilano address is to sell drugs to the Americans.

Environmental conditions and a relaxed attitude towards marijuana use have combined over the years to make British Columbia one of the world's primary exporters of high-quality weed. It's relatively easy to make great sums of money by bringing that weed across the border.

But there's a problem with that. The ease and huge profits of moving weed was like a modern-day gold rush. Competition grew fierce. And it drew the attention of organized crime, in particular the Hells Angels. They were determined to monopolize the market—as they had with strip joints a few years earlier—by force, if necessary.

The increased danger forced traffickers to band together to protect themselves. Now, instead of just money flowing over the border from the south, there was also a steady stream of firearms. Making matters worse, the same people who had been dealing weed were now dealing in even-higher-profit drugs like cocaine, methamphetamine and Oxycontin. That caught the attention of brutal Mexican and Colombian gangs.

Suddenly, what were sleepy little towns were bustling, impersonal metropolises full of desperate young men who had money, guns, enemies and addictive drugs. The violence was inevitable.

The Bacon Brothers stood out simply because they were definitive of the new-style gangster. They didn't come from any ethnic ghetto; they didn't come from poverty or an abusive or broken home. In fact, they came from exactly the opposite upbringing that many social critics say incubates crime. The Bacon Brothers lived in middle-class affluence in a nice house with their supportive parents. They went to good schools at which they excelled athletically and were popular socially.

They were not inner-city kids forced into crime because they had no other option. They were just some guys who thought they could get rich selling drugs.

And they were hardly alone. They represented a new kind of gangster—one who weighs the pros, cons and risks, and makes a conscious effort to make a career out of crime.

CHAPTER 1

THE SURREY SIX: OCTOBER, 2007

As soon as the SkyTrain stopped, Eileen Mohan was worried. She knew they didn't stop the SkyTrain between stations unless it was a major emergency. The unscheduled stop had happened just before her station. She immediately worried about her son. She called home, but there was no answer. She knew she couldn't get him if he'd already left home, as he had said he would, because the two shared a cellphone—she took it on weekdays and he had it on weekends.

Eileen had left for work at 8:00 a.m. and was on her way home at 7:30 p.m. Chris, her 22-year-old son, was at home. He had the day off from the liquor store where he worked and wanted to play basketball with some friends in the nearby city of Burnaby. The Mohans—Eileen, her husband and Chris— lived in Balmoral Tower, a luxury condo development at 9830 East Whalley Ring Road in Surrey. Although it's technically the second-largest city in British Columbia, Surrey is generally regarded as the most low-end of Vancouver's suburbs.

The Mohans, who had emigrated to Canada from Fiji 11 years earlier, had lived on the 14th floor of Balmoral Tower for a year, but when a penthouse suite on the top floor, unit 1504, opened up a week earlier, they'd jumped at it. But the penthouse would be temporary, as the family had almost saved enough money to buy their own house. Although the Balmoral was a condo building, many of its residents were renters because a number of units were owned by offsite investors who brought in tenants to pay their mortgages for them.

Chris was a normal kind of kid. He wore his hair jelled-up like the guys on *Jersey Shore* and loved to work out.

He was average-looking with a big grin and fashionable hip-hop–inspired clothes. He'd long since traded in his glasses for contact lenses. Since graduating high school, he had worked part time at a liquor store, but all he really cared about was lifting weights, playing basketball and eating fast food. And he would indulge in all three whenever he could. "He was really into working out," said an old high school friend named Nikkie Ewasiuk. "That was one of his main goals; he wanted to be big. The last time I saw him, I couldn't believe how big he had gotten." He wasn't too big for his Spider-Man bedspread, though.

Like most people of his generation, he expressed himself through online social media. Describing his personality on MySpace, he wrote, "I am an outgoing kind of person and I always want to be doing stuff because being bored out of your mind sucks. I like making people laugh by telling jokes or doing stupid things. But I know when to be serious." His mom, Eileen, ran a disciplined household, threatening to throw Chris's clothes in a garbage bag and him out on the street if the police ever came to her door looking for him.

On October 18, 2007, he accepted an invitation to go play basketball with some friends in nearby Burnaby but promised his mom he would stay home until the guy came by to service the unit's gas fireplace. At two in the afternoon, Chris called his mom to tell her that the gas guy and the building manager had arrived, and that he was leaving to play with his friends in Burnaby. "Mom," he said. "I've got to go—love you." She told him she loved him, too.

• • •

The gas guy was Ed Schellenberg. Originally from Coaldale, a small hardscrabble town in Alberta, Schellenberg's family moved to Abbotsford—another small British Columbia city that had been absorbed by the Greater Vancouver area—when he was 3. Schellenberg was from a very close family of strong Mennonite faith. In fact, after high school, he had served a mission for his church, working with kids at a youth detention center in Ohio, then traveled to Poland and lived in the Northwest Territories before returning to Abbotsford. Many would consider that kind of life dangerous, and Ed wasn't a very big or intimidating man. He stood just five foot eight. He was bald and stout, and did not carry himself like a tough guy. Because he wasn't. No, he was a charmer. His oversized red handlebar moustache, ready smile, twinkling eyes and quick wit had always been enough to get him out of trouble in the past. He didn't need to be tough.

Back in British Columbia, Schellenberg had started a gas installation and maintenance business at which he employed his brother-in-law, Steve Brown, and Steve's 21-year-old son, Zachary. Balmoral Tower was one of his biggest clients. Among the building's selling points was that every unit came equipped with a gas fireplace. Insurance regulations (and common sense) required that the gas systems be professionally maintained on a regular basis, and Schellenberg and his crew were generally regarded as the best in the business.

Schellenberg, Brown and his son had spent a week that October working on Balmoral Tower, starting on the bottom floor. Because they were so far ahead of schedule, Brown left early, sure that Schellenberg and Zachary would have no problem finishing the job. By the end of lunch break, the two of them had just the seven units on the top floor to do. At two o'clock, he and the building manager knocked on the Mohans' door. Chris let them in and they chatted while Schellenberg did his work. His nephew was supposed to handle the last unit, 1505, across the hall, but the building manager took Ed aside and asked him if he could do it instead. There were four young guys who lived in there, although they didn't seem like bad guys, but he'd just feel a little more comfortable if it was Ed who did their unit. It was, after all, the kid's first week on the job. Ed smiled and said it would be no problem.

• • •

The owner of 1505 was a man named Ceasar Tiojanco, but he didn't live there. A successful agent at Regent Park Fairchild Realty, Tiojanco and his wife, Myrna, actually owned six properties in the area and had rented out unit 1505 ever since they had purchased it for $82,000 in 2003. In the spring of 2007, he rented 1505 to a 20-year-old man who had run into a few problems with the law. When he took over the unit, Raphael Baldini was facing charges related to a break-and-enter incident. But Baldini soon moved out of the unit and sublet it to some friends.

Although it was a one-bedroom unit, in October 2007, a total of four young men lived in 1505. And they were, to use a shop-worn expression, "known to police." All of them had been charged with a number of serious crimes, and all of them had connections to known gangs. In fact, the foursome had become something of a gang themselves.

The de facto leader of the quartet was Edward "Eddie" Sousakhone Narong, 22. Trouble for him started early. Back in 2000, his buddy—then-14-year-old Quang Vinh Thang "Michael" Le—had been severely beaten by a gang of Korean youths. Ethnic biases learned from parents and grandparents often came with immigrants over the Pacific to the New World, just as they had come over the Atlantic for earlier generations. In places like Coquitlam, where they both lived, Southeast Asians like Le, who was Vietnamese, and Narong, who was Thai, frequently found themselves the targets of other bullies, who were almost as often of European descent, or Aboriginal Canadians, as they were from other parts of Asia.

Le decided not to let the issue drop. He assembled a gang of mostly Southeast Asian buddies, including Narong, to exact revenge. The little army invaded the Hi-Max karaoke club, which the original bullies frequented, and attacked their alleged leader, 16-year-old Richard Jung, as he headed to the men's room. They beat him so badly, he was dead before the ambulance arrived.

Le was charged with second-degree murder, a charge that was reduced on appeal to manslaughter. Narong, the only other member of the gang to face charges, also pleaded guilty to manslaughter. In 2002, both were sentenced to conditional terms of 18 months. The others walked.

Almost as soon he got out of Willingdon Youth Detention Centre, Narong started getting in trouble again. In fact, between his release in 2003 and October 2007, he faced more than 30 different criminal charges, mostly related to drug trafficking and weapons, but somehow managed to get most of them stayed for various reasons. One he couldn't shake involved assaulting a police officer back in May 2007. In October, he was still on probation for that. It was said that he was part of—in fact, the leader of—a shadowy street gang called the Red Scorpions, but that he had recently left the organization to branch out on his own. Other elements had wrested control of the gang from him, and he was no longer welcome there.

With him in suite 1505 were the Lal brothers. Twenty-six-year-old Michael Justin Lal and 22-year-old Corey Jason Michael Lal were alleged at the time to have been career drug dealers, working mainly for a rival street gang known as the Independent Soldiers, before joining forces with Narong. Just as Narong had experienced with the Red Scorpions, outside forces had taken over the Independent Soldiers, making most of the old guard uneasy, to say the least.

A year earlier, Michael had received a conditional 17-month sentence for trafficking, and Corey was facing charges for trafficking after having been arrested in the summer of 2007. One of Michael's closest friends, Mahmoud Alkhalil, had been murdered in 2003 when he was just 19. Police allege the killing was connected to the 2001 slaying of Alkhalil's older brother Khalil and the subsequent attacks on Phil Rankin, the lawyer defending Michael Naud, the man many accused of killing Khalil Alkhalil. The Alkhalil brothers were accused of being members in yet another street gang, the Indo-Canadian Mafia.

Rounding out the little group—which was becoming known on the streets as the Lal Crew—was 19-year-old Ryan Bartolomeo. He too had been arrested for drug trafficking. In December 2006, he was charged with four counts of possession for the purpose of trafficking and possession of a controlled substance, and two firearms-related charges, and was still facing those charges in October 2007.

He was close to his older cousin, Damon Bartolomeo, who in 2002 was one of four men accused of breaking into a Surrey marijuana-growing operation, beating its owner with brass knuckles and holding him captive. One of the co-accused was Juel Ross Stanton, a full-patch member of the East End chapter of the Hells Angels, arguably the dominant gang in Vancouver. The four accused got off the hook when witnesses refused to testify or were found unreliable and the victim, Alexander Goldman, died of a stroke in 2004. The incident happened just two blocks from Balmoral Tower.

At the same time that Chris Mohan let Schellenberg and the building manager into 1504, all four of the Lal Crew were inside 1505.

• • •

Eileen Mohan didn't know the guys in 1505. She had met only Baldini, whom she had judged to be an okay guy based on his appearance and external habits. "There was no traffic in and out of the suite. The only guy I saw was the tenant. He looked like a normal guy. He was dressed nicely—no tattoos, no bling-bling, nothing alarming," she said. "If they had told me the person living beside me was a drug dealer, do you think I would have stayed there?"

At about four o'clock on that Friday, the building manager noticed Schellenberg's truck in the parking lot. Since he should have left at least an hour before that, the manager chose to investigate. Getting out of the elevator on the top floor, he could immediately tell something was wrong. The door of 1505 was open, and so was that of 1504. It was eerily silent. He slowly approached 1505. He saw Schellenberg facedown on the ground. There was a pool of blood under his nose, but it was no longer flowing. He was clearly dead.

Although he couldn't smell anything, the building manager immediately thought there had been a gas leak, and that Schellenberg had asphyxiated. Scared the entire building could go up in flames, the building manager raced down the stairs and called 9-1-1.

The fire department arrived and evacuated the building, and as protocol dictated, authorities shut down the SkyTrain and blocked off the nearby highways. The firefighters went up to the 15th floor, and their gas detectors indicated there was no leak. They went into 1505. Inside, they found six corpses. It was no gas leak. All six men were lying in pools of blood, and there were visible holes in their heads. It was clearly not a job for the fire department. They called the police.

Despite its size and high crime rate, Surrey doesn't actually have its own police force. Instead, they have a 640-officer RCMP detachment. Alerted by the firefighters, the RCMP sent out a HAZMAT unit and members of the Integrated Homicide Investigation Team (IHIT), a unit formed by a number of police forces and RCMP detachments in the Lower Mainland region of British Columbia to investigate all homicides across city and town borders.

RCMP Superintendent Wayne Rideout was in charge of the IHIT, but he had already left for the weekend. And many of the other IHIT officers were investigating an incident earlier that day in which a small private plane, a twin-engined Piper Seneca, had flown into the ninth floor of an apartment building in nearby Richmond.

Overwhelmed by the massive amount of evidence at the crime scene, the IHIT officers at Balmoral Tower called Rideout at home. "I got the call from the plainclothes commander at the Surrey detachment," he said. "They were suspecting now that it was a multiple homicide. We called out multiple teams." Rideout drove out to Balmoral Tower. "I knew this was going to change IHIT forever," he said. "We had never had anything like this." Indeed, it proved to be British Columbia's biggest mass murder in recent history.

Before long, more than 100 investigators from the already stretched IHIT were on the scene. "It doesn't just impact that investigation. It impacts all investigations," Rideout said. "It has really drained resources."

● ● ●

On the stopped SkyTrain, Eileen Mohan started to hear rumors of a gas leak. She immediately thought of the gas guy looking at the furnaces in Balmoral Tower. At least, she thought to herself, Chris had left for his basketball game even if something had actually happened there.

She got off the train and walked the rest of the way home. The cops and fire department cordon was still in place. She could not go home. She knew something bad had happened but wasn't worried about Chris—at least, consciously. "I was looking to the very side of the building where my son lay dead. I had no idea," she said. "There was no fear in me." Unable to get inside and unwilling to stand out in the cold rain, Eileen headed to a relative's house nearby to wait for the authorities to declare Balmoral Tower open again. Still she couldn't get over the sick feeling in her stomach. "I thought, 'why am I feeling this way?' "

Unable to relax, she went back to Balmoral Tower after midnight. It was still closed, and the worry she had felt rose to the surface. "It began to register on me. My son hadn't called. It was one o'clock," she said. "He always called to let me know where he was."

She rushed back to her relatives' place. Unable to call Chris himself, she called the friends he had told her he was going to play basketball with. They told her that Chris had never made it to the game in Burnaby. Sitting on the couch in her relatives' house, Eileen heard on the news there had been a murder in Balmoral Tower. "It was then that my heart sank," she said. "I went limp."

The next morning, Eileen began to get calls from some of Chris's other friends. He was supposed to have attended the funeral of a close friend at ten o'clock that day, and they wanted to know why he hadn't shown up. She didn't know what to say. She returned to Balmoral Tower at four o'clock that afternoon. She was still not allowed in. She now knew that six people had been murdered in the building and had even heard people say that it had happened on the 15th floor. She went up to a detective, and begged him for any information about her son.

"Does your son have any tattoos?" he asked.

"No, my son does not have a single tattoo on his body," she answered, surprised by his question. "Christopher has a mole here." She pointed at her chin, where she too had a mole. "And he has a mole here," she pointed at her sternum, where she also had a mole. The detective said he couldn't help her.

Then Eileen asked a couple of RCMP officers if they had heard about her son; he was missing and had not called. She saw their faces drop. They asked her if she had a picture of her son.

• • •

A few hours before Eileen Mohan's heart was broken, concern started to wash over the Schellenberg house in Abbotsford. Ed's wife Lois had made pizza for dinner, but Ed had not returned to eat it. She got Kevin, their son, to call him. No answer. But that wasn't too strange; Ed would never pick up when he was with a customer or on the road.

She had heard on the TV news that night that there had been a gas leak at Balmoral Tower but didn't worry about Ed, even though she knew he was working on the gas lines in that very building. She was confident he knew what he was doing. The news of the small airplane crashing into the Richmond apartment building dominated the program. She hadn't heard the whole story, so she immediately called her sister who lived in an apartment building in Richmond to see if everybody was okay. Her sister was fine—it wasn't even that close to where she lived—but she brought up what was going on in Surrey, aware that Ed, his brother-in-law and nephew had all been working there. Lois said it was just a leak or something, nothing to worry about. Her sister disagreed. "Haven't you heard? It's been upgraded," she said. "It's a murder or a police incident."

Now it was serious. She called Brown, who told her he left Ed and the 21-year-old boy at the building to finish the job and had not heard from either of them since. Lois called their two other children and told them to return home immediately. Brown called his son. The boy told him that they had finished all the units except for 1505, but that Uncle Ed was going to take care of that one, so he went downstairs to get ready to go. Then the fire department and police arrived and took him from the building. They didn't answer any of his questions, but the other people they evacuated were all talking. They kept asking him if he was okay, if he was hurt. He was confused; he had no idea what had occurred. He was waiting in the parking lot when one of the other residents of the 15th floor called him. He asked the caller what was going on. "Something terrible has happened on the 15th floor, and your guy's van is still down in the parking lot, and his tools are still out in the hallway," the caller said. "Something horrible has happened in 1505."

CHAPTER 2

THE GANGSTER'S PLAYGROUND: 1907–1998

Chris Mohan, Ed Schellenberg, Eddie Narong, Michael Le, and the Lal brothers would soon be known as the Surrey Six, and the events at the Balmoral Tower in October 2007 would mark a turning point in the history of criminal violence in the Lower Mainland. But that history was long and deeply entrenched.

For most of the early part of the twentieth century, organized crime in Vancouver was largely under the radar of the media, but without realizing it, the combined governments of Canada, British Columbia, and Vancouver had put together a perfect incubator for organized crime. They called attention to specific ethnic groups (primarily the Chinese, but also immigrants from the Indian subcontinent) and passed laws that specifically targeted them. The government isolated these groups in their own segregated neighborhoods, which the city had declared high-crime areas, and the only official interaction with the government these groups had was with a police force that had a reputation for excessive and even unnecessary violence. And, as though that weren't enough, the government gave these groups an instant black market by banning opium, which was not only a major part of these ethnic groups' culture, but also a huge source of revenue for the otherwise poor Chinese neighborhoods.

It was the same kind of situation that has bred crime organizations around the world, most notably the Mafia in Sicily and Calabria. As with the Mafia, powerful Chinese men, mainly merchants, banded together for their own benefit, cooperating with one another to ensure mutual success. These groups, perfectly legal to form, eventually became known as "tongs," from the Chinese word for "meeting place."

Eventually, others in the Chinese community began to approach the tongs to acquire loans, to settle disputes and to get protection. And, just as the mafia had, the tongs began to act as a shadow government for Chinese communities around the world who felt alienated by their official governments. Of course, unelected leaders with extra-legislative powers are as prone to temptation as anyone, and many influential members of tongs used their prestige to become involved in loan sharking, extortion, human trafficking, prostitution and drug trafficking. Organizations within tongs that are dedicated to organized crime are called "triads," from a phrase that means "secret society."

The first triad to be discovered in Canada was the Hung Shan Tong (Red Mountain Society) in Barkersville, British Columbia, in 1863. Members of a much larger tong in San Francisco had come to the tiny mountain town after gold was discovered there and quickly set up businesses appealing to the Chinese community already there.

Tongs spread all over British Columbia and, to a lesser extent, Chinese communities in the rest of Canada as well. One member in Vancouver, Shi Mei (also spelled Shu Moy), rose to prominence after the 1908 opium ban, using an ingenious method. Opium was still legal in Asia, and many tourist boats traveled there, including Canadian Pacific's Empress Line. Shi bribed the line's mostly Chinese employees to smuggle opium back to Canada. After he became wealthy, he started a local string of gambling parlors catering mainly to Chinese patrons, who played a number of games, especially a dice game called "barboodey." He was part of the focus of McGeer's 1928 crime probe, which called him "king of the gamblers" and accused him of paying the police $50 a month for protection.

Police made crackdown after crackdown over the years, but had little success in stopping the vice trades in Chinatown. Before long, the people of Vancouver came to tolerate, even ignore, vice crimes in Chinatown, developing a "what happens in Chinatown stays in Chinatown" mentality.

In the late 1970s, competition for trade among gangs operating out of Chinatown was fierce. The Lotus Gang, also known as the Lotus Brothers—founded in 1976 by Ling Yue Jai (who also went by the name David So)—was young and aggressive, and began to upset the equilibrium that had been established. They especially annoyed another young gang, the Gum Wah (Golden Chinese), and the two came close to war. Outnumbered, the Gum Wah preemptively entered into a mutual relationship with the Hung Ying (Red Eagles), a smaller gang made up mainly of immigrants from Hong Kong and ethnic Chinese immigrants from a number of Southeast Asian countries, including Vietnam, the Philippines and Cambodia. Looking for more manpower to catch up, the Lotus Gang formed a loose alliance with Los Diablos, a street gang that was originally made up of Hispanic immigrants but, after a series of arrests and deportations, had become mostly made up of Indian Canadians.

War was avoided, but attrition through arrests and defections led to there being three prominent gangs in Chinatown: the Hung Ying, the Lotus Gang (by then led by a man named Park Shing Low) and the Viet Ching (made up primarily of ethnic Chinese immigrants from Vietnam and led by Hy Hang and Law Kin Keung, also known as Allan Law). The Gum Wah had been largely sidelined, having been eclipsed by the Hung Ying.

Throughout the 1980s, the Hung Ying and Viet Ching fought a war of attrition, leaving the Lotus Gang as the top crime organization in Vancouver's Chinatown. But they would soon see another rival, one with roots in China's Communist Party.

The Red Guard, established to prosecute Mao Zedong's bloody Cultural Revolution in the 1960s, established a number of prison camps, which were taken over by the Communist Party. The biggest of them—just outside Guangzhou (still known to many Westerners as "Canton")—was called the "Big Circle" because the barracks were constructed in a ring around the guardhouse.

Lots of prisoners managed to escape from the Big Circle and, accompanied by defectors from the Red Guards, they fled to Hong Kong, which was at the time a British colony. Hardened by their time in captivity and at odds to make ends meet in one of the world's most expensive cities, many of them turned to crime. They started with robbing couriers, then moved onto bigger targets. Their loose association became known as "the Big Circle Boys."

Fortuitously for them, the West fired one of its last blows of the Cold War by liberalizing immigration policies in many countries, especially for immigrants who had fled a communist regime. Because the people of Hong Kong were officially British subjects—and many were eager to leave, with the knowledge that Britain was due to turn the colony back over to Chinese ownership in 1997—many went to Canada. They regrouped in Chinese neighborhoods in many cities there, particularly Vancouver and Toronto.

The Big Circle Boys first came to the attention of Canadian law enforcement in 1988 when a rash of pickpocketings hit Toronto's Chinatown and adjacent subway stops. Credit cards were being copied and put into use, and phone cards—all but extinct now, but common at the time—were being run up to the tune of tens of thousands of dollars each month. Further investigations led law enforcement to believe that the Big Circle

Boys were importing drugs to Canada from East Asia and that they ran a number of brothels in Chinatown and Scarborough in which the employees had been trafficked from impoverished Asian countries with promises of legitimate jobs.

As they grew in strength, the Big Circle Boys expanded their repertoire. They would go into restaurants in large groups, eat and drink all they wanted, then leave. Any waiters or others who challenged them would be threatened with violence. And they also ran a "window cleaning" scam—in which shop owners who did not pay them a monthly stipend could expect to have their windows smashed.

Later, the gang specialized in home invasions, simply barging their way into the houses and condos of wealthy Asian-Canadians and taking what they wanted. They were also linked to counterfeiting cash and passports, as well as trafficking heroin into the United States. A 1996 report by the Criminal Intelligence Service of Canada (CISC) stated:

> There are clear indications Asian heroin traffickers such as the Big Circle Boys are co-operating with Vietnamese gangs, Laotian, Fukienese and Taiwanese criminals, Italian organized crime, [the] Hells Angels and with any criminal organization that will buy drugs.

But the nature of the Big Circle Boys, and the code of silence that is strictly enforced in Chinese Canadian communities, make their moves nearly impossible for law enforcement to monitor. So it came as a complete surprise on November 4, 2007, when a 10-year-old girl called 9-1-1 to report that her dad had been shot in front of their mansion in Vancouver's upscale Shaughnessy neighborhood. The victim was Hong Chao "Raymond" Huang. He was dead by the time emergency crews arrived at the scene. The 45-year-old had done his best to keep a low profile but was well known as a Dai Lo (Big Brother), a high-ranking member of the Big Circle Boys. Neighbors had been suspicious of the Huang family, who purchased the $3.7-million house with extra security in 2003. They told media they found it odd that the family had never learned to speak English and kept a number of large guard dogs—very rare among Chinese families—on the premises.

The case was never solved; an indication of just how easy it is for the Big Circle Boys and other gangsters to fade into the background when they have to.

• • •

In the 1960s, Vancouver experienced another mass migration. Rumors of abundant drugs, relaxed laws and cheap rent attracted a remarkable number of young people, most of whom were—correctly or not—described as hippies. By 1967, the area had become frequently described as Canada's hippie capital, and young people and their fashionable habits were commonplace in the area. Mayor Thomas J. Campbell referred to them as "a scum community" and added, "If these young people get their way, they will destroy Canada. From what I hear across the world, they will destroy the world!"

But the sheer numbers of hippies and others who thought like them had a remarkable effect on the city. Vancouver opposed freeways, became a forerunner of relaxed drug laws and even gave birth to Greenpeace in 1971. But while the people of Vancouver had different attitudes than the rest of the country when it came to drugs, they still had to abide by federal laws. That became abundantly clear in the summer of 1971. The city's chapter of the Youth International Party (better known as the Yippies) organized a "smoke-in"—a protest in which about 2,000 people openly smoked marijuana in defiance of the law—in Gastown's Maple Tree Square on August 7. Mayor Campbell, who had embedded undercover officers among the series of Yippie-inspired protests that summer, sent in the riot police. Although a CBC cameraman on the scene claimed that protesters were throwing bottles and pieces of pavement at officers to provoke them, the footage that was carried in the media was exclusively of helmeted officers without identifying badges beating what appeared to be helpless youths with long riot batons. Things got far worse for the cops' reputation when a 16-year-old from Ontario sued them, claiming that a cop had broken his leg with his baton and threatened to break the other if the boy did not stand up and leave. A total of 79 arrests were made in what are now known as the "Gastown Riots."

Mayor Campbell and the cops may have hated them, but to organized crime, the hippies were something of a godsend. Generally law-abiding people otherwise, they had an insatiable hunger for drugs and, as they became settled in the prosperous city, the money to pay for them.

But it was not always easy for the hippies—almost exclusively white English-speakers—to go to Chinatown and communicate a desire to buy drugs, especially with traffickers who were ever vigilant for undercover cops. That gap was filled by another cultural phenomenon that came to Vancouver in the 1960s—outlaw motorcycle gangs.

Like the outlaw motorcycle gangs in other parts of the world, the ones in the Vancouver area aped the fashions and lifestyle popularized by the 1955 Marlon Brando film *The Wild One* and codified by the Hells Angels. They rode chopped and stretched-out Harley-Davidsons with extra-loud pipes, they grew their hair long and wore leather jackets with their clubs' names and logos on the back. And they sold drugs. Most outlaw motorcycle gangs sold drugs they manufactured, like methamphetamine, while others relied on crime organizations like the Mafia to supply them with heroin or cocaine. In the Vancouver region, though, the outlaw motorcycle gangs were generally supplied by the Chinese and, as marijuana cultivation began to become widespread in the Fraser and Okanagan Valleys, from local growers.

There was no shortage of recruits. White kids in Vancouver had banded together as gangs for decades. Collectively called "the Park Gangs," each group was focused on the park they considered their turf. Before the bikers became the driving force in the area, the park gangs generally acted like a parody of 50s greasers with souped-up cars they'd race on city streets every Friday night, denim jackets, chains and switchblades. Their drug activities included drinking beer and sniffing glue.

Generally, they were into small-time crime. Jim Chu, Vancouver's police chief and a graduate of Sir Charles Tupper Secondary School, remembered his first experiences growing up near one of the Park Gangs. "The Riley Park gang was a product of the housing project by Ontario and 33rd Avenue. They were lower-income, often single-parent families living there. I didn't think of them that way at the time—they were just kids I went to school with," he said. "They wore jean jackets and jeans. Other kids wouldn't wear that—that signified you were a Riley Parker. They were tough guys who fought with tire irons and chains, and if you fought one of them, you had to fight them all."

He generally steered clear of the gang members but was confronted by them in 1973 when he was a 14-year-old paperboy. "Our shack at 26th and Main won recognition for the fewest complaints in the city. Our supervisor said, 'You guys did great, I'm going to buy you some burgers and pop,'" he recalled. "The day came, and he brought the burgers to the shack. And just as soon as he dumped them on the table, the Riley Park guys came over and said, 'These look good, and we're gonna help ourselves,' and ate them all. The supervisor didn't do a thing. He was too scared to get involved. To look back, it's sort of funny now. Whenever I see the character of Nelson Muntz on *The Simpsons,* I think of the kids who became Riley Parkers."

Though their appearance may cause him to grin now, Chu remembers that some Riley Park gang members were far from small-time miscreants. "I remember one student from my

Grade 5 class who was a hardcore Riley Park gang member," he said. "I later played rugby with him at Tupper before he was expelled. Then, in his 20s, he was arrested for murder. By that time he'd gotten pretty heavily into a life of crime and violence. He's dead now."

The most notorious of the Park Gangs was the Clark Park gang from the Kensington neighborhood. Through informants, Vancouver police discovered not only that they were selling drugs, but that they had also incited some hippie gatherings to riot and attack police. Constable Ken Doern went undercover and infiltrated the gang for five months in 1972. He was unable to prevent an attack on two police officers by Clark Parkers, who used dog chains with lead weights tied to them, but he did learn of a plan to violently disrupt a Rolling Stones concert at the Pacific Coliseum later that summer. The cops decided that the planned attack had political overtones far more important than proving who were the toughest guys in Clark Park, so they formed a strategy to prevent, or at least lessen, the effects of the assault.

Alongside the standard security, there were 50 uniformed officers present and another two dozen in full riot gear hiding in a nearby building. The doors opened at six, and things got ugly right away. About 2,500 angry people who had bought fake tickets were milling around the parking lot, many of them already drunk or high, or both. Police and security were still dealing with them when the Clark Parkers showed up at nine, as the Stones were into their first set.

Instantly recognizable in their checkered lumberjack shirts (what's called a "Kenora dinner jacket" in Ontario) and steel-toed boots, the Clark Park gang made their presence known by throwing a homemade smoke bomb into the crowd and then empty bottles at the Coliseum's glass doors. The police rushed in, and the crowd grew more aggressive, throwing bottles, planks from a nearby fence, rocks, pieces of concrete, and even Molotov cocktails. Aware that the riot would become uncontrollable once the 17,000 people inside the building came out at 11:30 p.m., the police called in reinforcements from the RCMP. Unable to quell the mob by other means, the RCMP executed a mounted charge at 11 p.m., which finally led to the combatants retreating.

The riot left 31 police injured, including 13 who were taken to hospitals. Among the 22 arrested was a man who was wielding a chain with a sharpened hook on one end and a leather handle on the other.

Keenly aware that the Clark Park gang was a serious threat to security, the police formed a new group called "the H-Squad." Made up of big, tough cops—the minimum height was said to be six foot four—the H-Squad hung out in Clark Park, posing as regular citizens. The official plan was that if any gang members tried to rob them, assault them or sell them drugs, the cops would arrest them. Others have told me it didn't exactly work out like that. The cops, said to be armed with baseball bats, were rumored to have sought out gang members and beat them or thrown them into Burrard Inlet. No matter what happened, the Clark Park gang ceased to exist after a while, and the other Park Gangs also calmed down. But those same bored, alienated white youth soon found another way to bond and make money—outlaw motorcycle gangs.

In Vancouver, as with the rest of Canada, outlaw motorcycle gangs started small—usually just a group of high school friends—and only succeeded if they were tough enough to protect their territory and smart enough to make powerful alliances. Perhaps realizing this, in 1977, two prominent Vancouver-area outlaw motorcycle gangs—the Gypsy Wheelers of White Rock and the 101 Road Knights of Nanaimo—decided to join a prominent East Vancouver outlaw motorcycle gang called "the Satan's Angels," becoming chapters of that club. Sensing their opportunity, the Satan's Angels did their best—through threats of violence and actual violence—to chase off other prominent clubs like the once-powerful Ghost Riders.

Suddenly, the Satan's Angels became the most prominent outlaw motorcycle gang in British Columbia. They became known for their annual summertime pilgrimage to the Okanagan Valley. A fruit-growing Mecca, the Okanagan invites thousands of migrant pickers every year. These days, many are from Mexico, but back in the 70s and 80s, they were almost entirely French Canadian. And they were not well-liked by the locals. Derisively called "Frogs," they had a reputation for wild parties and petty crime. And they had experienced run-ins with both the police and the bikers before.

After a few locals raided a camp set up by French Canadian fruit pickers on the night of June 26, 1980, causing damage and injuries, no charges were laid. But the local Osoyoos RCMP detachment promised to keep investigating. They also warned the French Canadians to leave town for the next week to avoid having a problem with the Satan's Angels, who were having a "run" in the area. Many pickers left immediately, and those who didn't pitched their tents in the safety of the orchards they worked in. "We heard a rumor the bikers were coming to clean up our French problem for us," joked RCMP Sergeant Lou Turcott.

The reputation of the Satan's Angels spread, and they were soon approached by Sonny Barger's Oakland chapter of the Hells Angels to become prospective chapters of the big club. The Hells Angels were eager to expand back then, especially into areas with lucrative drug markets. A few years earlier, in 1977, the New York City chapter had sponsored Canada's first Hells Angels chapter in Montreal, but they had no connections on the West Coast and—you can call this irony if you want—they were all French speakers.

The Satan's Angels jumped at the chance to be part of the big club, but the guys in Oakland had one condition: the Satan's Angels had to eliminate, chase off or subdue every other outlaw motorcycle gang in British Columbia. The Satan's Angels went to work, and by the summer of 1983, there were just three outlaw motorcycle gangs left in the province—the Satan's Angels, the Tribesmen of Nanaimo on Vancouver Island and the Highwaymen of Cranbrook in the mountains near the Alberta border. The agreement was that the Tribesmen would be a prospective Satan's Angels (and later Hells Angels) chapter, while the Highwaymen would become what outlaw motorcycle gangs call a "support club" and law enforcement calls a "puppet club"—a smaller gang that pays tribute to the parent club and performs various tasks for its members.

To celebrate, the newest chapters of the Hells Angels threw a huge party. Delegations from Oakland and Canada's other chapters in Sorel and Laval, in Quebec (along with their friends from prospective chapters in Sherbrooke, Quebec; Halifax, Nova Scotia; and Hamilton, Ontario) arrived. Oakland's brass and Canadian national president Yves "Le Boss" Buteau withheld the Satan's Angels' new patches until they got rid of some of their less dedicated members. Still, there were more than enough bikers to go around, and the Hells Angels opened chapters in East Vancouver—some of the most lucrative drug-selling territory in North America—on December 22, 1983; in Haney (now part of Maple Ridge, British Columbia) on June 13, 1987; and in Burnaby on July 23, 1998.

The Hells Angels soon emerged as the top dogs in the organized crime world in Vancouver. They trafficked drugs and prostitutes from the Chinese and also from Quebec—especially, law enforcement contends, from the Hells Angels new Sherbrooke chapter. Taking a cue from other successful crime organizations, the British Columbia Hells Angels were rarely ever caught doing anything wrong. Instead, they invested their money in legitimate business—often strip joints and bars—and hired, coerced or extorted others to do their work for them, often using prospective membership as a lure.

That gave rise to a large group of loosely associated young men who were unofficially affiliated with the Hells Angels but ready to do their bidding at the merest hint. Called support crews, they were easy to identify. Uniformly white—because non-whites could forget about ever becoming a full-patch Hells Angel—they tended to wear red and white, the club's colors, and have words like "Support 81" either on their clothes or tattooed on their skin. The number 81 is a none-too-sophisticated code for Hells Angels, derived from the fact that H is the eighth letter of the alphabet and A is the first.

But being on top did not make the Hells Angels invincible. Although, as is often the case with outlaw motorcycle gangs, the people the Hells Angels had most to fear were their own "brothers." And that also extended to their friends and associates. John Ginnetti, whom everyone called "Ray," was a flamboyant guy with a quick temper. Ginnetti met and befriended a number of Hells Angels and their associates when he was a successful car salesman on the Kingsway in East Vancouver in the 1980s. He quit that job and became first a direct marketer, then a stock broker and financial adviser, first working for Canarim Investment (Vancouver's largest at the time), then going independent. Police allege that a big part of his business came from legitimizing the investments of his pals in the Hells Angels. He made no secret of the fact he had friends in the club. He had run into trouble once, when investigators burst into his telemarketing company in 1986. Inside they found an illegal boiler-room operation with "sucker lists" of potential scam victims. Just as they were about to confiscate a bag alleged to contain $50,000, an employee threw it out the window. The investigators allege Ginnetti caught it and drove away.

Ginnetti was a temperamental man and once came to blows with volatile actor Sean Penn at a Vancouver restaurant (the pair had to be separated by waiters). He had hired Roger Daggitt—a former mixed martial arts fighter before he became an enforcer for the Hells Angels—as his full-time bodyguard. The position required that Daggitt quit his post with the Hells Angels, mostly because Ginnetti worked with other criminal organizations, including some Russians. Quitting the Hells

Angels is not always an easy thing, but Daggitt's size and ferocity made it possible.

On May 9, 1990, Ginnetti's wife opened a closet in their
lavish West Vancouver home to find his bloody remains. He
had been shot once in the back of the head with a .380 semiautomatic handgun. At the time, he had been actively promot-
ing a stock called Genesis Resources, a gold-mining company,
and making wild claims of future profitability.

Many people who were ready to accuse the Hells Angels
changed their minds when a dozen of them—including East
Vancouver sergeant-at-arms Lloyd Robinson—attended his
funeral. Seeing the bikers' seemingly sincere grief made it look
like they were not involved in his demise. Less than a week
later, a Russian-born cocaine dealer named Sergey Filonov
was heard to be drunkenly bragging about his involvement
with Ginnetti's murder. On their way home from a bar that
night, Sergey and his brother Taras were attacked in front of
Trev Deeley's Harley-Davidson dealership on Boundary Road.
Sergey was shot and died, while Taras was badly hurt when he
was beaten with a hammer. Two men—Shannon Aldrich and
Miroslav Michal—were arrested and charged with the attack,
but were released after Taras refused to testify.

It was later revealed that the Filonov brothers had stiffed the
Hells Angels on a $250,000 drug deal. According to police, the
Filonovs had made the deal, but once the cash was on the table,
they pulled out their guns, took the money and ran. Taras had
later been kidnapped and released when his brother coughed
up a $200,000 ransom, but it didn't end anything. Bad blood
existed between the Russians and the Hells Angels. Days later,
Eugeniy Alekseev, reported to be part of Vancouver's Russian
mafia, had just finished dinner with his brother, Aleksandr, and
Russian-born Vancouver Canucks star Pavel Bure when he used
a remote starter to fire up his Mercedes-Benz. The car blew up.

Two years after Sergey was killed, a student discovered
Taras's body in a forested area behind the University of British

Columbia. He was handcuffed, and a shotgun blast had obliterated his face. Aleksandr Alekseev went missing in 1994, and Eugeniy was found with a bullet hole through his head in a Mexico City hotel room in 1995. The always-obliging Mexican police reported his death as a suicide.

Ginnetti's murder remained unsolved until police tracked down a career criminal in California's notorious Lompoc prison in 1995. Jose Raul Perez-Valdez, a Cuban, was serving an eight-year sentence for kidnapping and trafficking cocaine. He could not be extradited until he had finished his sentence in the U.S. When he finally appeared in court in Canada, he admitted that he had killed Ginnetti for $30,000. And he said he was paid by Daggitt.

While it would have been fascinating to hear what Daggitt had to say about the accusation, he had long since been silenced. On October 6, 1992, his son and he had been enjoying the show at the Turf Hotel, a run-down strip club once frequented by serial killer Clifford Olson, when somebody put three bullets in his head. He died before he hit the ground.

The man who killed him was a professional hit man from Montreal named Serge Robin. After his first murder conviction back in 1977, Robin made a bid for freedom. While being transported to prison, he produced a rolled-up aluminum can he had hidden in his rectum and had threatened his guards and driver with it, claiming it was a pistol. As the van he was in stopped on a gravel shoulder, the cop car behind it radioed for help. By the time Robin emerged from the truck, he was surrounded by cops with their weapons drawn. One of them had the unfortunate task of taking his can away from him.

He had been busy on his trip to Vancouver. In the week before he offed Daggitt, Robin had killed small-time cocaine dealer Ronald Scholfield in his car out front of the Downtown Eastside's notorious Cobalt Motor Hotel, and on the following day he murdered another street-level dealer named Robert Pelletier. Although Robin pled guilty, he refused to give details as to who wanted Daggitt dead. It was up to the media and public to guess.

While all this was going on, one of British Columbia's most prominent Hells Angels met his own end. Michael "Zeke" Mickle was the popular president of the Nanaimo chapter for years when he stepped on a ferry to the mainland on the night of April 30, 1993. He was never seen in public again, and his cellphone account had been deactivated by an unknown party. When the RCMP went looking for clues, they were inundated with a number of anonymous tips that all claimed Mickle was beheaded by an unnamed Vietnamese gangster who had just moved to Vancouver Island and was out to prove he did not fear the Hells Angels. They didn't fall for it and later found more reliable sources who informed them that Mickle had started using the drugs he had been selling and had gone into considerable debt with his "brothers" in the Hells Angels. The case has never been solved, but nobody's looking for the Vietnamese kingpin anymore.

Despite their hard-earned reputation for xenophobia, the Hells Angels (at least, their close associates) did not mind dealing with the Italian Mafia from Montreal and Colombian cartel members when it came to cocaine.

• • •

If there is a Canadian dream, Eugene Uyeyama appeared to have achieved it. By December 1995, he had a brand-new luxury car and a gorgeous cliff-side house in Burnaby with a swimming pool and a deck that gave him views of Burrard Inlet to the west and the Coast Mountains to the east. More important, the woman he had loved and pursued for a dozen years had finally said yes and married him. His new bride, Michele, delighted him when she told him she wanted to start a family right away. After they returned from a two-week Caribbean cruise, they went Christmas shopping, and Eugene noticed that Michele was checking out baby clothes.

Somewhat less enviable was the life of Bobby Moyes. Addicted to heroin since his teens, Moyes was a career criminal. Despite 40 convictions, including many for violent crimes, and a string of bank robberies, the Victoria native was on day release after serving a sentence at the minimum-security Ferndale Institution for armed robbery. At night, he checked into the Sumas Centre halfway house, and by day, he shared a house in Coquitlam with a drug trafficker he met in Ferndale named Roberto Salvatore Ciancio. "It was very generous," Moyes said, referring to Ciancio's offer to put him up. "Sal allowed me to live there and never asked anything of me." That would change.

Ciancio was well known in the area as a bad dude, some-one you did not cross. A rough-looking guy with bad skin and worse teeth, Ciancio was intense and had a hair-trigger temper. He was hooked up with very powerful people, and many thought he had something to do with the 1983 contract killing of Joe Philliponi, a reputed made man and nightclub owner, that was eventually pinned on a drifter named Scott Forsyth and the man who would become Ciancio's father-in-law, Sid Morrissroe, a surprisingly wealthy plumbing contractor. Ciancio had been in prison for shooting at some cops who'd caught him stealing a tractor-trailer. He was also said to be close to Anthony "Big Tony" Terezakis, a drug trafficker with close ties to the Hells Angels.

And Moyes was no angel either. He had first been arrested in 1975 for armed robbery and been given a five-year sen-tence. While serving time, he was convicted of three counts of attempted murder when authorities learned he held down a sheriff named Gib Perry while a friend stabbed him 30 times but failed to kill him. With the escorting sheriff down, Moyes and his associate escaped prison, went to a nearby farm house, bound and robbed the family, and were finally taken down in a gunfight with police. Moyes and his friend were using guns stolen from the farmers. That sentence was for 15 years. But he was released on parole in 1980 only to be arrested weeks later in Montreal for violating his release conditions. The operation to find him uncovered enough evidence to sentence him to 15 more years for nine armed robberies. In 1986, he walked away from the fenceless Ferndale Institution and was caught some nine months later having committed more than two dozen bank holdups. That got him a life sentence. The Supreme Court judge said he had a "dreadful record involving crimes of violence" and that the life sentence was necessary "to put a stop to [his] predatory activities for as long as possible."

But he was out on the streets again in August 1993 with the condition that he attend psychological counseling and not consume any intoxicants, including alcohol. But when he was caught drinking and driving in October, his freedom was reduced to day parole, meaning he had to spend his nights at the Sumas Centre. Years later, Moyes admitted that he had lied repeatedly to the parole board, including feigning an interest in Native Canadian spirituality, even though he is not a Native Canadian. "I know how to make the rules work for me, just like a lawyer," he boasted.

Through what later became contentious court testimony, Moyes brought to life a grisly murder.

By December 1995, Moyes was working steadily for Ciancio, who had opened up an auto body shop, and did odd jobs for him. Moyes said that Ciancio's shop was partially bankrolled by his friend and fellow trafficker, Peter Chee.

On one occasion, Moyes said, Ciancio told him he needed him to do a job. Moyes thought that meant beat someone up (something Moyes later testified he had done for Ciancio several times before), so he agreed. They then agreed to talk in one of Ciancio's cars, a Fiat Spider convertible. Moyes said that the pair then drove to a restaurant in New Westminster and that Ciancio told him that a large quantity of drugs had been confiscated and that there was a rat in "their group" who would have to be eliminated before Christmas.

Moyes told the court that the following day he met with Ciancio and Chee. They told him, he said, that the target was Uyeyama and that they knew he was a rat because "nothing had stuck to him." He said they gave him an address, told him that Uyeyama's wife worked at a nearby grocery store and that Uyeyama had a brother who hung out at the house and occasionally slept over. They made it clear that anyone in the house would have to be killed. Chee, he said, did not want it to look like a home invasion or robbery, but that it should look like an assassination.

Moyes said that Ciancio then introduced him to an old friend whom he didn't completely trust but wanted to go with Moyes, named Mike Samardzich. The trio, Moyes said, then moved to Samardzich's old Cadillac because they couldn't fit in the two-seat Fiat, then drove by Uyeyama's house.

On December 20, 1995, Moyes had done it again. He had managed to have his day parole changed back to full parole effective the following day under the condition he attend an Alcoholics Anonymous meeting that night. He didn't.

That day, he drove Ciancio to the airport. Ciancio was going to Montreal to visit his father. His wife, Tammy, later said in court that Ciancio told her "a couple of people had to be taken out, and if I'd been around, I'd have been a suspect." Ciancio left a gun and some money in their shared laundry hamper. Moyes also claimed that Ciancio told him that if they found any money or drugs in Uyeyama's house, Ciancio would share it with them.

At the same time he was supposed to be at the AA meeting, Moyes claimed that he and Samardzich rang the Uyeyamas' doorbell. Moyes described himself and his associate as "impeccably dressed" and said they were holding wrapped gift boxes. Michele answered but did not unchain the door. Moyes was disappointed to see her. "I thought at the time that this was a really screwed-up thing," he said. "The woman wasn't supposed to be there. It changed everything."

He told her he had some Christmas presents from "the boys." Michele was no gangster, but she was also not naive enough to mistake what her new husband did for a living. "The boys" clearly indicated someone the visitors thought she would be familiar with, but I have also been told that in the Lower Mainland's crime circles, it usually refers to the Hells Angels. Still, she was cautious. Michele told the pair to leave the gifts outside. Moyes said that normally he would, but there had been so much rain that the porch was soaking, and the gifts would be ruined.

As soon as she reluctantly unchained the door, Moyes dropped his box and thrust a handgun under her chin. Once they were both inside, Moyes told Samardzich to "take care of" Michele. He knew she was not the target. Instead he began to search the house, finding Eugene asleep in the master bedroom. Thinking quickly, he pointed his gun at Eugene and shouted "Police!" before ordering him out of bed. As soon as Eugene was standing, Moyes grabbed him by the hair and forced him to the ground, face down. Pulling him arms behind him, Moyes tied him by the wrists with an electrical cord.

He called Samarzdich into the bedroom. According to Moyes, Samardzich, with a gun up to Michele's head, told Eugene he'd kill her if he did not tell them where the money was. Moyes kicked Eugene to encourage him to talk. Then he unwrapped one of the "gifts" to reveal a curling iron, which he threatened to "shove up his ass" unless he talked. It did not take Eugene long to give in, telling the invaders that the cash was in a nearby closet. Moyes searched the closet and pulled out a bag of cash. But it didn't save Michele's life. Moyes claimed in court that Samardzich saw the loot, and then used an electrical cord to strangle her, throwing her lifeless body at Eugene's feet. Eugene began to struggle. According to Moyes, Samardzich tackled him and grabbed his feet, holding him down as Moyes strangled him. At their trial, Moyes' version of events was rejected by the court and Samardzich was acquitted.

With both of the Uyeyamas dead, Moyes then unwrapped the other box they had brought. That Christmas gift was a red plastic can full of gasoline. Moyes then drenched the corpses and left a trail back to the front door. Throwing the can inside the house from the porch, Moyes then lit the trail and closed the door as the house erupted into an inferno.

Eugene Uyeyama was indeed an informant. In fact, he was the RCMP's most highly paid informant in British Columbia history at the time. The order to assassinate him came from the then-mighty Cali Cartel in Colombia. His death was part of what the RCMP called "an internal security review" by the cartel and their allies.

On October 5, 1995 (less than three months before he was killed), Uyeyama had proved his worth to the RCMP when he brought them an ordinary-looking 11-inch aluminum frying pan. He revealed to them that the Colombian-made pan—which he had spirited away from a shipment earlier that week—had a false bottom that was covering a disc of tightly packed powdered cocaine. Now aware of how the drugs arrived in Canada, all the cops had to know was when.

Their source of information was silenced just before Christmas when Uyeyama and his wife were killed, but not before his disclosure that, on February 12, 1996, a new shipment would be arriving. Inside a 40-foot container aboard the *MV Los Angeles* was a huge number of pots and pans from Colombia, all of which, the police discovered, had false bottoms concealing cocaine. The RCMP didn't manage to arrest any major players, but they did get almost 1,000 pounds of coke off the streets.

In March 1997, Moyes was arrested in Matsqui, British Columbia, for driving while intoxicated and leaving the scene of an accident. Despite his almost absurd number of arrests and convictions, it did not land him behind bars. Instead, his parole was reduced to day parole, meaning he had to go back to the Sumas Centre every night.

Even with those restrictions, Moyes told the court, Ciancio hired him and another man, a hulking friend of Moyes' from Ferndale named Mark Therrien, to kill again.

Ray Graves was a 70-year-old drug trafficker who lived with his 56-year-old wife, Sonto, and her son from a previous relationship, 37-year-old David Sangha, on a farm in Abbotsford. They were trouble. Graves, despite his age, and his wife were out on bail at the time fighting an attempted murder charge after another reputed cocaine dealer, Balbir Singh Sandu of nearby Chilliwack, was shot at on the Graves' farm.

Moyes claims that Ciancio told him that Graves and his wife had fallen $500,000 in debt with "Carlos," a mysterious Colombian who ran the Cali Cartel's operations in the Lower Mainland, and had to be eliminated. There was also a rumor circulating at the time that the pair had turned police informants.

Moyes recognized Therrien as another guy who had to sign in every night at Sumas. What he did not know is that Therrien had previously worked for the Graveses on their grow op and had left on bad terms. He had a score to settle.

On September 9, the murderous pair drove to the Abbotsford farm and ran into Sangha outside. Therrien said he had to speak with the Graveses, so Sangha led him inside. They immediately drew their guns and quickly overpowered the family inside. They then tied all three of them to kitchen chairs with duct tape. With the family at their mercy, Therrien and Moyes began to demand they reveal where their cash and drugs were hidden. They wouldn't talk. Therrien then took matters into his own hands and slashed Sangha's throat. Panicked and watching her son bleeding out, Sonto told them they could find what they wanted in an upstairs bedroom. Therrien ran up the stairs, returned with both cash and drugs, and then executed both of the Graveses with throat slashes.

As they were killing the Graves family, Moyes and Therrien heard a knocking, then a banging on the door. After it subsided, they looked out the door to find that their car had been blocked in by another. Clearly, the people who had been knocking on the door were still on the property. A quick search located Daryl Klassen and his wife Teresa in the nearby shed, taking drugs. Both worked for Graves as dealers. Therrien recognized them and ordered them to the floor, face down. He then grabbed a nearby crowbar and bashed both of their heads in, killing them.

After the murders, the pair split up the loot (Moyes had also grabbed jewelery and other valuables from the house) and threw their weapons and the duct tape off the Mission Bridge into the Fraser River. Then it was back to the Sumas Centre to fulfill their parole requirements.

At the time, police and media appeared to think that the mass killing at the Graves farm was an act of revenge from Sandhu's people. But evidence soon linked it to Moyes, who was returned to prison in January 1997. As the Crown failed to make a sufficient case against him and he managed to mount a deft defense based on guilt by association, Moyes was again released on day parole in November 1999. After two weeks, his parole was again revoked when he tested positive for heroin. In January 2000, he was released yet again on day parole but returned to prison in September after his parole officer called his behavior "problematic." A week later, he wrote to the RCMP admitting his role in both the Uyeyama and Graves killings.

• • •

While the Chinese (particularly the Big Circle Boys) and the Hells Angels were undeniably at the top of organized crime in Vancouver, they were hardly the only major operators. In fact, the best known gangsters in Vancouver history before the Bacon Brothers were the leaders of rival multiethnic, but predominantly Indian Canadian, gangs.

Bhupinder "Bindy" Singh Johal was born in India and moved to Vancouver in the late 1970s when he was still a small child. Even while still very young, he was identified as something of a "problem child" and did not take well to discipline. But, just as with many others like him, Johal's temperament was not something officially reported, teachers had to learn it for themselves. "When he came into Grade 8, it didn't seem like he had any problems," said Rob Sandhu, who taught him at the same Sir Charles Tupper Secondary School Jim Chu attended. "It seems these kids are not being flagged. But teachers are raising these issues, so why aren't we acting on it?" Johal's character traits grew worse and more dangerous as he grew older, and his sudden bursts of anger and violence earned him a reputation on the streets of Central Vancouver and in the halls of Tupper. On one occasion in 1989, 18-year-old Grade 12 student Johal was called to the school's office. While the vice-principal intended a closed-door discussion on his behavior, Johal took the opportunity to give the man a brutal beating, sending him to a hospital emergency room.

Caught, Johal did not deny the beating, but in an act that smacked of cold-blooded cynicism, tried to rationalize his behavior by claiming he assaulted the vice-principal in a fit of rage brought on by the discrimination he had endured as a minority (although by no means were people of Indian descent uncommon in his neighborhood or school). Neither the judge nor school board were fooled, and Johal received a 60-day sentence and expulsion from the school.

After his sentence was completed, Johal moved to nearby Richmond and enrolled in Matthew McNair Secondary School, but was expelled after he was caught smashing the window of a car and charged with possession of a dangerous weapon. Out of school and not prepared for any other work, Johal quickly fell into organized crime.

As has been true of other immigrant groups like Serbs and Croats, many Indian arrivals brought their biases, rivalries, and bitter feuds over to Canada with them. Particularly divided was the large and generally prosperous Sikh community. A gulf between the hardliners, who supported the establishment of an independent Sikh state, Khalistan, in India's Punjab region (by violence, if necessary), and the moderates, who were more than happy to leave such politics back in India and move ahead as a community in Canada.

The Sikh community around the world was enraged in June 1984 when Indian Prime Minister Indira Gandhi ordered the violent takeover of the Harmandir Sahib (Golden Temple) in Amritsar. The violent response came to Canada in June 1985 when an Air India Boeing 747, Flight 182, took off from Montreal's Mirabel Airport with 329 people on board, headed for London and then Delhi. Over the Irish Sea, a bomb in the plane's forward hold exploded and the jumbo jet disintegrated. Less than an hour later, a similar bomb intended for Air India Flight 301 exploded in Tokyo's Narita Airport, killing two baggage handlers. One prominent Canadian Sikh, miner-turned-journalist Tara Singh Hayer, editor-in-chief of the *Indo-Canadian Times*—North America's oldest and most popular Punjabi-language newspaper—condemned the attacks. In 1988, he was shot in the back by a 17-year-old Sikh extremist. Hayer was paralyzed and wheelchair-bound for the rest of his life.

It was against this backdrop of violence and suspicion that Johal and his friends—primarily drawn from Vancouver's large Sikh community—sold drugs, broke into cars and committed other petty crimes in a loosely tied group. Many of them attended Tupper and had been involved in a gang with ties to the newly emerging gang that had previously been called "Los Diablos." Originally mostly Hispanic, Los Diablos became increasingly multiethnic, especially after much of its original leadership had been arrested or deported. At the time Johal arrived on the scene, the gang had become almost entirely Indian, mostly Sikh, and was by then more widely known as the Indo-Canadian Mafia or the Punjabi Mafia.

The Indo-Canadian Mafia split into factions when one of its regional leaders, Jimsher "Jimmy" Singh Dosanjh, was charged with the October 14, 1991, murder of Colombian cocaine trafficker Teodoro Salcedo. Jimmy was eventually acquitted due to a lack of people willing to testify against him, but while he was behind bars, Johal assumed leadership of his men. Johal and his friends made money not just by drug trafficking, but also by exporting stolen car parts and selling goods, mostly electronics, stolen from transport trucks, often with the cooperation of the trucks' drivers. A CBC documentary at the time estimated that Johal was making about $4 million a year. He was as flamboyant as he was temperamental, and his regular appearances on local media angered many in the Lotus Gang, who had a history of cooperation with Jimmy Dosanjh and Los Diablos, but were not impressed by the mercurial Johal.

One of Johal's friends, a 21-year-old named Parminder Chana, was driving home at about nine o'clock on the evening of October 11, 1991, when he received a call from a mutual non-Sikh friend, Faisel (also reported as Faizal) Ali Dean. Dean told him to meet him at the Insurance Corporation of British Columbia's salvage yard in New Westminster right away. Chana worked there as a night security guard and frequently used it as a spot to meet with friends and make deals.

When he arrived, he saw Dean and another old friend, Rajinder "Little Raj" Benji. Chana was surprised to see Benji, as the two had experienced something of a falling out since Chana had started dating Benji's 17-year-old sister Kulwinder (better known as "Jassy"). As soon as he was close enough, Dean wrestled Chana to the ground and held him down. Police said Benji loomed over Chana, then produced a knife. Law enforcement officials allege that Benji began berating Chana for going out with his sister, then repeatedly slashed and stabbed him, eventually cutting off all of his fingers before slashing his throat. The two men then carried the body to a nearby drainage ditch and threw him in the water. He had been cut 54 times.

Four days later, Jassy leapt to her death into the Fraser River from the Pattullo Bridge that connects New Westminster and Surrey. She left behind a note that read "When Parmar died, I died."

Benji was quickly arrested for Chana's murder, and so was Dean after someone overheard him bragging about holding the victim down while Chana was sliced up. At the trial, it was determined that the Benjis had been a law-abiding family in northern British Columbia until the father died, an older sister ran away from home never to be heard from again, and the family moved to Vancouver. Soon "Little Raj" and his older brother—also named Rajinder, and known as "Big Raj"—were both involved with the Indo-Canadian Mafia, selling drugs and committing other small-time crimes. Little Raj admitted at a trial for another matter that he not only sold cocaine, but also had a network of dealers and drivers in the area—and that Dean was one of them. It was also revealed that Little Raj had three previous convictions for armed robbery in which he had threatened to kill his victims (one of them a 5-year-old boy) if they went to police.

In December 1991, the body of Sanjay Narain—a 21-year-old who many believe witnessed the Chana murder—was found at the bottom of North Vancouver's Cleveland Dam. After that, no witnesses dared testify against Jimmy, and he was acquitted. Dean, however, had already implicated himself and was found guilty of second-degree murder.

When Jimmy Dosanjh was released from jail, he was disturbed to learn that his men now answered to Johal. He was so upset, in fact, that he hired a man to kill Johal. But the assassin instead went to Johal, told him of Jimmy's plan, and cut a deal with Johal. For a little more money, they agreed, the assassin would kill Jimmy instead. On February 25, 1994, the double-crossing assassin told Jimmy that he had some stolen electronics he wanted to sell him, lured him into an Eastside alley, and shot him dead.

Jimmy's brother, Ranjit "Ron" Dosanjh swore revenge—
on camera. Highly political, Ron had been president of the
Vancouver Chapter of the International Sikh Youth Federation,
and as a strong supporter of an independent Khalistan, he was
suspected of ordering the assassination attempt on prominent
Sikh Bakhar Singh Dhillon for speaking out against political
violence. Years of experience had made him something of a
slick operator. So it came as a surprise to many when he told
a television reporter that if Johal came to his house, he would
"shoot him between the eyes." Johal fired back, also in front of
TV cameras, saying, "Basically, I just want these guys to know
you got another thing coming, bitch. I'm still here."

In a strange twist, the "thing coming" was a bullet between
the eyes. During the afternoon rush hour on April 19, 1994,
Ron Dosanjh was sitting in his customized red pickup waiting at a stoplight on the Kingsway when a car pulled up beside
him. The passenger in the car pulled out an AK-47 and shot
him in the face. Dead, Ron Dosanjh's foot fell from the brake
pedal, and the pickup lurched into oncoming traffic. As other
drivers screeched to avoid it, the truck kept rolling up onto the
sidewalk until it collided with a tree.

Johal was questioned by police and released. On April 24,
1994, a neighbor of Johal's, Yukon native Greg Olson, agreed
to walk his landlord's dog in a nearby park. While with the
dog, Olson was shot and killed. It was later revealed that the
gunmen mistook him for Johal, who was about the same size
and age, and wore similar clothing.

The next day, during Ron Dosanjh's cremation service,
police announced that Johal was under arrest for Jimmy's
murder. Also charged were Preet "Peter" Sarbjit Gill, Rajinder
"Big Raj" Benji, Sun News Lal, Michael Kim Budai and Ho-Sik
"Phil" Kim, who was alleged to be the triggerman.

At the trial, the Crown alleged that Johal had paid Kim
$30,000 to kill Ron Dosanjh because Johal had heard that Ron
Dosanjh was going to kill him to avenge his brother Jimmy.

Despite what was then the longest criminal trial in Canadian history, the accused were all acquitted, much to the surprise of many in the media.

A few months after the verdict, a Vancouver police officer who had been involved in the case saw Gill dancing at a nightclub with one of the jurors, Gillian Guess. Suspicious, the police initiated surveillance on Guess and recorded phone conversations in which she admitted having a romantic affair with Gill while sitting on the jury of his murder trial.

Guess was charged with obstruction of justice—in fact, it was the first time in North American history that a juror had been caught sleeping with an accused murderer on trial—while Gill, Budai and Kim were ordered to be retried. Guess went out of her way to engage the media and public, and even set up a website for her fans, but was found guilty and received an 18-month prison term. Gill was not retried for murder but was sentenced to six years for his role in the obstruction scandal.

While in jail awaiting trial, Johal met and befriended a man named Bal Buttar. Johal assessed the 150-pound Buttar and started feeding him steroids and encouraging him to work out. Soon, Buttar was a 250-pound monster, able and willing to knock out just about anyone. The two became so close, in fact, that Johal offered Buttar a leadership role in the Indo-Canadian Mafia. Buttar recalled to a reporter, "When I was in jail with Bindy, Bindy told me, 'You are going to be the one underneath me. You listen to me. If you take care of things at your end, I'll be happy with you, brother. If you fuck me over, I'll kill you. Right?'" He then told Buttar about a crew he had assembled called the Elite. They were five Indo-Canadian Mafia members whose job it was to assassinate Johal's enemies.

After both Johal and Buttar were released, they went to work. They started with extortion and debt collection before getting back into trafficking. On October 26, 1996, Johal's close friend, Roman "Danny" Mann, was buying two kilos of cocaine from Randy Chan. After he sampled it, he declared it impotent, watered down with baby powder or some other adulterant. Angered by the perceived attempt to swindle him, Mann forced Chan outside and into his car. Perhaps suddenly aware he had made a big mistake—Randy was younger brother of Lotus Gang member Raymond Chan and well connected—Mann drove his hostage to Johal's house. Undaunted, Johal quickly came up with a plan. He called Raymond Chan and went into negotiations. Raymond played tough—Randy was in their hands for 56 hours in total—but when Johal shoved his little brother into the trunk of his car and drove him around Vancouver while negotiating over the phone, Raymond relented. It was finally decided that Randy's life was worth five kilos of coke.

After that, Johal started settling some old scores. The first to die was Amarjit Singh Dheil. As he left the Marpole-Oakridge Community Centre after a floor hockey game with friends on January 19, 1997, Dheil was gunned down. Johal believed he had been in cahoots with the Dosanjh brothers.

Buttar began to notice that Johal used the Elite for his own purposes, almost at his whims, and not always for the overall strategic plan. On October 21, 1997, Gorinder Singh Khun Khun was shot and killed as he was exiting his home. Khun Khun had been an old friend of Johal's, dating back to the Tupper days, but Johal was convinced he was involved in the blundered assassination attempt that had killed Olson. On July 1, 1998, Johal ordered Buttar to arrange for the Elite to kill another old friend, Vinuse News MacKenzie, saying that he had been holding out from the organization. Buttar went ahead but had a sneaking suspicion that the real reason MacKenzie died was because a certain girl Johal fancied actually preferred MacKenzie.

Those killings disturbed Buttar, but the one that really turned him around was that of Derek Chand Shankar. Buttar sincerely liked Shankar, a good kid and a solid earner, and when they went out clubbing on September 19, 1998, they called Johal to come and join them. But the boss begged off, saying he was too tired. Shankar, already drunk, called Johal an "idiot" and a "baby," and mocked him for not being willing to have a few drinks with his crew. Johal snapped, reminding Shankar who he was talking to. A few hours later, Johal showed up at the nightclub with his old pal Mann and asked where Shankar was. Buttar told him he was sleeping in his truck. Johal suggested they go for a drive. Buttar could not gather the courage to oppose him. The men drove under New Westminster's Queensborough Bridge, a few yards from the salvage yard where the Chana murder took place. Throughout the trip Buttar kept telling Johal that Shankar was just a drunk kid and that he didn't mean any harm. They stopped under the bridge. Johal shot the barely conscious Shankar. Buttar briefly considered killing Johal then and there, but instead helped him throw Shankar's corpse into the cold Fraser River.

But Johal was hardly the only source of violence in the Indian Canadian community. A friend of his, Vikash Chand, was told he could get a free stolen car to chop up for parts if he met some guys he knew at Rags to Riches Motorcars in Burnaby on the afternoon of October 7, 1998. When he arrived, a meticulously planned assassination was put into effect that resulted in Shane Shoemaker (who was paid $7,000) shooting and killing Chand while he was screwing a stolen license plate onto the car he had been promised. As planned and rehearsed, Shoemaker then ran to a minivan driven by his friend Haddi Binhamad, who spirited the shooter away to what they thought was safety.

They would have gotten away with it, too, if it hadn't been for a sharp-eyed witness who reported the license plate number of the minivan, which belonged to Binhamad's mom. Caught, Binhamad traded testimony for immunity. He confessed he had tried to kill Chand a couple of times before but had failed, and had been given the gun by George Wafsi, the mastermind behind the assassination. Binhamad later gave the gun to

Shoemaker. Chand was a drug dealer supplied by Wafsi and had run up some major debts with him.

On November 29, one of Johal's oldest friends, Mann, told him he wanted out of the gang. It was just too dangerous, he said. Johal punched him in the face, cutting his lip. Later, Mann's body, with a single bullet wound to the back of the head, was found in a vacant industrial lot in Burnaby not far from the Queensborough Bridge. When Buttar asked about what had happened and what he was going to do about it, Johal told him, "Blame it on the HA [Hells Angels]." Then he asked Buttar if he wanted to go out clubbing that night.

A few weeks later, the pair did go out. They were headed down Scott Road in Delta to a club in Surrey when Johal pulled a surprise 180-degree turn. A cop saw them and turned on his lights. As the police car approached, Johal showed Buttar a gun, which surprised Buttar because he knew the boss rarely carried a weapon. Buttar convinced Johal to hide the gun, but the cop saw it and called for backup. Johal told Buttar to say it was his gun, to take the blame and the jail time. Buttar agreed, but not out of loyalty. He realized that Johal had to go. Johal had lost it. He was killing innocent kids like Shankar, and even his best friends like Mann. Buttar knew he could persuade the Elite to kill the boss, and he knew that being behind bars would be the perfect alibi. He rationalized the order to himself by the belief that if he did not kill Johal, Johal would soon kill him.

Johal was partying at the Palladium nightclub at 4:30 in the morning of December 20, 1998. A lone gunman approached him on the dance floor and shot him in the back of the head at extremely close range. Despite the presence of about 350 revelers in the club at the time, not a single person came forward to describe the assailant.

The death of Bindy Johal did not end the violence in Vancouver's Indian community. In fact, bloodshed increased as the gangsters underwent a Balkanization process, as the Indo-Canadian Mafia splintered into bitter factions.

• • •

And that was the Vancouver the Bacon Brothers grew up in. It was a place with spectacular wealth just blocks from ridiculous poverty. It was a place with almost unprecedented diversity that had self-segregated itself into a set of insular, paranoid communities. It was a place with plenty of idealists and entrepreneurs—and lots of people who were prepared to take advantage of them. It was also a place in which organized crime was based on ethnicity. But that was about to change.

CHAPTER 3

UNITED NATIONS: 1997–2001

Times were changing. The old models of who associated with whom were breaking down. Ethnicities began to stop self-segregating as the children and grandchildren of immigrants started hanging out with anybody they liked, regardless of where their families came from.

One of the people who grew up thinking that ethnicity was a lot less important than friendship and shared experience was James Coulter. He had it rough growing up in the Lower Mainland, but nothing like the kids he saw in Central America. When he was sent down south, he was appalled at the conditions in which the people there lived. He knew why they were so bad off, and he knew he was part of it. He saw how their economy, their culture, their families and any sense of normality they had were ruined by the drug trade. It was enough to make him give it all up. The money, the cars, the clothes, the friends: he would miss it all, and he knew there was no way he could have gotten it without being a gangster. But he just didn't want to be part of something that was ruining so many lives all over the world.

While not as rough as those of the kids he saw in Latin America, Coulter certainly had a disadvantaged start in life. He came from a family with severe addiction issues. In fact, when Coulter was born, his heroin-addicted teen mother, Bobbi Smoker, was in prison, and his father, also a drug user, was absent. Smoker admits that both she and Coulter's father robbed banks, even though that's not what she was behind bars for. Corrections Canada let Coulter's mother keep him until he was 6 months old, and then he was taken to a foster home. He was handed from foster home to foster home until his mother earned the right to get him back when he was 5. But their home life was far from ideal, and she lost custody of him again when he was 12. Coulter says his mother was abusive; Smoker denies that, saying Coulter liked foster families because they spent more money on him. Over the next three years, he was again shuffled from one foster home to another—15 of them. Tired of them, he struck out on his own at just 15 years old.

By his early 20s, he was leading a dissolute life. He had moved to Abbotsford in 1996 and was running through a series of dead-end jobs, including cooking at a Keg restaurant and manning the kill room at a Lilydale poultry processing plant, before settling in at a warehouse. He liked to party and would go to nightclubs and raves as often as he could. Many of the friends he met there were involved in the drug trade, and he quickly came to admire them and their wealth. "I just got caught up," he said. "I started hanging out with kids with nice cars. And you know, they would go to the gym in the day, and that really conflicted with my warehouse hours. And they had a couple of jobs here or there for me, and they would say, 'Hey, do you want to learn how to grow [marijuana]? Do a week of work, and you'll get a couple of grand.'"

Before long, he found himself selling the weed his grower friends supplied, and eventually, he moved up the dealer food chain. At the very beginning of 1997, at a rave in Chilliwack, some friends introduced him to a big guy with tattoos named Clayton Roueche. He wasn't handsome, but he was very charismatic and always surrounded by lots of friends.

A little older than Coulter, Roueche came from more settled surroundings. His dad, Rupert "Rip" Roueche, owned a scrapyard and metal recycling business in Chilliwack that he told people made in excess of $1 million annually. He also said that he planned to hand it over to his son when he retired. Clayton graduated from high school in 1993 and went through a variety of retail sales jobs before becoming a sales manager. He gathered his resources to fulfill his dream of opening a restaurant, but it was unsuccessful and soon closed.

The two hit it off and became close friends. Even after everything that happened, Coulter would always hold Roueche in high regard. In fact, Roueche showed him a type of tough love that had been missing in Coulter's life when he stayed with him through the horrible withdrawal symptoms Coulter suffered when kicking his drug habit.

Coulter and Roueche also became business partners. Roueche had been in the drug trade for a long time. The first time he came to police attention was back in 1994, when he was 18. He paid a visit to a known drug trafficking house in Chilliwack, and the police questioned him. They reported that he was cooperative, even friendly, and showed them a recent tattoo on his back that he said read "blood brothers forever" in Chinese characters. They had nothing to charge him with and let him go.

By the time he met Coulter in 1997, Roueche had access to all kinds of drugs, much better drugs than Coulter could get on his own. And he always had tons of cash and admirers. But Roueche also had a steady girlfriend, later his wife; he was helping her raise her son from a previous relationship and was eager to start a family of his own. His girlfriend happened to have an uncle who was reputedly very well-connected with the highest reaches of Vancouver's Asian gangs.

That would explain why Roueche had access to seemingly infinite amounts of high-quality drugs, while Coulter's other friends were small time. Because of the Hells Angels' drive to monopolize the drug trade on the Lower Mainland, the best anyone outside their circle could usually hope for was a small amount of weed, furtively grown by another friend desperate to stay under the bikers' radar. Growers and dealers who did not kick a portion of profits up to the Hells Angels could expect violence until they did. And that intolerance for others in the trade was hardly limited to growers; even street-level dealers who did not cooperate could expect a visit from someone working on the bikers' behalf.

Although they had a great time partying night after night, not everything was as idyllic for all of Coulter's friends. They were hardly the only group attending the nightclubs and raves on the Lower Mainland. Most groups of friends, even gangs, had always done their best to keep the peace, let everyone have a good time and a share of the market. In those days, with a few exceptions, Indians hung with Indians, Vietnamese with Vietnamese, and everyone else with "their own kind." And that's also usually whom they sold to.

But things were changing. Second- and third-generation immigrants were far more likely to hang out with and befriend people of other ethnicities. And if the Korean kids had the best connections for ecstasy or some white guy was plugged into a steady weed supply, the power of economics would eventually overcome any fear of outsiders or racism. Everyone's money was the same color.

But there was one group who didn't want the old ways to change. The Hells Angels were on the top of the heap, and they sold to anyone. But they did not include everyone in their ranks. Although the organization tends to be coy about it, everyone in the Lower Mainland knew that you had to be white to get into the Hells Angels. Historically, there has never been a non-white full-patch Hells Angel (although there is a persistent rumor of one in London's East End, he has yet to show himself if he exists). Their supporters will eagerly point to Greg "Picasso" Wooley as an example of how a non-white can be a Hells Angel, but he is actually a good indicator that one cannot. Wooley, born in Haiti and black, was an outstanding soldier for the Montreal Hells Angels. He made millions selling drugs for them, he beat dozens of people up for them, and even allegedly killed some. He was best friends with the notorious Maurice "Mom" Boucher, and could be seen at every party and event thrown by the Hells Angels. But he never spent a single day wearing the winged skull. Despite all he had done, despite his connections, his wealth and his obvious capability, Wooley was barred from the club because of the color of his skin. Instead, he was made president of the Rockers, a Laval-based puppet club who did the Hells Angels' dirty work for them. And he was the only non-white Rocker. Notably, Wooley's previous gang experience came with Master B, which was all black; and Boucher's was with the SS, which was not only all-white, but avowedly racist.

From time to time, Hells Angels members and supporters will argue that their club is not all-white, but nobody has ever shown me a full-patch or prospect Hells Angel who was black or Asian. It doesn't really matter if someone ever did produce evidence of a non-white Hells Angel, and not just because he would represent just one of several thousand, but because my opinion or theirs doesn't actually matter in this context. The fact is that every kid in the Lower Mainland in the late 1990s knew that non-whites had no chance to be Hells Angels there.

But lots of white kids did think they had a chance, and they did what they could to prove their worth. They sold drugs (kicking much of the profit upstairs), collected debts, and intimidated witnesses—anything they could to catch the eye of a full-patch member who might one day sponsor them. It's a fool's game, of course, to risk your freedom and life for a chance at illegal riches, but it's one with no shortage of players, especially back then.

You saw them everywhere. Some kids called them Hells Angels or, more often, just Hells or HA, but they were not actually Hells Angels. Nor were they prospects or even hang-arounds. In fact, it would be a stretch even to call them associates. They were wannabes—kids who believed if they showed enough toughness and cunning, they would get picked for a shot at the big time. The Hells Angels and the kids themselves called them "support crews."

They were easy to spot. They wore what the clubs call support gear. Because the Hells Angels forbid non-members from wearing their logo or name, the alternative is to wear clothing with the phrase "Support 81." The clothes—mostly T-shirts and hoodies—are sold by the Hells Angels and indicate the wearer's affiliation to the club. These clothes are almost invariably black, with the text and any images in the Hells Angels' familiar red and white.

And, since they were aligned with the top dogs, the support crews had a sense of entitlement. Being a member of a support crew conferred certain powers and privileges. It wasn't merely because they were a largely tough group of young men who traveled in packs, but it was also because it was hard to tell how connected any of them were. If you had a dispute that culminated in a fight, under normal circumstances, you could expect it to end there or your opponent might bring back some of his buddies to try to win back some credibility. But—accurate or not—the belief among many in the club scene on the Lower Mainland was that if you messed with a support crew member, you were taking on the Hells Angels and could wind up at the bottom of Burrard Inlet.

It was a reputation that was not just well earned, but well publicized. A videotape of an East Vancouver Chapter associate and dealer named Anthony "Big Tony" Terezakis torturing a debtor was discovered after his arrest. In it, an addict known as Tommy sits on a filthy couch as Terezakis—a huge, ugly man covered in tattoos and wearing a massive gold crucifix—asks him for his money. When Tommy (who was high at the time) demurs, Terezakis pummels him with his fists and repeated kicks to the head. All the while, Terezakis is spitting on Tommy and repeatedly shouting, "Praise the Lord!" Later, Terezakis claimed that the tape was part of a reality-show idea he had called *Bible Thumpers.*

It was also revealed at about that time that Mickie "Phil" Smith, a former insurance salesman turned contract killer, had been contacted by a mysterious Asian businessman named Brian who hired him to kill a man for the East Vancouver chapter of the Hells Angels. The man in question was Paul Percy Soluk, a 33-year-old who made the mistake of stealing from a Hells Angels–associated grow op. Smith quickly located his prey in a Downtown Eastside crack house and forced him into his car. Smith drove Soluk to an empty garage and shot him dead. Smith testified at his trial that he then called a man called Yurik to help him chop up the body and dispose of it. When the Crown asked if Yurik was a Hells Angel, Smith replied, "He's not an Angel, but he works with the Angels. I know he's done lots of hits."

While that news may have made the general public more aware of the Hells Angels reach and ferocity, anybody already involved with the drug trade already knew that crossing the Hells Angels was extremely dangerous and often meant a death sentence. The support crews had no compunction about taking advantage of that fear and used it to intimidate and belittle anybody who got in their way or even crossed their path. The majority of the guys Coulter and Roueche hung out with were East Asian—Chinese and Vietnamese. Coulter and Roueche sincerely admired their cultures, particularly martial arts, which they both practiced. The Asians among their little group were often physically slight and frequently found themselves targets of bullying and intimidation from members of support crews.

But it was more than just friction over dance-floor space at the nightclub. The Hells Angels are very intolerant of other people selling drugs in their territory. While not all support crew members sold drugs for the Hells Angels, it was expected that they would at least report any unauthorized drug sales they saw and, if possible, put the offending dealer out of business.

Many young club-goers on the Lower Mainland took ecstasy. Also known as "X" or by its scientific name, "MDMA," ecstasy was originally a clinical drug used to fight depression. It became popular—first in gay clubs, where it was known as "adam" or the "no-calorie martini"—in the 70s and was outlawed in most countries, beginning with the United States in 1985. Increasingly popular, ecstasy gives the user a euphoric feeling mixed with heightened confidence and a feeling of goodwill toward others. It became synonymous with all-night parties and raves in the 90s.

In truth, ecstasy is not seen as one of the more dangerous illicit drugs. Its potential for user dependence is fairly low (about on par with marijuana and lower than caffeine), and overdoses are very rare. The big problem with ecstasy as a recreational drug is its purity. Unlike most other recreational drugs, ecstasy must be manufactured in technically advanced laboratory conditions and is consequentially rare and costly. To overcome that, many dealers adulterate their ecstasy pills with similar-looking powdered substances like ibuprofen, caffeine, and even baby powder. As an illegal, non-regulated product, ecstasy pills may have as little as 1 percent MDMA or even none at all. In order to give the pills a little kick, dealers will often substitute for MDMA with another, cheaper active ingredient—methamphetamine. Unlike MDMA, meth can be made anywhere by just about anyone. It can give the user similar euphoric feelings but with an aggressive element and, perhaps more important, is one of the most addictive of all illegal drugs. Since meth, and cutting ecstasy with meth, were (and are) both rampant on the Lower Mainland, it's very likely that many of Coulter's friends had taken meth at least occasionally.

Few of the club kids had legitimate sources of income, and even those who did often supported their drug, fashion and party habits by selling drugs. Most of them started in high school, distributing weed to their friends for a few bucks, but by the late 90s, they were supporting their relatively hedonistic lifestyles selling weed, ecstasy and crack in Lower Mainland nightclubs. In a move eerily reminiscent of how a group of drug dealers in Montreal—sick of the Hells Angels' attempts to monopolize the drug market there—banded together to form the Dark Circle (which aligned with the Rock Machine, starting the Quebec Biker War) in 1991, Coulter, Roueche and their friends in May 1997 formed a gang they called the United Nations.

Roueche was firmly in charge and modeled the UN after his own beliefs and ideals. The gang's motto was "Honor, Loyalty, Respect." Members used the phrase when addressing one another and were also expected to have it tattooed on their bodies, usually in Chinese characters. "I liked honor, loyalty and respect. I thought those were good virtues," Coulter said. "You honor your family, you respect others—you treat others the way you want to be treated."

Eastern mysticism (which fascinated Roueche) was a key factor in almost all parts of the United Nations. The standard uniform was a hoodie bedecked with East Asian–style imagery like tigers and dragons, and jewelry with similar images or the gang's motto. Members were required to learn and practice mixed martial arts, especially kickboxing and jiujitsu. And Roueche developed some rituals based on Buddhist and Shinto practices that he performed on special occasions.

Using the template so historically effective with outlaw biker gang tradition, the United Nations had a set hierarchy and a strict set of rules. Punishments for breaking club rules were usually group beatings, with the accused returning to good standing once the beating was complete.

Before long, the United Nations was a cohesive group, with members hanging out together at nightclubs, particularly Animals in Abbotsford. Coulter appreciated the group as a surrogate family. "You go to a club with 20, 30, 40 guys, and as soon as you get there, you give hugs to everyone. It is like a family, right?" he said. "And that is something I never had. I never had a family. So that was my family."

As much as it was like a family, the United Nations was also like a corporation. There was money to be made, and everybody had his job. Coulter's was as an enforcer or, as he prefers, "mediator." When someone had a problem—usually about money—with the club, Coulter was one of the members who would be sent to straighten things out. To facilitate this, he started taking his first drugs stronger than weed, steroids. With them and daily visits to the gym, he eventually packed 220 well-muscled pounds on his formerly slight five-foot-ten frame.

By 2000, bigger trouble was in store. One Friday night, while the United Nations were partying at Animals (the club later renamed itself the Luxor before going bankrupt after a license suspension), they noticed a few Hells Angels support crew in their midst. It's very unlikely they were there by accident. The Hells Angels, particularly in Canada, are notoriously intolerant of drug dealers in their territory, and the UN was beginning to make a name for itself in trafficking circles.

Usually, the presence of a few muscular young men in Support 81 gear is enough to scare off opponents, or at least get them to start negotiating. But the United Nations did not knuckle under as so many had before. After a brief scuffle, the support crew guys were turfed. Coulter, who admits his memory of those days is hazy at times, distinctly recalled them yelling back, "You guys are dead! We're coming back next week."

So the United Nations leadership rallied the membership. The next Friday night, there were about 70 members of the United Nations at Animals, all ready to fight for control of the nightclub. Before long, about 15 support crew guys showed up.

Assessing the situation, they called for reinforcements. Coulter distinctly recalls hearing one shouting into his cellphone, "There are a bunch of Asians here and a bunch of guys here, and they started shit with us." Reinforcements did indeed come, some from as far away as Haney, but there were only 30 or so of them. Badly outnumbered, the support crew stood their ground, probably thinking the Hells Angels' violent reputation would prevent a brawl.

It didn't. Coulter recalls the melee:

> I'll never forget. There was the big fight inside. It lasted maybe five minutes. Then everyone started running outside. I remember I came out the front doors, and there were probably about five or six different fights happening out on the street. And I seen an Abbotsford police officer pull up, and he gets out of his car and he's on his walkie-talkie and he's like: "There's HA! There are fights everywhere!" It was like he had never seen anything like this before. Nor had I.

When the dust cleared, the support crew were gone. The United Nations had won. But it was more than just a bar fight they had won. It was their right to exist, their right to sell drugs in the Lower Mainland without paying the Hells Angels. It was, as history has pointed out time and again, a dangerous position to be in.

• • •

Richard Shatto saw Roueche's rise in power from a great vantage point—right next door. The consultant was at home one day in 1998 when an elderly Vietnamese couple dropped by. They introduced themselves and told him they had just bought the house next door for their children.

Shatto didn't think much of it but was quite charmed by the couple's daughter and her 2-year-old girl. "She was just the cutest thing," he said. "And so nice."

But things started to change as more people moved into the house, including the daughter's boyfriend and father of her little girl, Clayton Roueche. Clayton, the only one of the group who was not Vietnamese, "floated in and out," according to Shatto, and kept mainly to himself. He wasn't rude or standoffish, he just didn't go out of his way to make friends with the neighbors.

Things started to change very quickly at the house: bigger, better vehicles, numerous home renovations (including a 10-foot-long aquarium), and two massive Neapolitan mastiff puppies imported from Italy. Those changes and frequent interruptions with electricity led Shatto to believe the couple were running a grow op in the house. Grow ops are common in the area, and most people know to look for certain signs— young people with excessive, quick wealth, massive electrical consumption, guard dogs, and lots and lots of young visitors.

And then the parties started. Roueche's house was constantly being visited. There was a steady stream of guests and well wishers who invariably dressed alike. "They wore black and white with white bandannas," Shatto said. "When they were going out to a club or a party, they always wore black or white fedoras." They all had fancy SUVs or "souped-up sport cars." Often, when they would go out partying, they would all ride together in a limousine.

When they partied at home, they partied loud and late, with lots of drinking and sex. One day, his interest was piqued when he saw an unmarked trailer parked in front of the Roueche house. There was one of their more raucous parties that night. Shatto stayed up to see what was going on. At about one in the morning, the music stopped, and Roueche shouted, "Let's go!"

At his command, the partygoers marched out of the house single file and approached the now-open trailer. Each person took a single item (Shatto could not make out precisely what they were) from the trailer and carried it back into the house. Convinced the strange parade had something to do with the grow op, Shatto called the Abbotsford police. "If you come right now," he told them, "you can catch them in the act." They didn't come.

In fact, several people had called the police about goings-on at the Roueche house, but the police never showed up. Discouraged, Shatto started to do his own investigating. He first warned his own kids to keep an eye out for the people who lived at and visited the house and report anything odd they saw there. Then he spent a lot of time watching the house on his own, collecting the license plate numbers of everyone who visited.

Oddly, Shatto had heard Roueche's name in the news and read it in the paper, but he had never matched it to the guy next door.

The police refused to visit, and most neighbors did their best to avoid confrontation. On one occasion, a neighbor—who Shatto said was a former member of the band Loverboy and hated drug dealers because he worked with kids whose brains had been affected by drugs—confronted them. The youngsters threatened him but eventually backed down. When someone later broke the mirror off the neighbor's car, Roueche's girlfriend visited a number of neighbors, including Shatto, to apologize for what her friends had done.

After about three years, a "For Sale" sign went up for one day (probably to gauge the house's worth), and about a week later, Roueche's girlfriend told Shatto that they had sold the house to a friend for cash. The new couple had much less in the way of obvious wealth and acted nervous and afraid. The man lost his rather modest car and then his motorcycle. The couple began arguing loudly enough for Shatto to hear. "They'd scream things like, 'We're dead now,'" he said. Then one day they just ran, returning a month later to tell Shatto and some other neighbors that they had been foreclosed on and that if there was anything inside that they wanted, they could have it.

Shatto entered the house out of curiosity and saw how drug dealers live. There were holes in the walls for ventilation and a hidden trap door to the basement since the stairs had been blocked off and built over. More chilling, however, was something he found in the front closet—a baseball bat embedded with about 200 drywall screws. "It looked like some kind of medieval weapon," he said.

• • •

It was around this time that another new multiethnic Vancouver gang took shape. For their part in the murder of their alleged tormentor Richard Jung, teenagers Michael Le and Eddie Narong, who in half a dozen years would find themselves in suite 1505 at the Balmoral, were sentenced to the notorious and now repurposed Willingdon Youth Detention Centre. If the hope was to rehabilitate them, it was in vain. The two remained close for mutual protection and also made a number of new friends with serious drug connections.

Though still just teenagers, Le and Narong collected their new group and presented them with a plan. They would form a new gang. It would be multiethnic (though predominantly Southeast Asian), have the same hierarchy and rules as an outlaw motorcycle gang, and embrace Eastern philosophies and martial arts, and members would be identified by a tattoo on their wrist or neck. And, in a move that could only have come from teenagers, the name of the club was to be the Red Scorpions.

It's unclear whether they were aware of the success of the United Nations or not, but their blueprint was remarkably similar. And it set them on a course that would lead to all-out gang warfare on the streets of the Lower Mainland.

• • •

Although the brawl at Animals had established the United Nations as a force to be reckoned with, the streets of the Lower

Mainland were still a very dangerous place for individual dealers, especially those not affiliated with the Hells Angels. To combat this, the United Nations came up with a simple, yet very effective, strategy. Called "dial-a-dope" by the cops and media, the plan limited the amount of exposure dealers and their employees had to law enforcement and rivals.

An associate would go to a nightclub or bar and hand out cards, much the same way promoters do for concerts and other special events. The cards would then be marked with a name chosen by the local distributor—one well-known one was "Dark Alley"—and a telephone number. The numbers led to prepaid cellphones, which were changed every three to four weeks to escape detection. The phones would be answered by the distributor or another associate and the order taken. Then another associate would deliver the drugs to the customer.

It was so effective that it was widely imitated. By 2003, there were dozens of competing dial-a-dope lines in the Lower Mainland. Of course, any plan is only as good as its talent, and many less careful and sophisticated dial-a-dope operations quickly attracted the attention of law enforcement and, even worse for them, rival dealers. Usually, it was only the delivery guy who'd get caught, and if the distributor could depend on him to keep quiet and even take one for the team, the operation could survive.

And that's why the fanatic loyalty Roueche instilled in the members of the United Nations (as Le and Narong would later among the Red Scorpions) proved essential to their survival.

● ● ●

Later, yet another gang was forming in response to the stranglehold the Hells Angels and their allies held over the drug trade on the Lower Mainland. At first, it was just a bunch of Indian Canadian (mostly Sikh) friends who hung out at the Sunset Community Centre and Sunset Park. They began to get into the usual amount of trouble boys that age do. They had spray-painted walls, gotten into fights, gotten drunk, and smoked weed. The Sunset Boys, as they came to be known, were considered small-time until they gained the notice of some of their old idols—the surviving members of Bindy Johal's old Indo-Canadian Mafia.

Connections with these older, more established gangsters didn't just give the Sunset Boys jobs to do and drugs to sell, but it also emboldened them.

Unlike so many other gangs of young men who met their idols and, out of awe or fear, yielded to become their vassals, the Sunset Boys dealt with the Indo-Canadian Mafia if not as equals, then at least as independent contractors. In fact, as the Sunset Boys matured as an organization, they assumed the name "The Independent Soldiers."

• • •

And it was into this environment that a family moved from Edmonton. The father, David Bacon, was a special education teacher who had recently been hired by the Abbotsford School District. His wife, Susan, quickly found a job as manager of property and premises for Prospera Credit Union, meaning she was responsible for the Abbotsford-based company's maintenance staff. They appeared to be a typical middle-class Canadian couple who (like many others) came to the Lower Mainland for its climate, physical beauty and financial opportunities.

And they brought three boys with them: Jonathan David (born in 1981), Jarrod (1983) and James Kyle "Jamie" (1986). I managed to speak with two women who knew Jonathan, though not well, at Abbotsford's W.J. Mouat Secondary School. Neither wants her name published because both still live in Abbotsford, and as one said, she knew how brutal it could be for people who talked. For the purposes of the book, let's call them Stephanie and Amy.

Stephanie described Jonathan as popular, with a number of friends. Other published reports from high school contemporaries have called him "normal," as being "well liked" and even "mild mannered." Amy agreed, saying that it did not seem to her as though Jonathan had any one particular best friend, but that he was always with a group of kids.

Amy said that she and most of the girls she knew considered him decent-looking, if not actually handsome, and that Jonathan was not very big, though athletic. Mouat is a school that takes its sports very seriously, and Jonathan simply did not have the size to compete in football or basketball. They were surprised, both said, that he went into wrestling and even succeeded. But since wrestling is a sport divided into weight classes, Jonathan's overall lack of size was negated because he would only face guys his own weight.

Amy, who lived close to the Bacons' first Abbotsford residence, noted that they seemed like a normal enough family and were considered fortunate to have both parents living at home and enough money to go around. She was "vaguely aware of" Jonathan's younger brothers and knew that both were considered "bad news" in the neighborhood, despite their youth.

Both women noted that charming, personable Jonathan became a little less open, friendly and polite as he advanced through school. "It's not like he became mean and nasty, or like a bully or anything," said Amy. "It's just that he became less friendly, more of a tough guy." Stephanie agreed, and added that as Jonathan gradually changed, he started running around with a different group of friends. "They were older, some of them in their 20s," she said. "They all had cars and expensive stuff like jewelry and watches. When [Jonathan] started to hang out with them, he started acting like them, talking like them, dressing like them." When I asked if any of Jonathan's new friends had tattoos, Stephanie said that many of them did "and that wasn't anywhere near as common back then." When I asked them if they ever saw any tattoos that said "UN" or "Honour, Loyalty, Respect," neither could remember specifically, but Amy did remember that many of them, including non-Asians, had tattoos made up of "Chinese writing."

Neither woman could definitively say if they knew Jonathan was involved in the drug trade while in high school, but both had their suspicions. "When you see a kid start to have more money all of a sudden," said Stephanie, "You immediately figure it's drugs."

Jonathan graduated from W.J. Mouat in 1999 and did not attend college. He did, however, get into trouble quickly. He was arrested in 2000 for possession of a controlled substance and again in 2001 for possession of stolen goods with a value of less than $5,000. For each conviction, he spent one day in prison.

Although Jonathan's criminality was clearly emerging, his younger brothers were not quite as well-mannered, polite and polished as he was; especially Jamie, the youngest.

In 2001, the family moved into a far ritzier neighborhood in Abbotsford. The house—at 35475 Strathcona Court—was massive, with seven bedrooms. A colleague of David Bacon's told me that it was a topic of conversation at school as to how a special-ed teacher and a maintenance manager could afford such an impressive home.

Jarrod, 18 at the time of the move, and Jamie, 15, were enrolled in nearby Yale Secondary School. Like Jonathan, Jamie was an accomplished high school wrestler. But unlike Jonathan, Jamie was huge and had the requisite mean streak to put him on top. In 2002, he wrestled in the 84-kilo (185-pound) class, moving up to 110 kilos (242 pounds) the following year, and winning the provincial high school championship.

But while Jonathan may have been remembered as a popular kid who began to hang out with a rough crowd, Jarrod and Jamie actually were the rough crowd. Stephanie, Jonathan's contemporary from W.J. Mouat, remembered Jarrod well. "He was a tough guy, pushing his weight around," she said. "While Jonathan could be quite charming at times, Jarrod was more like a thug. My little brother and all his friends would avoid him at all costs. They were scared of him."

As with Jonathan and W.J. Mouat, the people who knew Jamie from Yale and agreed to be quoted for this book did not want their names used. Andrea and Christine attended school with Jamie and remember him as aggressive and boorish. "He was a jerk," said Andrea. "I never liked him. At that age, lots of guys can be immature, but Jamie was mean; like, over the top, like he seemed to enjoy pissing other people off." Christine has similar recollections. "I couldn't believe it when I heard he was a teacher's son," she said. "He was disruptive in class and seemed not to care at all about the work."

But both admitted that he was, in his own way, popular. "Oh yeah, he had a whole bunch of kids who hung around with him, like an entourage," said Andrea. "He totally influenced them. They would dress like him and act like him. One day he called someone a 'knob,' then all his friends started calling each other 'knobs.' It was like that. He would do something, and they would all follow suit."

Christine pointed out that Jamie always had lots of money and flaunted the affectations of wealth. "He always had new fancy things, like clothes and jewelry, and he had a car when he was very young—a big car, an expensive one." I asked her if she knew how he got all that money, if he had a job or not, and she told me: "I just assumed it was drugs."

Not long after moving to the big house on Strathcona, Jamie got into trouble. At the age of just 15, on May 12, 2001, he was arrested for assault. This subsequently came out in court when he was tried as an adult, but details of the incident and trial have not been made public.

But the Bacons were still very small-time compared to some of the bad dudes out there—bad dudes who would eventually become their friends and business partners.

PART II

THE PATH TO WAR

While in Vancouver, I always listened to a lot of talk radio because a lot of it was about crime. The consensus among the experts and the callers alike was that the root cause of crime was economic and social disadvantage. The thinking is that if we, as a society, give youth career and leisure-time activities, they will choose a different path.

There is good logic behind this idea, and even some real-world evidence to back it up. It's a well-documented fact that a lack of realistic or desirable career opportunities can very easily make a young man or woman seriously consider crime as a career option. And strict schools, cooperative employment and programs like midnight basketball have done wonders in poor, crime-ridden neighborhoods in the United States.

But like all conventional wisdom, it's a half-truth at best. While the factors people normally associate with disadvantaged upbringings can indeed make a career outside the law an appealing option, that does not mean that if we could get every at-risk youth a job and something to do in their free time, we would have a society free of crime. Crime becomes attractive to a larger number of people as the profits gets higher and the risks become lower. A perfect example of this occurred in Canada in 1994. The Jean Chretien Liberal government passed a massive tax increase on the price of cigarettes. Hundreds of Canadians reacted by smuggling cigarettes over the border from the United States. While much of the smuggling was limited to people hiding cartons in their cars and not declaring them to customs, a group of professional smugglers emerged almost immediately. Many of them were ordinary Canadians who just saw a chance to make a quick buck. They would buy cigarettes in bulk over the border (often from tax-free Native American reservations), then spirit them over the St. Lawrence, Niagara or Detroit Rivers in speedboats under the cover of darkness. It became so common that law enforcement was compelled to act. In response, the smugglers began to arm themselves, and occasional firefights took place. They also attracted the attention of organized crime—particularly outlaw motorcycle gangs—who provided them with vehicles, distribution, contacts and weapons. It was a billion-dollar industry almost overnight.

The situation was out of hand. Later in the year, the Chretien government repealed the tax in hopes of curbing the rampant and increasingly dangerous smuggling epidemic and to get back the tax revenue they were losing. By their own estimates, the federal government admitted that 70 percent of all cigarettes sold in Quebec and 35 percent in Ontario had been smuggled in from the United States.

What was remarkable about that debacle was how quickly ordinary Canadians were willing to break the law when their idea of how expensive a cigarette should be was challenged. And it wasn't just the smugglers, but also the consumers who knew what they were doing was illegal.

A similar analogy can be observed in the advent of Apple's iTunes Store. Before the iTunes Store, people downloaded songs illegally because they believed that it was not worth paying a record company $20 for a CD when all they wanted was one song. There were risks associated from malware and other nasty things from the Internet (and a more vague threat from law enforcement), but millions started doing it, claiming that they were only getting back at a recording industry that had been stealing from them for years. So when the iTunes Store came out in 2003 offering individual, legal song downloads for 99 cents, most of those same people adopted it very quickly. It did not end illegal downloads (nor did Chretien's admission of defeat stop cigarette smuggling), but it moved the mainstream user to legal downloads by providing a safe, reputable service.

The situation in British Columbia was very much like Ontario and Quebec in 1994 or the music business before 2003. There was an abundance of marijuana in the province. Everybody wanted it, and the Americans were willing to pay top dollar. The risks from law enforcement were slight (at least, north of the border).

It was a dynamic, booming industry that attracted thousands. Some, like James Coulter, came from predictably disadvantaged circumstances, but many were simply attracted to the idea of fast, easy money.

CHAPTER 4

Bumps in the Road: 2001–2004

As rough as the UN's James Coulter's youth had been, that of Red Scorpions associate Anton Brad Kornelius Hooites-Meursing may have been worse. Born to a Canadian father and Australian mother in Calgary in 1971, Hooites-Meursing was the second of three boys. As he later testified on a number of occasions, their home life was anything but idyllic. His mother, he said, was schizophrenic, prone to violent outbursts that his father would often respond to with brutality. Anton said the police visited frequently, but did little other than to tell the family to settle down.

The Hooites-Meursing family moved to Australia when Anton was still very young, then relocated to Los Angeles when he was 8. His dad set up a very successful construction business there, and the family lived on the edges of Beverly Hills. But his parents split up, and Anton lived with his mother until he was 11, when she left him a note saying that she was no longer able to take care of him and his brothers. He and his younger brother went to live in a foster home, then with some friends of the family, before moving in with his father and his new wife.

But it wasn't a happy home there, either. The father forbade the boys from talking about or communicating with their mother and made it clear he resented their presence in his new life. According to Anton, the family's fortunes took a nosedive when the IRS found that Anton's dad had not been honest on his tax returns. The ensuing garnishments and penalties drove the family into relative poverty, moving them from their enviable address to a small house on the border between Long Beach and the notorious Compton.

It was a poor, violent neighborhood, and Hooites-Meursing claims, as one of a very few white kids in the area, he was a frequent target for abuse. He quit school in the ninth grade and, with some friends, started stealing from cars before stealing the cars themselves. Like many other youth in the area, he sought the protection and camaraderie of a gang. But the dearth of white gangs in the area—they do exist in Los Angeles, but not in South-Central—led him to a Hispanic one. "I had no love or anything close at home, but rather was hated by my family and dad especially," he said. "So it was, as I look back, a natural seeking out acceptance and love which was mine to be had joining...a Mexican gang."

The following decade did not go well. At 17, he moved in with his best friend only to return from work one day to find a shot-up apartment and his friend murdered. He moved back in with his father, who by then had managed to restore his finances enough to buy a small house in Compton. But that modicum of stability did little to help young Hooites-Meursing, who spent the next few years in and out of trouble. Looking back, he called it a "decade of gladiator school in the Los Angeles County jail system, which for anybody that is white is a total nightmare."

By the time he was 29, the United States had had enough of his law-breaking ways and on December 7, 2001, deported him to Canada—a country he barely remembered. He ended up in Vancouver's Downtown Eastside.

But he was determined to start a better life in his new country. Within weeks, he managed to get two jobs—one as a data entry clerk for the British Columbia Automobile Association and another as a floor attendant for Home Depot. He used the proceeds from them to rent a small apartment in New Westminster and to enroll in a night school course that taught him to sell cars. He eventually landed a salesman job at Jim Pattison Auto Group, the largest car dealer in B.C., and claimed to be very successful at it.

Despite his deportation order, Hooites-Meursing would occasionally drive back to Los Angeles to visit his girlfriend. She was the reason, he said, that he went straight. But when she broke up with him, he was shocked, which led to depression and suicidal thoughts. In an effort to quell those feelings, Hooites-Meursing started taking ecstasy and going clubbing every opportunity he could. To afford that lifestyle—and also put his feelings for his now-ex-girlfriend behind him—he dove back into the gangster lifestyle.

It was a pretty easy transition. He knew people in Los Angeles who had money and wanted drugs, and he knew people in the Lower Mainland who had drugs and wanted more money than they could get for them in Canada. The product was high-quality BC Bud, which was like gold in the United States. At first, he did not actually export or even handle the drugs, but served as a broker, introducing interested parties to one another. He also helped friends build hydroponic marijuana grow ops.

But as is commonplace, Hooites-Meursing was attracted to the definitive life of a drug dealer—the cars, the flashy clothes, the tattoos and the guns—and he started trafficking large amounts. On regular driving trips, he would bring marijuana from Vancouver to Los Angeles in modified propane tanks and cocaine from Mexico through a Los Angeles supplier he had met in jail back the same way. When he had an excess of cocaine, he would send it to connections in Australia—who paid a much higher price—in custom-made compartments in briefcases.

He also started taking his own products. In exchange for the BC Bud he could get, his friends in Los Angeles would supply him not just with cocaine and guns, but also with steroids and more exotic drugs like Percocet and Oxycontin. It did not take long for Hooites-Meursing to become huge with muscle, and as so often is the case with steroid users, he became unpredictable and violent, earning a reputation for assaulting rivals in public and bright daylight. He specialized, he said, in disarming opponents with his bare hands, keeping their guns—three or four a month, he recalled—and, if he liked them, their watches.

Though not actually a gang member early in his career, Hooites-Meursing worked with a number of organizations and was particularly close to the then-fledgling Red Scorpions. Early in 2001, a Red Scorpions member whom Hooites-Meursing will not name asked him to kill street-level dealer Randy McLeod. Still depressed, profoundly affected by steroids and now addicted to Oxycontin, Hooites-Meursing agreed, noting to himself that it might be a good opportunity to grab some of McLeod's drugs and cash.

The conspirators agreed to meet McLeod in the parking lot of a Surrey Canadian Tire. As soon as they saw him, Hooites-Meursing grabbed the 22-year-old McLeod in a headlock and threw him into the back of a cargo van. Hooites-Meursing then held McLeod down by driving his knee into McLeod's spine and bound his hands and feet with nylon straps. They then drove to McLeod's townhouse on 66th Avenue, broke in and ransacked the place. Inside, Hooites-Meursing discovered some cocaine and heroin, and about $10,000 in cash. But it wasn't enough. Enraged, Hooites-Meursing went back to the van and began punching the helpless McLeod in the face repeatedly.

They then drove their captive to 0 Avenue—which serves as the ridiculously porous border between Canada and the United States—where Hooites-Meursing argued with the driver over the need to kill McLeod. Hooites-Meursing lost the argument and strangled the bound man, removing some of the victim's clothes that he decided could potentially be used as evidence. Once he was sure McLeod was dead, Hooites-Meursing instructed the driver to take him a few blocks north, to a wooded area away from the busier border, and disposed of the body there. It was found 11 days later, a black inch-wide nylon strap still around its neck.

Some months later, Hooites-Meursing was asked by his friend, Edward "Skeeter" Russell, a Red Scorpions member, to keep a mutual friend safe. On the night of December 22, 2002, Hooites-Meursing took the man and another friend to the Luxor nightclub. Once inside, the man Hooites-Meursing was expected to protect got into a fight with James Thiphavong, a United Nations associate. The fight expanded to include a couple of Thiphavong's brothers and their friends. The Red Scorpion whom Hooites-Meursing was protecting was hit in the forehead with a bottle and began to bleed. As the fight spilled into the parking lot, Hooites-Meursing pulled out a knife and stabbed BonLeuth Thiphavong and his brother Souskavath Thiphavong repeatedly. BonLeuth later died from his injuries.

A month after that, Anton's friend Russell was killed. The Red Scorpions believed his murder was in retaliation for the death of Thiphavong. When an audiotape of a United Nations associate named Gupreet "Bobby" Rehal talking and laughing about the planning of Russell's murder emerged, the Red Scorpions decided he must have been involved and decided to kill him. Hooites-Meursing was at the meeting and was chosen to be part of the mission.

On March 13, 2002, the conspirators stole a nondescript Honda Civic, drove to Rehal's house on Saturnia Crescent in Abbotsford and knocked on the door. Hooites-Meursing was waiting in another stolen car two blocks away. When 19-year-old Rehal answered the door, the Red Scorpions shot him in the face, then ran away to where Hooites-Meursing was parked. Rehal lingered in Royal Columbian Hospital for a few hours and died the following morning.

A close associate of Hooites-Meursing—one might even say a friend—was 24-year-old John Lahn (which was an alias for Laurent Jean-Guy Rahal). Lahn was a drug dealer operating out of the notorious Bonanza Motel, but his specialty was as the head of a home invasion squad frequently employed by the Red Scorpions. Hooites-Meursing worked for him as supplier, dealer and hired muscle.

But things were going bad for Hooites-Meursing at this point. According to Marlin "Marlo" Aburto, one of Lahn's alleged lieutenants, Lahn had intended to fire him because of his unpredictable, often violent, behavior. The last straw came at a 2003 birthday party in Victoria for another alleged Lahn lieutenant, Robert "PDog" Padley. One of the guests made a joke at Hooites-Meursing's expense. While the rest of the party was laughing, Hooites-Meursing punched the man, knocking him to the floor, then pulled out a gun, cocked it and stuck it in the man's mouth. The rest of the party convinced him to put the gun away, and Hooites-Meursing, now twice admonished, left.

Later, Lahn told Aburto and others that he was upset over the incident and that he planned to fire Hooites-Meursing. Aburto later testified that Lahn had no intention of beating up, let alone killing, Hooites-Meursing and that it was commonplace for employees and contractors of Lahn's organization to be fired without violence or further incident. Lahn set up a meeting with Hooites-Meursing in front of the Orkideh Beauty Salon, in a strip mall at the corner of 10th Avenue and 6th Street in Burnaby, where they both got their hair cut.

In the parking lot in front of the Starbucks, the two had words, which quickly escalated into a scuffle. In the struggle, Lahn was shot and died. Hooites-Meursing was arrested and charged with murder, though he claimed self-defense.

• • •

Just as the loss of the crude effectiveness of Hooites-Meursing affected the Red Scorpions' ability to do business, the United Nations had their own problems. One of their most prominent members, Jing Bon Chan, heard that his girlfriend of the last two years, Christina Hyun Oh Yoon, was stepping out on him. On August 2, 2003, he received a call informing him that a guy had just been seen entering Yoon's downtown Richmond apartment. Enraged, Chan sped to 6331 Buswell Street and ran up the stairs to Yoon's third-floor place. Inside, he found her in bed with a guy named Winston Thieu Anh Bui. Chan pulled a knife and stabbed Bui several times. Nude and bleeding, Bui ran to the balcony. In an attempt to jump his way to freedom, he lost his footing, fell and hit the pavement with his head. He was taken to a nearby hospital and placed in a medically induced coma. Chan was charged with attempted murder, possessing a prohibited firearm with ammunition and carrying a concealed weapon.

• • •

And the Hells Angels were feeling their own bumps in the road. Robert Molsberry was a big man, big enough to hold down a bouncer's job at Number 5 Orange, a notorious Downtown Eastside strip joint that has seen Italian porn star–turned–politician Ilona Staller (La Cicciolina), Hugh Hefner's wife Kimberly Conrad and singer Courtney Love perform on stage and played host to luminaries like Sylvester Stallone, Bill Murray, Charles Barkley and Wayne Gretzky. And it was popular with bikers.

Molsberry not only befriended the Hells Angels, but went into business with them. He ran an after-hours club they frequented and used as a drug-retailing store. And he started and tended a marijuana grow operation supplying the Hells Angels with product. It was a pretty lucrative deal until someone raided Molsberry's grow op, stealing all of his plants. He told his contact with the Hells Angels that he would not be able to make his ordinary shipment because of the theft. In response, the Hells Angels fined him $10,000. Without any product, he was unable to pay that—and the $1,500 he owed them for an ounce of cocaine he had been fronted earlier—on time, so they took him behind Number 5 Orange and beat him up.

That was it for Molsberry. He went to the police and offered to tell them everything he knew. "Fuck these guys," he told them. "I made them so much money over the years, and they do this to me. Well, fuck them." He agreed to become a paid informant in exchange for immunity. The investigation, called Project Breakpoint, yielded no arrests, but evidence from it led to another operation called Project Nova. In it, Molsberry made deals for cocaine with several members of the Hells Angels, and surveillance recordings determined that Hells Angels and members of the Regulators—a Burnaby-based puppet gang that had originally been a boxing club—were dealing in a variety of illegal drugs including GHB, the so-called "date-rape drug."

Just weeks after Hells Angels spokesman Rick Ciarnello appeared on a radio show and dared the police to prove they were a criminal organization, they did. A total of 76 people were arrested, many of them members and associates of the Hells Angels and the Regulators. Among the arrested were full-patch Hells Angels Francisco "Chico" Pires, Ronaldo "Ronnie" Lising and Vincenzo "Vinnie" Brienza. Also arrested was Brienza's brother, Romano, who had been president of the Regulators. He was charged with possession of a kilo of cocaine, 30 pounds of marijuana and an illegal handgun. One Hells Angels hang-around, Rob Alvarez, was arrested after police overheard him being told to remove anything potentially incriminating from Lising's house. Police also seized more than $12 million worth of drugs, cash, property and weapons.

In July 2003, police spotted full-patch Hells Angel Glen "Kingpin" Hehn and his close associate Ewan Lilford loading boxes from a Public Storage unit he had rented at 5555 192nd Street in the Cloverdale section of Surrey into a truck. They arrested the two men and found $1.5 million worth of cocaine in boxes both in the truck and the storage unit. As is often the case with Hells Angels, brotherhood broke down quickly, and both men blamed the other. Hehn said that Lilford had a key to the unit and had let himself in and that Hehn rarely used the locker himself. He had happened to come by, he said, and saw Lilford loading the boxes and decided to help him without asking what was inside them. For his part, Lilford made basically the same claim, transposing the names, and pointed out that he did not have a key on him. The police charged them both with trafficking, but they stuck to their stories at the subsequent trial.

• • •

The other major crime organization in the Lower Mainland, the Independent Soldiers, was also still gaining in prominence. Their top guys would hang out in a Gastown nightclub called Loft Six. The club had something of a past. It had been owned by Hells Angel Donald Roming, who made a name for himself in the 1990s as an enforcer when the club was taking over all the strip joints and stripper agencies in the Lower Mainland. Although he was never arrested because witnesses were always reluctant to talk, it was well known that he had brutally beaten several holdouts in the industry, including one 67-year-old man who had to be hospitalized. Roming, however, was murdered on March 9, 2001, when two men began to argue with him just before closing time at a Yaletown nightclub called Bar None, shooting him after the dispute had spilled over into the parking lot.

The club reopened under the same name with new management and a $200,000 renovation. But while the Independent Soldiers frequented Loft Six, it was not exclusively their turf.

Members from other gangs would often show up there with little or no problem. But things changed on the night of August 16, 2003. Not only were the Independent Soldiers and their associates in the bar, but there were also Hells Angels and their supporters. Despite the use of metal detectors, many of the patrons at Loft Six that night were armed.

There are varying stories of what happened next, but I have heard from reliable sources that sparks started to fly when one of the Independent Soldiers recognized a guy named John "JJ" Johnson. Apparently, Johnson had worked at a Hells Angels–associated strip joint called Brandi's and had so much trouble with one loud mouthed customer that he decided to beat him into the hospital. When he later found out the guy was an influential Indian gangster, he went into hiding. And when he showed up in the midst of the Sikh-dominated Independent Soldiers, it was only a matter of time before trouble erupted.

Despite there being about 200 people in the club, most of them innocent bystanders, at just before 4 a.m., shots came from every direction. "A fight broke out, and all of the sudden bullets started flying," one witness said. "We just ran. We were right in the line of fire. We couldn't see anybody; we didn't know who was shooting, and people began crawling over top of each other to get out of the way."

When the smoke cleared, three people were dead, and eight, mostly innocent bystanders, were injured. Gerpal Singh "Paul" Dosanjh—cousin to two of the original Indo-Canadian Mafia members, Jimmy and Ron Dosanjh—was shot in the head but survived. Not as lucky were Johnson, whose presence sparked the melee; John Popovich, an innocent DJ visiting Vancouver from Windsor, Ontario; and Mahmoud Alkhalil, a member of the Independent Soldiers and little brother of Khalil Alkhalil, who was murdered in Surrey in 2001.

• • •

After the Loft Six murders, things began to change among the criminal organizations on the Lower Mainland, particularly the Indian Canadian ones. The Independent Soldiers—who had always been predominantly Indian—began working with more and more white guys, many with connections to the Hells Angels.

And as the region was still reeling from the November 28 murder of Mao Jomar Lanot—a teenager who had a glass soda bottle broken over his head when a mob outside Sir Charles Tupper High School attacked him—it was shocked by two murders of young Indian Canadian men in two days.

On December 12, the Richmond RCMP unit received a call from the New Westminster police about a shooting. When they arrived, 20-year-old Naveen Shiv Daval was already dead. He had been shot in an apartment and managed to get to his vehicle before passing out and dying behind the wheel. The other occupants of the East Richmond apartment he was shot in—a 20-year-old Indian Canadian and a 19-year-old white kid—were questioned but eventually released. The case was never solved, and police told media that Daval's death was most likely a case of mistaken identity.

On the following morning, at about 9:20 a.m., a couple had just finished a pleasant walk in Surrey's Bear Creek Park when they planned to return to their car. On their way to their car, they noticed a late-model Mercedes-Benz sedan with its engine running and its lights on. Moving closer, the couple described what they saw as an Indian-looking man behind the wheel. He appeared to be unconscious, so they called 9-1-1. When paramedics arrived, they determined that the man in the car—36-year-old Gurwinder Singh Bath—was dead.

His death was eerily reminiscent of the May discovery of Karmen Singh Johl, who had also been found shot dead behind the wheel of his car in the same neighborhood. In fact, Bath and Johl were both involved with a company called "R&S Trucking," which had been the subject of a major investigation involving shipping marijuana over the border in tractor-trailers. Despite the fact that Johl had a long series of drug-related convictions, both men avoided charges by claiming they did not know what was in the trucks they were driving.

But while many people in the Lower Mainland had come to regard Sikh-on-Sikh violence to be a problem limited to that community, those minds changed at the start of 2004. On the night of January 2, Rachel Davis—a pudgy 23-year-old blonde who looked a lot like her mother, Janet Wright, one of the featured actors on the Canadian sitcom *Corner Gas*—went to the Purple Onion nightclub with some friends. On the way out, she noticed an Indian Canadian man involved in a fight with a group of other Indian Canadian men. As the man, 25-year-old drug dealer Imran Saff Sharif, was thrown to the ground, Davis intervened, putting herself between Sharif and the men who threw him down. As she was attempting to calm the situation, Sharif pulled a handgun and started firing wildly. He shot and killed Davis and a passerby named Richard Hui. It came out in Sharif's trial that he was running a dial-a-dope operation and had strong gang connections, but the authorities would not reveal which gang or gangs he worked with (they often keep this information to themselves because it's something the defense would make them prove in court).

There were a few more suspicious murders in the Lower Mainland with no obvious connection to established gangs, until March 6. At 5:00 a.m. that morning, Paul Dosanjh and an associate, both armed, were engaged in a summit meeting with a pair of rival drug dealers—one Indian Canadian, one white—over a territorial dispute at the Gourmet Castle, an East Hastings Street Chinese-food restaurant. Shots were exchanged, and Dosanjh was killed. "Because he is well-known to police and because of the family connections that are well-known to police, we are obviously looking at the gang link and the drug link," a Vancouver police spokesman said. "But at this point, we don't have any idea why he was targeted." Still, they did issue a media release indicating they would have an armed presence at his funeral.

• • •

By this time, of course, everything was changing. The organized-crime landscape looked very different on the Lower Mainland in 2005 than it had just a few years earlier when guys like Bindy Johal were acting all "gangsta" on local television newscasts.

The big players were still the Hells Angels and the Chinese, but—more than ever before—they were working behind the scenes, operating the street-level drug and other vice markets by proxy. There was no shortage of young men (and, to some extent, women) who wanted to be involved in the drug trade, particularly because of the ease and relative safety of dial-a-dope operations.

The only problem was getting the drugs to supply. For decades, dealers would have to connect with the Chinese or the Hells Angels for cocaine, heroin or meth, but could get marijuana from any of the thousands of independent growers in the area. But—just as they had with independently owned strip joints, escort agencies and other vice-related businesses—the Hells Angels had used violent, one might even say terroristic, methods to gain control of growers who did not want to play ball by selling exclusively to Hells Angels–associated dealers at a price determined by the bikers. Independent growers could expect to be robbed, beaten or even murdered if they tried to stay independent.

Of course, there were holdouts—small-time suppliers flying under the radar of the Hells Angels—but their output was small and the methods they used to stay out of the Hells Angels' way often led to them being invisible to other potential dealers as well.

So, despite all the talk of loyalty and honor and brotherhood, dealers went where dealers have always gone—to established organized crime. The United Nations—the very gang whose original stated reason for existence was to protect its members from the Hells Angels—began to play both sides of the fence. Roueche had connections with East Asian drug importers through his girlfriend's relatives, but other notable members and associates of the United Nations began buying marijuana and other drugs first from Hells Angels associates and then members themselves. The United Nations never really became a puppet gang, as they have been characterized in the media. Some UN members continued to deal without any connection to the Hells Angels or their allies, and continued their antipathy toward them. But many of them they did leave their original ideals behind for the sake of easy money and started dealing for the Hells Angels and kicking profits upstairs just like everyone else. Still, it was at best a tenuous relationship, and many members of the UN retained their loathing of the bikers.

Of the other two major youth gangs on the Lower Mainland—the Independent Soldiers and the Red Scorpions—both were becoming increasingly diverse and territorial. After the Loft Six shootings, many of the original members of the Independent Soldiers quit and were replaced by more Hells Angels–friendly members who rapidly rose through their ranks and eventually swayed that gang, as well, from anti- to pro–Hells Angels. Whether this was an intricate plan of infiltration by the Hells Angels or just a coincidence, a result of the Independent Soldiers evolving in the face of the same contemporary zeitgeist as the United Nations has been the subject of intense debate. Either way, the Independent Soldiers steadily became less and less independent.

The lone holdout at that point were the Red Scorpions. Although I have been told by their supporters that it was because its members had more integrity and were made of sterner stuff, I have also been told by others that the Hells Angels rejected them as small-timers. Since that kind of rationalizing—my group is right no matter what it does, and all other groups are wrong if they are in opposition—is rampant, an essential part of the culture among gang members, the truth is anyone's guess.

• • •

But few were guessing at what the Bacon Brothers were doing. Like pretty well everyone else who agreed to talk to me for this book, the guy I will call Nelson asked me to protect his identity. Originally from the Toronto area, Nelson moved to the Lower Mainland with his graphic-designer wife and later shifted from a mid-level job at TD Bank to setting up his own business as a broker of a (legal) commodity he also won't let me name, but one that he will admit draws an entirely Asian market. The extra income allowed him to move into a much better house on Strathcona Court, not far from the Bacons.

When Nelson moved to Strathcona, the Bacon Brothers were all in their early 20s and, to his mild surprise, living at home with their parents. He did not like the family and, in his opinion, neither did anyone else. He described the neighborhood as "nervous" because of the Bacons' presence. "Nobody wanted to run into them because they were obnoxious and rude," he told me. "It started with the old man. He was not just rude, but aggressively so. I have no idea how he had a job as a teacher." Nelson explained that he did not know the boys' mother very well but said he "had a pretty good handle" on the brothers themselves.

He characterized Jonathan, the oldest, as "a pretty normal-looking guy" and also noted that he was the most approachable of the family, the least likely to be belligerent. He said Jarrod, the middle boy, was "flashy" and "tried to look like a gangster" in dark suits and expensive sunglasses. "He looked like he had more money than taste," Nelson mused.

But the two of them appeared gentlemanly, in Nelson's opinion, compared to Jamie, the youngest. "He was the size of a moose and seemed about half as smart," he said with a straight face. "While the other two had macho swagger, Jamie looked like a psycho." He made it a point to steer clear of the young man, in case he experienced a "'roid rage."

The Bacons, he said, tended to consider the street to be theirs and would park and hang out wherever they felt like. They were loud and kept late hours, often coming home or "partying" well into the morning, to the consternation of neighbors.

All three boys had late-model luxury cars, which they traded in, according to Nelson, annually. He told me about their other conspicuous signs of wealth—including clothes, jewelry and huge parties—and I asked them where he thought three boys could afford such as ostentatious lifestyle. He looked at me like I was crazy. "They sold drugs, of course," he said.

The police, too, were aware of the Bacons, and their alleged drug sales operation, but could not acquire enough evidence to receive a warrant or even to mount a surveillance operation. Those in the know, though, have told me that the Bacons were selling drugs they had received from the United Nations, which could be traced back to the Hells Angels.

But things changed very rapidly in 2004, when Jarrod Bacon was charged with attempted murder after an altercation in the seedy Fraser Valley Inn. He went out back with two men, presumably to straighten things out, and shot one of them. The other fled. Nelson recalled, "Jarrod got into an argument with a guy at the pub about who could do what where and shot him. I guess it must've been bad because I know he was charged with attempted murder."

But, just as the people who I spoke with were loathe to allow me to reveal their identities for this book for fear of retribution, the man the Crown alleged Jarrod was trying to kill refused to cooperate with police. Although the Crown continued to press the charge, the judge had no choice but to stay the case due to a lack of evidence, allowing Jarrod to walk free.

It was a valuable lesson for the Bacon Brothers: if nobody talks, you have nothing to fear.

CHAPTER 5

GOING GLOBAL: 2005–2006

While the Bacon Brothers and others like them didn't think they had much to fear from law enforcement if they could convince the people around them, including the victims, to stay quiet, competition on the streets of British Columbia for product, territory and customers was leading to widespread violence. And, as they had in the past, the Hells Angels did their best to intimidate the competition, often through the use of puppet gangs and support crews.

One of the most violent of them was simply called the Crew. In fact, it was something of an oddity—a puppet gang of a puppet gang. Prince George, tucked away in British Columbia's mountainous interior, is a hardscrabble timber-and-mining community and has been named "Canada's most dangerous city" twice by *Maclean's* magazine because of its disproportionate rates of murder and other violent crime.

With prosperous markets for drugs and other vices, Prince George is a vital part of Canada's underground economy. And, as such, it could not be ignored by the Hells Angels. "The north has always been an expanding field. There are a lot of drugs consumed in the north," said Inspector Gary Shinkaruk, head of the RCMP's Outlaw Motorcycle Gang unit. "They [the Hells Angels] want to tap into that lucrative market."

But operating there and living there are two very different things. In the early 2000s, the Hells Angels visited and recruited some of the local tough guys to form a gang, the Renegades, to act as their representatives in the city, moving product and preventing anyone else from trying. They did their job with gusto, flooding the city with drugs. But they quickly realized they needed to enforce their dominance in the city.

To accomplish this, the Renegades recruited guys they knew to act for them on the streets, both as dealers and enforcers. Called the Crew, these guys acted viciously, conducting severe public beatings and worse. One such case occurred when a local (and, it would appear, uncooperative) drug dealer named Patrick Patriquin struggled into a convenience store covered in blood. When the shocked clerk saw that Patriquin was missing his left hand, he called 9-1-1. Patriquin regained consciousness in a hospital bed the following day but refused to cooperate with police. The hand was never found. Law enforcement officers on the street were convinced that the incident was the work of the Crew, but they could not get enough evidence to make any arrests.

Prince George, even more than most such places, has a voracious appetite for crack. One frequent user was a Shawn Giesbrecht. In order to have enough money to buy crack, he also sold crack. And like everyone else in Prince George who sold crack, he got it from the Crew. In fact, he got it from the Crew's president, Scott Payne.

Payne was a particularly nasty fellow. Abandoned by his mother at the age of 5 to a father who was constantly in and out of prison, Payne was found wandering the streets of Maple Ridge at the age of 8 and taken into foster care. As later revealed in his trial as an adult, his first convictions, when he was 15, were small time and netted him just probation. But in January 2000, he was caught with crack and sentenced to one day in jail. Less than two weeks later, he was arrested again, for assault and carrying a concealed weapon. In June 2000, he was caught fencing stolen goods. In 2001, it was assault with a concealed weapon again. In 2003, he was caught with an illegal handgun, and in 2005, he was found to be carrying crack again and added resisting arrest to his list of charges.

Giesbrecht was, quite reasonably, scared of Payne. And on November 14, 2004, he was absolutely terrified. For various reasons, he had fallen into arrears with his supplier. He was $170—a fortune in crackhead terms—short. It might have made sense to lay low, but Giesbrecht didn't have that option. Not only did he need more product to sell if he wanted to make the money back, but he also needed crack for his own addiction— and there was no place else to get it. So he headed to Payne's crack shack and explained to his boss what had happened.

Payne calmly told him to put his left hand on the table that was between them. Giesbrecht complied. Payne then pulled a long, serrated hunting knife out of his pocket and sawed off the little finger on Giesbrecht's left hand. He then put the severed digit in a cardboard box with a lid, telling Giesbrecht and the others in the shack that he'd use it as a warning to others.

Payne was also present when his close associate Alia Brienne Pierini—a 21-year-old mother of a toddler—attacked Alphonse Holtz, another addict–turned–street-level-dealer who couldn't pay his bills, with an axe in an apartment the pair often used to process crack.

But arrests of various members of the Crew, including Payne and his right-hand man Joshua Hendrick, led to an intolerable amount of bad press and police surveillance, and the Crew was shut down. To replace them, the powers that be collected the remaining worthwhile members of the Crew, a couple of new recruits and some tough guys from Kelowna and formed them into the Prince George chapter of the Independent Soldiers.

It was a telling strategic move. Law enforcement now realized that the Independent Soldiers were no longer controlled by the gang's old Indian Canadian founders, but were actually just another club taking orders from the Hells Angels. And they had no problem recruiting in a city where fewer than half the provincial average attend higher education, despite the fact that its few visible minorities are almost entirely Native Canadians with almost no South Asians in the area. "Some of these guys think, 'What the hell. I'm going to give it all I got because I don't think I'll live past 30,'" said one RCMP officer in Prince George. "In one check stop that we made on Highway 16 West, we stopped an 18-year-old kid who had $8,000 cash in his pocket. He just looked at me and said, 'If you think I'm going to work for minimum wage when I can make this kind of money, you're crazy.'"

But while the Hells Angels and their underlings were gaining ground in their desire to monopolize the drug market, there were, as always, internal tensions. When the RCMP let Renegades president William "Billy" Moore know how much evidence they had collected against him, he elected to turn paid informant rather than face trial.

It was a bad career choice. On March 25, 2005, responders to a raging fire at his home found him just outside the flaming house. His corpse, full of bullet holes, was sitting in the front seat of his car. The Hells Angels who attended his funeral— under the watchful eye of media and law enforcement—praised him as "a nice man." His replacement, Romano Brienza, who had just beaten trafficking charges, died of natural causes a month later.

And there were other leaks. Michael Plante was a bodybuilder who occasionally worked as a bouncer to pay his way through college. He'd never been in any real trouble before—he was charged once for assault when an argument at a gym got out of hand, but it never went to trial—but the first bar he worked at, in the North Burnaby Inn, was owned by Hells Angel Bob Green. Alarmed by the amount of crime he saw, Plante moved to Medicine Hat, Alberta, for a year but came back when he saw it was no different when it came to how bouncers had to work for criminals. Back in B.C., he took a job loading trucks for Costco to get away from shady dealings but eventually found himself working as a bouncer again.

He worked at a series of bars, often connected to the Hells Angels. At one location, the Dell Hotel in Surrey, he was sometimes asked to watch over a room the Hells Angels used to stash cocaine. He worked the door at a couple of strip joints, the Marble Arch and the Cecil Hotel, both of which were owned by Hells Angels associates. It was at the strip joints where he met and became friends with a number of gang members who frequented the spots. He was surprised, in fact, at how many different gangs would socialize at the Cecil Hotel, an indication of how many allies the Hells Angels had on the streets.

Eventually, Plante started ferrying drugs and cash for Randy Potts, who owned the Cecil Hotel, ran a stripper/escort agency and had just been elevated to prospect status as a Hells Angel. As a hang-around, the level below prospect, he was given a leather vest that indicated his status on the front. The vests are a Hells Angels prized possession and hang-arounds are instructed upon receiving one never to allow a non-member to even touch it. Potts was wearing his vest proudly in 2003 when he was set upon by an old rival named Audey Hanson. Not only did Hanson beat him up and black his eye, but he stole Potts's vest.

Embarrassed, Potts went to see his sponsor, full-patch Hells Angel Lonnie Robinson, to let him know what happened. For moral support, he brought along Plante, a mutual friend. It didn't do much good. Robinson knocked Potts to the floor with an open-handed slap to the face and instructed him to get the vest back at any cost.

Potts recruited Plante to help him stake out Hanson's house. After two months of watching, Potts determined that Hanson would be alone, and he and Plante paid him a visit. But Plante quickly found out that Potts had more on his mind than simply beating Hanson up and taking the vest back. He handed him an Uzi, .38 handgun and a balaclava and told him to shoot Hanson. Plante did shoot, but intentionally missed him with the .38 and claimed the Uzi had jammed. Potts was angry, and gave the job to another friend who managed to shoot but not kill Hanson.

Plante, who was initially reluctant to get involved with the gang, was upset that they'd expect him to kill over a leather vest and appealed to the police to become a paid informant. But it was not just his desire to be a good citizen that motivated him. After it got rolling, Plante's deal paid him $14,000 a month, along with a 1997 Mustang, the lease of a Harley-Davidson, dinners out with bills of up to $2,000 and vacations to Mexico.

But Plante—later known as the million-dollar rat in the media—was the only way the police had to get inside any of the drug trafficking organizations. And because the Hells Angels had since become linked with the Independent Soldiers and the United Nations, the potential was there to disrupt a lot of trafficking.

Over the next several years, Plante acted as an informant for the RCMP under a project known as Operation E-Pandora. He learned and relayed who the players were and how they operated. For example, a gesture simulating turning a car's ignition key indicated a "key" or kilogram of drugs in conversation. His account of working in the underworld all came out in testimony against his former associates.

One of his primary suppliers was a Hells Angels associate named Kerry Ryan Renaud, who cooked and sold methamphetamine for full-patch Hells Angels Ron Lising and the unfortunately named Johnny Punko. Since both believed they were working with Plante and Renaud exclusively, Plante had yet another secret to keep.

The cops hit the mother lode on September 6, 2004, when Plante received a phone call instructing him to meet Lising and his friend Nima Ghavami at 8 Rinks sports center in Burnaby. It was, he said, going to be a big deal. The cops tailed Plante, who was driving the black Mustang they bought him. At the meeting, Lising told Plante to drop off a pound of meth on the counter of a deli in Vancouver's Champlain Mall. Despite the obvious danger, the police okayed the plan.

They followed along and filmed him making the drop off. Later that day, Plante received text messages from Lising asking to visit so he could tell him where he could pick up the cash for the meth. He was then instructed to go to a restaurant in Hope, sit at a table, read a newspaper and wait for a man from Kelowna to give him $10,000. He also handed Plante a note that he was instructed to hand over to the bag man. Apparently Lising was upset that the guy from Kelowna was using a phone Lising had given him for personal calls when it was intended just for drug transactions. "I don't care if you are calling taxis or pizzas, don't use that fucking phone," Lising threatened.

Plante went to the restaurant and met the money man. He handed Plante $5,000 in cash hidden in a rolled-up newspaper. Plante texted Lising with the news. Lising answered with a message to the guy from Kelowna: "Hey fuck face, that's not what you promised." The guy didn't have any more money, so Plante left with the $5,000 and let the other two work out how the rest would be paid.

But it didn't matter in the larger sense. Plante had done the job the RCMP had paid him in excess of $1 million to do. He gave them enough evidence to storm in and arrest 18 men, six of them full-patch Hells Angels and the rest associates. Their defense pointed out that, while an undercover informant, Plante sold drugs and committed several assaults. But that didn't matter, either. Plante's defense was that since he was posing as someone auditioning for the club, he had to act the part, and committing crimes on a regular basis was part of that. The Hells Angels were guilty and Plante, as bad as he was and as many tax dollars as he took with him, had brought at least a few of them down.

• • •

"It was like Grand Central Station up there," Jeremy Enright told me when asked to describe life around 2005 and 2006. "All you had to do was wait a few minutes and another airplane or helicopter would go by. It's a wonder none of them ever crashed into one another." Enright, who lives in Bellingham, Washington, likes to hike and camp in the North Cascades, near the Canadian border.

But for a while, he could get no peace in his beloved mountains because of the huge amount of air traffic. "It was especially bad at night," he said. "I go up there for peace and quiet, and I might as well have camped out by the airport." Interestingly, Enright was certain that the government was behind all the action in the skies. "To tell you the truth," he said. "I thought it was the DEA looking for weed." In fact, what was flying above his head *was* weed.

It was a crazy time. Sure, there was money to be made in dial-a-dope. But it wasn't the big time. The abundance of weed had driven the price way down. Operating a dial-a-dope operation could easily net you the lease of a nice Acura SUV, but if you wanted to pay down a fully loaded, customized, armor-plated Cadillac Escalade with hydraulic gun racks and an innards-shaking stereo system—and many, many young men did—you needed to branch out from the Lower Mainland.

There was an absolute surfeit of weed. A tradition of locals growing pot for themselves and their friends had morphed into a huge and sophisticated industry as organized crime pushed growers for more profits. Using methods like hydroponics, aeroponics, grow lights and artificial daytimes, British Columbia farmers had found the way to get not only the highest yield of marijuana, but also the most potent. In fact, the best of the local strains—known collectively as "B.C. Bud," set the smoking world alight. It was so prized, so valued, that in some places, it was actually bartered kilo-for-kilo with cocaine, a feat unimaginable with any other strain of marijuana.

The provincial government estimated there were 22,000 marijuana grow operations in B.C., and in 2005, *Forbes* magazine estimated these harvested $7 billion in product. That was just too much weed for the province, and prices reflected that. Weed was cheap, competition was fierce and profit margins began to get thin.

But people were willing to pay a premium for weed elsewhere, especially the now world-famous BC Bud. Most of the sophisticated Lower Mainland and Okanagan traffickers already had systems in place to export drugs to Australia and Japan—in fact, the United Nations (the New York City–based multinational organization, not the Abbotsford-based street gang) has determined that one of the leading suppliers of cocaine, methamphetamine and ecstasy to both countries is Canada.

But while trafficking easily concealable drugs like cocaine, meth and ecstasy is one thing, moving marijuana is quite another. While very small quantities of stimulant drugs can yield a high profit, there's no way to make money hiding weed in the fake bottoms of frying pans. No matter what the selling price, to make money moving weed, you have to have significant volume. Even when dried and vacuum-packed, weed is bulky and cumbersome.

But across the border, they would pay through the nose for BC Bud. And if you could get the stuff as far away as Los Angeles or Chicago, you could get very rich very quickly. And that's what traffickers did. Like French wine merchants who serve the locals their worst and save the best for export, many drug traffickers in the Lower Mainland collected their best weed for the United States—where the real money was.

Getting it over the border wasn't hard. At first, they drove it over, but after 9/11, the Americans worked much harder to secure their borders. Driving over frequently opened the traffickers to increased scrutiny and the potential for arrests and the stiff sentences given out by U.S. courts.

But while the official crossings presented something of a challenge, the security along most of the border was a joke. For the most part in the Lower Mainland, the border itself is little more than a two-lane road, called (depending on which town it's in) 0 Avenue, Townline Road or Boundary Road. On the Canadian side, there are farms and scattered suburban housing tracts, while the American side is mostly wooded, with a few raspberry fields. Getting over is simple. Look both ways, cross the road and you're in the other country.

Naturally, traffickers took—and continue to take—advantage of this. The primary method for cross-border trafficking was to hire some teenager or twenty-something, give him (or her) a backpack full of weed and send him over the border.

But there are a few problems with that. The most weed a backpacker can usually take over the border is just a few pounds. The road is patrolled by police, and backpackers crossing the border—especially if they are in large groups—are liable to be apprehended. And they can talk. After arrest, backpackers can save themselves by turning in their contacts, and some have even been known to implicate their bosses by bragging in front of the wrong people about what they do and who they know.

There are other methods, of course. Canoes and kayaks are popular on the coast, but they are prone to federal scrutiny on both sides of the border. Some people use dirt bikes or ATVs, but the noise they make tends to invite unwanted attention. A few people have tried giant slingshots and makeshift catapults with limited success. Tunneling is an expensive, time-consuming and dangerous option, but it has been taken. A pair of Canadians built a tunnel from a Quonset hut in Langley that opened up in a friend's living room in Lynden, Washington, but they were arrested before they could complete a single shipment. The men, who were given nine-year prison sentences by a U.S. court, said they expected to move at least 300 pounds a day through the tunnel.

In order to move large amounts of product over the border quickly and safely, more and more trafficking organizations took to the air. Even the smallest Cessna can carry as much as 300 pounds of weed and can fly literally under the radar, spend a couple of undetected seconds on the other side of the border, land briefly or even just drop a package, and return.

As more people realized how safe and efficient the method was, the airways over the British Columbia–Washington border became very busy, especially at night. Drugs were being ferried over the border constantly. Law enforcement knew it was happening but could do little about it. It was such a commonplace activity that in 2006, when Jane Gerth was driving on Highway 17, 15 minutes away from the Canadian border, and saw a black-and-gold backpack in a ditch beside the road, she slammed on the brakes. The wife of a retired U.S. Border Patrol agent, she knew what was in the bag. When she unzipped it, it almost burst as the $20 and $10 bills packed tightly inside started pouring out of it. After a night of excited counting, Gerth had found $507,270 in U.S. currency. Since it was used as evidence in a raid that netted the arrests of three men who grabbed a replacement bag set out by police, Gerth was allowed to keep her prize, plus the interest that accumulated as the trial went along.

It was so easy to get mass quantities of weed over the border this way that it became very popular, and private pilots were in huge demand. Helicopters, which did not require airports and their complications, were extremely prized, and their pilots were worth their weight in gold.

One of them was Dustin "Princess" Haugen. Though only 24, the doughy, weary-looking Haugen was an experienced helicopter pilot and drug trafficker. He had never been caught red-handed, but had spent a few days in jail as a suspect in a helicopter-based trafficking ring and was released when a case against him failed to coalesce. A reporter for *Playboy* magazine rode along with some helicopter traffickers—many people I spoke with believe that Haugen was one of them—and quoted them as boasting they were more efficient than FedEx.

Haugen met Jonathan Bacon, and the two quickly became friends. At the time, Bacon was just another small-time dial-a-doper, but he was one with big plans. In fact, Bacon was so sold on the idea of helicopter trafficking, he started to take flying lessons in Langley. To get things started, Bacon rented a serviceable helipad in Abbotsford, near the border, from which Haugen flew a leased Bell JetRanger frequently. Despite the fact that the JetRanger could carry four passengers or up to 1,300 pounds of cargo, Haugen's flights never listed any cargo and rarely any passengers.

In March 2005, Haugen took his girlfriend—aspiring hairstylist Christina Alexander—on one of his flights. But he landed poorly, wrecking the helicopter and killing Alexander. Police investigated, but could find no drugs, large amounts of cash or witnesses willing to deny Haugen's story that he had been taking Alexander on a sightseeing trip (in the dark), so no charges were laid.

But the incident had an effect on Bacon. He stopped taking flying lessons and more or less fired Haugen, letting his lease on the helipad expire without financing any more trips.

Haugen, though, was less affected and went right back to work for other clients. On May 9, 2006, as part of Operation Frozen Timber, police on both sides of the border watched and photographed as Haugen and an associate named Daryl Desjardins took off in Canada and landed in the woods just over the border.

Desjardins had a long history as a drug trafficker and was a close associate of the United Nations. He had actually once run afoul of the group back in 2003, when Roueche found out that he had been overstating his status in the gang, claiming he was one of the big bosses when he wasn't. After a "talk" with gang enforcer James Coulter, Desjardins continued to traffic in association with the UN and presumably snapped Haugen up as soon as he heard that Bacon had let him go.

Agents from U.S. Immigration and Customs Enforcement (ICE) also photographed Haugen and Desjardins land and hand over five hockey bags to three young men with a large blue GMC pickup truck. They allowed him to take off and arrested the men in the pickup. Inside the hockey bags, ICE agents discovered almost 300 pounds of BC Bud shrink-wrapped into one-kilo packages. Desjardins and Haugen were arrested when they returned to the helipad near Desjardins' home after a brief stop near Chilliwack.

After Haugen served time in Canadian prison, he was extradited to the United States for trial there. Traditionally, that meant a much longer sentence, so when the Washington judge sentenced him to time served, rumors that he had made a deal, probably ratting on someone higher up, abounded.

●　●　●

While Jonathan Bacon may have abandoned the helicopter plan, he did not stop trafficking. The Abbotsford police—like pretty well everyone else—knew very well that Jonathan was a major source of drugs in the area. Though still keeping very close ties, he had moved out of his parents' house and rented another one on Winfield Drive ten minutes to the south to live with his girlfriend, the blonde and apparently surgically enhanced Rayleene Burton. Neighbors have told me that there were "expensive-looking" cars and trucks coming to and from the house at all hours and that "tough-looking guys" always seemed to be hanging around.

But his neighbors weren't the only people whose attention Jonathan had aroused. The police broke up a home invasion at a grow op and arrested him under suspicion of breaking and entering, and robbery. They were shocked to find that not only was he wearing a bulletproof vest, but it had been stolen from the RCMP.

A lack of cooperation from the victims of the break-in led to the Crown's case falling apart, and Jonathan was convicted simply of possession of stolen goods.

But the evidence gathered in that case allowed police to put Jonathan under surveillance, and in the spring and summer of 2005, officers watching the house saw as many as 15 transactions in which Jonathan exchanged a package with various other men. They never actually saw drugs or cash change hands, just packages. Eager to put him out of business, the Abbotsford police requested a search warrant for the house. It was denied. The local Judicial Justice of the Peace who reviewed the application declared that the reasons the police gave for the warrant fell "short of supporting reasonable grounds to believe that the items to be searched for [would] be at the requested location."

Constable John Forster, who was leading the investigation, was actually in the process of revising his search warrant application when he received a telephone call on August 4 from one of his officers watching the house. He was informed that Bacon was meeting with a friend named Godwin Cheng.

Forster knew that Cheng was no choirboy. He had been arrested in February 1996 along with Jaswant "Billy" Rai and

Rabinder Ahuja for a massive gang beating in which they had uttered death threats. All three were also suspected of being drug traffickers and UN members. He also happened to be out on bail after an April 19, 2005, arrest in which police found marijuana, cocaine and a loaded handgun at his Hawksview Place townhouse, less than a mile from the Bacons' house.

He and Jonathan were in Cheng's car, the officers on the scene told Forster, and it looked like they were making a deal. Forster told them to make an arrest.

The cops stormed the car, and the two men inside surrendered without incident. Inside the car, police found eight ounces of marijuana, 92 hits of meth, 15 ecstasy pills, 4 small packages of cocaine, $2,600 in cash and a number of cellphones.

Upon seeing the bust go down, Burton fled from the house and sped away in an SUV. She was stopped two blocks away. After she was arrested, a brief search of the vehicle yielded $88,000 in cash.

On the strength of the arrests, a warrant to search the house was issued. Inside, the police found a lot of what they expected from a drug dealer. There were 24 pounds of pre-packaged marijuana, score sheets, cellphones and four illegal handguns, two automatic and the other two semiautomatic, with matching ammunition. But the police were more disturbed by the fact that Jonathan also had a police scanner, a bulletproof vest and, most damning of all, a complete police uniform.

The three were granted bail, and were released to await trial.

• • •

While Jonathan was bedeviled by helicopter crashes and police raids, the Lower Mainland underworld continued to play out like a violent soap opera. While Hells Angels' influence had effectively taken the Indian leadership away from the major Indian Canadian gangs like the Independent Soldiers, others had emerged to take their place.

One of them involved three brothers who had formerly run with Bindy Johal and his Indo-Canadian Mafia. Balraj, Sandip and Paul Singh Duhre were alleged to have run an Indian Canadian gang that involved itself in drug trafficking and other illegal activities. Balraj was the oldest and supplied the muscle. He'd been arrested a few times before, including once for escaping police custody and another for assault. All three brothers—along with Johal—were arrested in 1997 for obstruction of justice.

No matter what they did for a living, the Duhre brothers led dangerous lives. In 2003, Balraj was walking down a Surrey street when someone shot at him from a moving car. One bullet grazed his face, but it was not a life-threatening injury. No arrests were made. On May 13, 2005, Sandip decided to stop at a Mac's convenience store on Scott Road in Surrey with his friend, Egyptian-born Dean Elshamy. As they prepared to exit Sandip's car, they were met with a hail of shots from inside an SUV. Elshamy died in the driver's seat, but Sandip was not hit. That summer, Balraj leased an armor-plated BMW from a friend in the car business. It was a worthwhile investment. On July 7, Balraj was stopped at an East Vancouver stoplight when an unknown assailant opened fire just inches away from his face. The car's special windows proved their worth as the bullets ricocheted harmlessly off the glass. At the time, many in the Lower Mainland thought the shots were supposed to be for Sandip, who was considered the leader of the Duhre Brothers gang.

After two attempts on his life in less than two years, Balraj left town to lay low for a little while. His father, Baldev—who works as a court interpreter—said that Balraj was taking some time to put his life back together and leave the gangster world altogether. Sandip chose to accept an offer of police protection. "They are at a stage where they want to change, but managing to do it is very hard," Baldev said of his sons. "They are at a stage where they want to walk away."

But in the fall of 2006, Balraj returned to the area and started living with his cousin, Ravi Sahota. On October 25, the pair went to lunch at Phở 66 on East Hastings. Even though it was in the Sunrise neighborhood where both grew up, it was an odd choice, as the men rarely ate Vietnamese food. At approximately 1:15 or 1:20 p.m., an East Asian man who had been sitting in the restaurant opened fire, hitting both Balraj and his cousin. The assailant then fled out of the restaurant and hopped into a silver four-door sedan driven by what witnesses called a "dark-skinned man."

Both men were badly hurt, but neither died.

"The people that were shot are known to us as gang members," said Vancouver Police spokesman Constable Tim Fanning. "It looks like a targeted attack that had no relationship to the neighborhood or the restaurant." Police also indicated they believe that the two men were lured to the restaurant specifically to be shot as part of an ongoing conflict. But they did not want the incident to cause anyone to panic, denying there was any kind of war on the streets.

• • •

But while Canadian law enforcement was busy on the streets trying to keep the violence down, it was the Americans who started taking strategic initiatives. Made aware of the details of the magnitude of drugs coming over the border and by which methods, ICE and other American law enforcement increased their efforts in the region. It was revealed later that one of their primary goals was to prevent the flood of Canadian marijuana from being exchanged for Colombian or Mexican cocaine, drawing potentially dangerous cartel members to American soil.

After a number of arrests—including successful projects like Operation Frozen Timber, a multi-force project aimed primarily at combating helicopter-borne smugglers—the

Americans learned through turned informants and other means that the vast majority of the weed being moved over the border could be linked directly back to the United Nations. Roueche's name came up particularly often.

The Americans used sophisticated methods, including motion-activated video cameras in the woods, shooting the trails they knew smugglers used, but the majority of their information came from informants. Many of them were scared Canadian kids who were anything but career criminals, and having heard horror stories about American cops and sentences, they were quick to turn.

In March 2005, the Americans learned of a pair of Canadian drug smugglers who were making repeated trips across the border. Finding the pickup truck they used in Washington State, ICE agents covertly equipped it with a GPS transmitter and an ignition kill switch. The cops tracked them going over the border frequently and then in June activated the kill switch on the Washington side of the border. Cops swarmed in and arrested Trevor Schoutens and Brian Fews, and charged them with trafficking. Later, the same informant who led ICE to the pickup truck—Ken Davis, the UN's top guy in the United States—received a call from Roueche himself asking him to help Schoutens and Fews get out of jail.

The next big one to go down was Roueche's personal friend, Alexander Swanson, who was caught pulling bags of weed out of a pickup truck in Blaine, Washington, on August 12, 2005.

About a month later, ICE received a tip from an informant that a deal was going down in Puyallup, Washington. As instructed, a multi-force team followed a Toyota Tundra with Colorado plates and a GMC Spartan with Washington plates to a house in Puyallup. When they saw the men carrying large black hockey bags into the house, they arrested them. A drug-sniffing dog confirmed their belief that the men had massive quantities of marijuana. In fact, it was 1,000 pounds in 23 bags. Two of the men—Zachary and Braydon Miraback—were UN members from Calgary. Zachary thought he'd play tough with the officers, refusing to give his identity and saying he had no identification with him. The ICE agents added a charge of crossing the border without proper identification.

They were followed on December 1, 2005, by Greg Fielding, a B.C. resident with UN ties who was observed collecting 325 pounds of marijuana from a white floatplane that landed on Soap Lake, a health resort high in the mountains. Fielding was arrested; the pilot escaped.

And it wasn't just federal and Washington State forces that got involved. Federal agents alerted local police forces about a white floatplane that had been seen dropping off large quantities of weed. They said it would be easy to spot because the identification numbers had been covered by duct tape.

The following day, March 14, 2006, they received a call from the Colville Indian Reservation tribal police. They had intercepted the plane, with 314 pounds of marijuana and 24,000 ecstasy pills on board, when it landed on tiny Omak Lake in their jurisdiction. They arrested Courtney, B.C., resident Kevin Haughton when they saw him walk away from the aircraft. He initially denied knowledge of the plane, but relented under questioning. He was, he admitted, ferrying the drugs over the border for Duane Meyer, a notorious trafficker and UN member. When he was presented to Okanogan County Sheriff Frank T. Rogers, the sheriff actually complained about how many suspects the new efforts were bringing in. "We're running ourselves ragged," he said. "It's like an epidemic up here. We're running from call to call."

He'd get no rest. On March 23, two Canadian women were seen picking up hockey bags full of weed near the shores of Soap Lake and throwing them into their SUV. ICE agents knew about the bags and had been watching and videotaping them the whole time. They arrested Sharmila Kumar and Shailen Varma, both of Vancouver, and brought them to Rogers. "It's almost like this is nothing to us. It's happening so much, it's ridiculous," he said with obvious exasperation. "They come any way they can. It's well-orchestrated, and they plan this well in advance. It's a daily event."

But they were small fry. People like Kumar and Varma were just transporters—"mules" in the parlance of the business—and were more valuable for information than anything else. The feds were after the big guys. And a few months later, on September 25, they got a couple. Acting on a tip, ICE watched the single strip at Tieton State Airport just outside of Rimrock, Washington, when the plane they were looking for landed.

Unfortunately for them, the items they unloaded were obscured by some nearby bushes and trees, but they did manage to apprehend two men—UN associates Joshua Hildebrandt and Nicholas "Nick" Kocoski—and arrest them for entering the United States illegally. Kocoski happened to be carrying a handheld GPS device that indicated the flight had begun in Chilliwack. Its history also showed that he had made many such flights and that Rimrock was just a stop on the way to other destinations, particularly Montana. A few days later, Kocoski's older brother Alexander (also an alleged UN associate) and Roueche's friend and real estate agent Mike Gordon drove over the border. They told customs and immigration officers they were going to bail out Nick and Hildebrandt.

As if to prove traffic also went the other way, B.C. native and UN associate Daniel Leclerc was stopped at Yreka Rohrer Field airport just outside Montague in northern California on September 27. Inside the plane was 315 pounds of cocaine, and his itinerary indicated he was headed for Chilliwack.

The informant Davis then visited Roueche in Abbotsford. Roueche outlined a plan in which Davis would regularly organize the transport of up to $500,000 to some friends in California and bring back 25 kilograms of cocaine. He also asked for his help in finding street-level dealers for San Jose,

California, and drivers who'd get BC Bud and ecstasy to some new clients he had in Texas.

He also told him, on tape, that since the feds were already onto the helicopters, he'd planned "something a little different, a little cool" that was "flatter" and would go deeper over the border and that negotiations were "brewing up."

At the start of 2006, Davis started transporting UN cash from Seattle down to Los Angeles to a Roueche contact there known as "Pitbull," who had also turned informant. He turned over two payments—one $109,555, the other $118,980—to ICE agents.

But Roueche was not happy with how long the payments were taking to get to Pitbull and told Davis that if they didn't speed up, he'd send someone down to beat up the guy who'd been driving them down for him. Davis also claimed he was told that if Roueche was on one of his many trips out of the country, his contact would be Dan Russell, Roueche's right-hand man.

The Americans knew exactly who they wanted. It was just a matter of how and when they'd get him.

• • •

But it's not as though Canadian law enforcement were sitting on their hands. While the Americans were intent on tearing down the UN because they trafficked marijuana into their country and attracted more dangerous elements from the south, the Canadians had their own agenda.

Sure that the drugs and violence could all be linked back to the Hells Angels and their allies, the police in Canada put particularly heavy pressure on them. After Plante's testimony led to the arrest of Lising and 17 others, the police used evidence gathered from that investigation to fuel new ones.

One of the major players who had not been arrested in Operation E-Pandora was Kerry Renaud, the meth cook and street-level dealer who worked with both Lising and Punko.

Based on what they had learned in E-Pandora, police were given permission to wiretap his residence.

It was not exactly his first run-in with the law. A few years earlier, a man who lived on the ninth floor of a 20-floor Surrey high-rise noticed a strange "chemically" smoke coming from the apartment below and called 9-1-1. When the police, who responded first, entered the eighth-floor apartment, they found Renaud on the balcony cooking methamphetamine on a cheap, two-burner hotplate using kitchen utensils. They also found more than 13 pounds of high-quality meth—with a retail value of about $500,000—and the ingredients to make much more. Renaud tried to flee but was apprehended. Since it was a first offense, he was given a particularly light sentence.

Since then, he had become more sophisticated and more cocky. He looked like a meth cook. He had tattoos, a shaved head and that tilted-head stance guys who think they're tough always take. Police heard him talk about how he outwitted them when they raided the Abbotsford barn he used as a lab by moving all his product—nine buckets of high-grade meth— elsewhere just hours earlier. They also heard him instruct the people who worked for him how to cook. "I'm the one running the show," he boasted. "This is how it's going to work. This is how we are going to make our money."

After he was arrested, the judge in his trial ordered a publication ban. It was made clear that he was cooking meth for a particular Hells Angel. The judge attempted to protect the identity of the biker in question, but since Plante had already testified that Renaud cooked for Lising and Punko, and Lising was already behind bars, it didn't take a brain surgeon to make an educated guess.

Unable to infiltrate their ranks because of strict new entry requirements, the police knew it was necessary to turn another informant. And they found one in the Prince George puppet gang the Renegades. This as-yet-unnamed source bought more than nine kilos of cocaine on several trips to the Langley house of East End full-patch Cedric Smith's house. He also managed to get Smith on tape telling him that the coke had come from East End president Norman Krogstad. Both Smith and Krogstad were arrested, the first time a chapter president had gone down in B.C. Both were sentenced to four years. In the raid that brought them down, police also seized 14 kilos of cocaine, 11 kilos of BC Bud, four handguns, a sawed-off shotgun, a civilian version of an AK-47 assault rifle modified for automatic fire, some $100,000 in U.S. currency and three lawn tractors recently reported stolen from a nearby golf course.

But while both were released after one-third of their sentences, they were only allowed to walk under the condition they not associate with people involved in the drug trade. That, of course, made the Hells Angels clubhouse and all of their haunts absolutely off-limits. The concept—arrest as many as you can and release them under the condition they essentially leave the club—was not new. Police in Ontario had used the same plan to take the teeth out of the once-powerful Outlaws, reducing them both in number and effectiveness.

To those other than perhaps his Hells Angels brothers, Robert Thomas was considered an egregious individual. Ugly, pig-nosed and flabby, Thomas was originally from Sarnia, Ontario—a dead-end chemical-industry town with particularly high crime rates. When he was bumming around southwestern Ontario, he was arrested several times for petty crimes, mostly B&Es, in Sarnia, Guelph and Windsor.

In 1986, Ontario was glad to see him go as he moved to Kelowna and graduated to drunk driving and assaults (sucker punches, from what I've heard). At one of the assault arrests, he was found to be carrying an illegal handgun, a mistake that would net him a lifelong gun ban.

But shortly after Smith and Krogstad went down, police found Thomas in possession of a stolen handgun with ammunition nearby (not to mention several other stolen items).

At his trial, Thomas said that he bought the gun from what he thought was a reputable dealer and that he had forgotten about the gun ban he'd been handed. He also went so far as to say he purchased the weapon to hunt in "the woods" in an effort to connect with his aboriginal roots, although hunting with a handgun is not only extremely unusual and difficult, but illegal in B.C. As for his membership in the Hells Angels? Well, that was because of his enthusiasm for motorcycles and to promote his burgeoning tattoo business.

In the end, Thomas was sentenced to four months for the gun and two more for the other stolen property. In the ruling, Justice P.V. Hogan did not issue any restriction on him after his release and explained it by writing, "I suppose I could be cute and pretend that he was being rehabilitated by being kept away from the Hells Angels, but I think that is just a twist of wording more than anything else."

And sometimes the police did not even have to work to catch a Lower Mainland Hells Angel. On April 28, 2006, White Rock sergeant-at-arms Villy Lynnerup was at Vancouver International Airport headed to a 4:45 afternoon flight to Edmonton. At 4:30, he threw his black canvas carry-on bag on the conveyor belt to go through the X-ray machine. The image that showed up onscreen in front of security was very obviously a Bryco .38-caliber handgun. Lynnerup was immediately arrested. The gun was illegal in Canada because of its barrel length.

At his trial, Lynnerup acknowledged that the bag and the other items in it were his, but he had never seen the gun before. The judge told him he might have believed that he had forgotten that he had put the gun in his bag (despite the obvious bulge and extra weight it caused), but to deny any knowledge of it was ridiculous. He was sentenced to 18 months and eight days, and received a lifelong firearms ban. He later appealed the judgment after serving his prison term—in hopes of getting the government to lift the firearms ban—but lost.

More important than the gun, though, was something else in Lynnerup's bag of tricks. He was carrying official club documents that indicated that the recently formed Outcasts were a puppet club for the East End chapter and that the Surrey-based Jesters were applying for the same position under the sponsorship of the White Rock chapter. Rick Ciarniello, who has acted as something of a spokesman for the Hells Angels in the Lower Mainland, denied that on a radio talk show, claiming the other clubs were simply informing the Hells Angels of their formation as a professional courtesy.

The Hells Angels weren't exactly reeling after the arrests, but they had lost a significant chunk of their manpower, at least temporarily. More important, however, they realized they were the number-one target of law enforcement in the region and that the police were willing to go to great lengths—including paying a low-level functionary like Plante more than $1 million—to turn informants.

At the same time, the United Nations had taken on a more powerful enemy than it had ever seen before—the U.S. government. As Roueche and his allies were becoming increasingly aware, federal agents were just beginning a series of increasingly sophisticated operations against their activities south of the border and sharing information with their Canadian counterparts.

At the same time, other gangs like the Duhre Brothers—natural heirs to the Indo-Canadian Mafia—were shooting each other in the streets.

It was a perfect opportunity for someone—perhaps an intelligent, crafty gangster with ice water in his veins like Jonathan Bacon—to take control.

● ● ●

Strathcona Court looks like an ideal place to raise children. It's quiet, tree-lined and pretty. The houses are big, and there's plenty of room for parking. It's designed in such a way that you'd never be there unless you had a specific reason to be there. Cars come along rarely, except when the parents are going to work or coming home, so the street itself is often used by kids playing games and parents socializing. There's an elementary school near the end of the street. And of the 16 houses on the cul-de-sac in the summer of 2006, just two of them were without school-age children. One of those housed the Bacons.

Most of the other families did their best to steer clear of the Bacons, especially—as one former neighbor told me—when there was a "lineup of expensive-looking cars there."

Thursday, September 21, 2006, was pretty much like any other late-summer day. Kids were playing outside after dinner and before bedtime (it was a school night), trying to enjoy the last bit of late sunshine and warmth before October brought its gray skies and cool rains.

The last of them were hustled into their homes, complaining that it was still light out, at about eight. About 15 minutes later, a strange car turned the right-hand corner. It was an unfamiliar car, something that made most of the neighborhood look out of their windows out of curiosity. Of course, strange cars came to visit the Bacons at all hours of the day and night, but none of their friends would be seen in this thing, a refrigerator white, rusting mid-80s Toyota Camry. Those who bothered to look probably decided it was just someone who was lost and went back to their business.

Until the shots silenced everything else. There were dozens of them. Six went into the home of the Bacons' next-door neighbors, including one right through the front door. "They just kept coming and coming," said one neighbor who would not be identified. "It was a nightmare." Children, thrown to the ground for cover by concerned parents, were screaming and crying. It was chaos. One resident told the media: "They didn't care who saw them. They didn't care who they hit. My kid could have been riding her bike up the hill at that time.

I won't let my children play out front. My son asked me, 'Are they going to come back?'"

When the shooting was over and the piece-of-crap car burned rubber and sped away, some of the neighborhood dads ran out to see what was going on. They saw a man—and they all knew who he was—laying in an increasingly spreading pool of his own blood. Jonathan Bacon had been shot four or five times, including once in the head and neck.

As a neighbor held him, waiting for the ambulance to come, Bacon said the same thing over and over: "I'm dead. I'm dead."

CHAPTER 6

NEW FRIENDS: 2006–2007

Jonathan Bacon was wrong. He was not dead. In fact, quick medical attention and poor aim had combined to get him back to relatively normal health very quickly.

But the shooting was something of a wake-up call. Up until that point, the Bacon Brothers had been operating more or less independently but in conjunction with the United Nations. They received their drugs from the UN, but they were far from members. They didn't have the requisite tattoos, and they didn't go for any of Roueche's juvenile faux-Asian, semi-religious rituals.

And they could see the writing on the wall. The UN was being decimated by arrests, mostly in the United States, but also in Canada. It could be time, the Bacons thought, to look for new friends, new partners who could give them what the UN had given them, but with more personal security and a more secure future.

While Jonathan recovered, many of his duties fell to little brother Jamie, the monstrous, childish, monosyllabic body-builder and wrestler.

Jamie had been in a little bit of trouble of late, though. On the night of October 25, 2005, he and his new friend Dennis Karbovanec—a close associate of the UN's biggest rivals, the Red Scorpions—got into a shouting match with some small-time dealers in front of a townhouse on Sandy Hill Road, and when police came to quiet things down it had escalated to the point at which they were both charged with pointing weapons and uttering death threats.

In January 2006, Jamie and two other friends—arsonist-for-hire Steven Porsch and armed robber James Potgieter, both of whom also had ties to the Red Scorpions—were caught robbing a grow op in nearby Mt. Lehman and terrorizing its owner.

• • •

Every large community has at least one. Loud, frenetic spots where parents can bring (or leave) kids for a day's amusement playing video games, driving go-karts or slapping out a few grounders at the batting cage.

In Abbotsford, it's the unimaginatively named Castle Fun Park. With a vaguely medieval theme, Castle Fun Park is something of a dumping ground for Lower Mainland kids to burn off energy or stress. It's around the corner from the house Jonathan Bacon lived in with Burton.

As with most of these places, it's rare to see anyone other than frenzied kids, annoyed parents or exhausted grand-parents. So on December 7, 2006, when a group of thickly muscled, densely tattooed 20-somethings were gathered in a recreation area usually reserved for parents and grand-parents to catch their breath while their kids ran around, it drew some attention. There were a number of topics on the agenda of the 20-somethings, not the least of which was what would be done about the Lal Brothers, who had recently left the Red Scorpions and become competitors. And when one of the thugs attending the meeting just happened to expose a handgun under his jacket when he extended his arm, a couple of concerned parents called 9-1-1.

A SWAT team arrived and rounded up the gangsters. They were surprised by whom they got. The Bacon Brothers' representative was Jamie, wearing a sleeveless shirt to show off his mighty arms and intricate tattoos. He was on bail, awaiting trial on a number of charges stemming from a 2005 home invasion at a reluctant marijuana supplier's grow operation.

Then there was Randy Naicker, who was also out on bail. He—along with Harpreet Narwal, his brother Roman Narwal and Sarpreet Johal—had, in January 2005, participated in the kidnapping, extortion and beating of Harpreet Singh. He just also happened to be one of the founding members of the Independent Soldiers—one who was not entirely unhappy about the Hells Angels' takeover of his old gang.

Another man, Barry Espadilla, was also out on bail—on a charge of manslaughter. Espadilla trafficked cocaine, meth, heroin and ecstasy for the Independent Soldiers. Back in May 2003, some friends ran into a group of Red Scorpions in a nightclub. A brawl broke out, and the fight spilled out into the parking lot. The next day, the leader of the rival gang's brawl contingent was murdered. Espadilla was originally charged with first-degree murder, but the judge preferred to believe his portrayal of himself as a frightened errand boy. He eventually was sentenced to two years and given a firearms ban.

And there were some other bad dudes at Castle Fun Park that day, too, representing the Red Scorpions. Among them were drug dealer and murderer Anton Hooites-Meursing, Jeff Harvey, Justin Prince, and Jamie Bacon's close friend Dennis Karbovanec, who had recently become a fully fledged Red Scorpion.

After the cops rounded up the summit participants, they found several to be carrying handguns, and three actually were wearing bulletproof vests. Although the logic behind having such a meeting at a kids' amusement park would appear to be that the participants would be much less likely to shoot, it was clear that all three sides came prepared to do so if they had to.

• • •

Although the cops busted it up, the Castle Fun Park meeting was significant because it showed that alliances in the Lower Mainland were constantly in flux and that the Hells Angels were always somewhere in the background of the picture. At the meeting, Jamie Bacon was representing the Bacon Brothers, who had previously had close ties with the United Nations but were edging closer to the Red Scorpions. He was meeting with veteran gangsters who had once been with the Independent Soldiers, a gang that had once been all Indian Canadian, but had since become just another Hells Angels puppet club. And also there were the Red Scorpions, a mostly Asian gang that were bitter, even deadly, rivals of the UN. The Red Scorpions were no longer a few prison buddies who banded together for mutual protection. They had morphed into a major crime organization with powerful connections and an enviable distribution network.

Clearly, the landscape of organized crime in the Lower Mainland was changing, and the Bacon Brothers wanted to be part of it.

• • •

Despite the arrests, business was booming for just about everyone, especially the Hells Angels. On January 13, 2007, they improved their strategic and corporate standing by opening up yet another chapter in the Lower Mainland.

On 3910 Grant Street, in an industrial area of Burnaby, the Hells Angels established the Burnaby Nomads chapter. In the highly stratified Hells Angels caste system, the Nomads are at the top. Their job is to tell Hells Angels what to do, just as members tell prospects, prospects tell hang-arounds and so on down the chain. Originally, Nomads were to be elite members of various chapters who could travel freely among all chapters, but would have no specific Nomads clubhouse. That has evolved over the years, and now many Nomads have dedicated chapters and clubhouses of their own.

It's interesting to note that the company that owned the building, Grant Street Holdings Ltd., was owned by known Hells Angels Bob Green, Gino Zumpano and Frank Amoretto, and was acquired from 666 Holdings, which was also owned by Green and Zumpano.

Green, the chapter's president, was best known as the former manager of the North Burnaby Inn, where police had broken up an illegal gambling ring and where a man named Terry Hanna—wielding a knife and hammer, and high on cocaine—died after being tasered by the RCMP.

Zumpano was well known as the unofficial manager of the notorious Brandi's Show Lounge strip club. It was a rough place known for fights, drug trafficking and the fact that both Hells Angels and UN members hung out there. It was a far cry from the early days in which UN and Hells Angels supporters fought on sight.

And Zumpano, in fact, may have been responsible for the change in heart the UN had experienced regarding the Hells Angels. Taped conversations between informant Michael Plante and Hells Angel Johnny Punko indicated that it was Zumpano who first reached out to the UN. In one conversation, Punko said that Zumpano "took a walk" with UN leader Clayton Roueche, which Plante testified he took to mean the two had an important meeting. Punko also indicated that he could see the UN becoming the Hells Angels' allies, but that he wasn't happy about it and would rather not see them at his favorite hangout, Brandi's. "If we walk in there and they're in Brandi's," he said, "They're going to get pounded out."

But whether Punko liked it or not, UN members did start to show up in Brandi's with greater and greater frequency. And their relationship with the Hells Angels became closer and closer.

How close they had become was made very clear to law enforcement in the spring of 2007. By then, Ontario biker cops had managed to turn a full-patch Hells Angel into an informant. This was Stephen "Hannibal" Gault, who had been treasurer of the powerful Oshawa chapter, and had taken pride in the fact that he had once bitten off a rival's ear in a fistfight. Naturally, he provided a wealth of information that led to many arrests.

One of them occurred on April 4, 2007. Gault had heard that Merhdad "Juicy" Bahman, a Hells Angels prospect from the Downtown Toronto chapter, had bought 600 pounds of GHB, the notorious date-rape drug, from some guys on the West Coast. After a thorough investigation, it was determined that the GHB came from an interesting pair. The two-man team who sold the illegal substance to Bahman were Haney chapter full-patch Hells Angel Vincenzo "Jimmy" Sansalone and his partner in crime, high-ranking UN member Omid Bayani.

Though hardly a typical UN member, Bayani was a definitive one. Born in Iraq, he was constantly in trouble for armed robberies and other crimes after his family emigrated to Alberta. In and out of correctional institutions, Bayani earned a reputation as an extremely violent individual, striking out at both fellow prisoners and guards whenever possible.

When he was released, he was ordered deported but continued to live in Canada—he had relocated to Abbotsford—and made a living trafficking drugs and stolen goods. Eventually, he caught the attention of the UN and quickly rose through the ranks.

While out on bail for the GHB charges, Bayani disappeared and has not been seen since. I have been told he now lives in Mexico.

The arrest was a milestone in some ways. It was later discovered that the executive team of the Downtown Toronto Hells Angels chapter—Larry Pooler, Douglas Myles and John Neal—had stepped into the situation because they had heard that Bahman owed the "B.C." Hells Angels and the UN $100,000 for the GHB, and were encouraging him to pay rather than face severe consequences, even murder. They did this, they maintained, not because the chapter was involved in drug trafficking, but because Bahman was their friend and they did not want to see anything happen to him. They did not extend that same courtesy to their "brothers" on the West Coast, testifying that Bahman was dealing with the Haney chapter and the UN as organizations, not with Sansalone and Bayani as individuals.

What that arrest did was prove to the public that the UN— so defiant in the past—were little more than vassals to the mighty Hells Angels crime empire.

But the alliance was not news to law enforcement on the Lower Mainland. They had known that individuals from both clubs had helped each other for a while. And while the Hells Angels were certainly the dominant of the pair, their members were anything but too proud to take on jobs from their former enemies.

Wiretaps from the Plante investigations revealed that David Giles, a full patch from the Hells Angels' East End chapter and a friend of meth cook Kerry Renaud, was hired by UN leader Clayton Roueche to collect debts from a pair of his dealers, known only as "Joe" and "B." Since the judge in the resulting extortion trial ordered a publication ban, few were aware of the connection.

But the Hells Angels' little empire had some soft spots. Villy Lynnerup, the White Rock sergeant-at-arms who was caught at the airport with a gun and plans to adopt puppet gangs, could not stay out of trouble. On January 17, 2007, he was arrested for a home invasion and assault at what I have been told was a grow op with a not entirely cooperative owner. Two weeks later, he was arrested again for assault, confinement, uttering death threats and mischief after a night that began with him smashing the victim's car windows with a baseball bat.

And law enforcement were doing their best to keep a sharp eye on the members, or at least the leadership, of both organizations. When there was a double shooting in downtown Vancouver on February 24, 2007, police were unsurprised to see Roueche and Jing Bon Chan—who many believed shared control of the UN with Roueche—show up just after they did. They were questioned, but had nothing to say to police, who drew their own conclusions. "In this instance, two known associates of the gang were shot—one in the head and one in the leg," was the official word. "It is believed Roueche and Chan were there to 'interview the victims' in order to determine the gang's response to the shooting."

• • •

The sudden shifts of alliances in the Lower Mainland's underworld were not limited to those gangs in league with the Hells Angels. The Bacon Brothers, perhaps sensing the impending legal trouble with the UN, switched alliances. Instead of getting product from the Hells Angels, they started getting close to their rivals, the Red Scorpions.

In fact, they became very close. While the Hells Angels/ UN ties had been discovered through wiretaps, informants and arrests, the Bacon Brothers' ties with the Red Scorpions were more obvious than that.

Under scrutiny from police and neighbors, the Bacons left Abbotsford on February 21, 2007, and moved into a rented but very luxurious house at 15830 106th Avenue in Surrey. It's interesting to note that while much smaller than Surrey, Abbottsford has a distinct police force, while Surrey is patrolled by an RCMP detachment. The feeling among many youth in the area was that it was easier to get away with crime in Surrey because the RCMP were fewer in number and more transient, caring less about the community than their career options.

Often in either house's driveway when the Bacon family was in residence, one could see a gigantic GMC Suburban. At least, police did. It was owned by Dennis Karbovanec. The same Karbovanec who was not only a convicted killer, but also one of the longest-serving members of the Red Scorpions. But he had been in jail since a December 14, 2006, drug and weapons arrest, a week after his appearance at the suspicious Castle Fun Park meeting.

Knowing the massive SUV belonged to Karbovanec, the RCMP were watching it and even managed to get a judge to agree to allow them to covertly install a tracking chip in it. While Karbovanec was behind bars, police frequently saw it driven around variously by Jamie and Jarrod Bacon. And in the spring of 2007, they found it at the site of a crime not committed by Karbovanec.

Jamie Bacon didn't even see the two guys on the street in front of the Surrey house at about one in the morning on April 13. He was just returning home in his Corvette and was more intent on getting home to his girlfriend, Chalsi Sylvestre, and his parents than anything else. But as he drove into the driveway, the two men sent a cascade of .45-caliber shells at him. Five shells hit the Corvette, seven penetrated the garage door and one of them ended up in one of the Surburban's tires.

Jamie instinctively leapt from the car, which continued to roll until it hit the house. As the two assailants ran away, Jamie pulled out a Glock handgun and fired four shots at them.

His mother, awakened by the noise, called 9-1-1. She later reported that she could hear her son screaming "I've been shot!" over and over again. She then ran to her son, who was bleeding from where a bullet grazed his scalp, and tried to help him. She later reported that Jamie told her, "Tell Dad not to go outside," before everything "blurred for [him] after that."

An eyewitness reported that two figures—he could not identify them, but they appeared to be male—came out of the house's front door to see what was going on. According to later testimony, the only two men in the house at the time were David and Jonathan Bacon. The eyewitness then said the two men appeared to be looking for something, returned an object to the Corvette and reentered the house through a different door.

Police arrived after neighbors called 9-1-1, searched the house for potential victims (without a warrant) and took Jamie to the hospital to be checked out.

Susan Bacon was shocked at the way the officers treated her sons. "They didn't treat Jamie like a victim at all or Jonathan," she said. "When we were leaving the house, I made the boys put them [bulletproof vests] on. I was terrified."

Actually, thanks to the fact he was wearing level-3 body armor at the time of the attack, Jamie was bruised and had a gash on his head, but was not severely hurt. One of the officers who rode with him in the ambulance, helped remove his bulletproof vest and then later drove him home from the hospital, Constable Byron Donovan, had an informal conversation with Jamie that shed some light on how gangsters operate.

When Donovan asked him about the shooting and how he felt about it, Jamie just shrugged and told him it was "part of the lifestyle." Donovan then asked him about his bulletproof vest. "Mr. Bacon made a comment that he was lucky to be wearing his level-3 vest that night, otherwise he'd be paralyzed," Donovan later said. "Mr. Bacon told me that it was a level-3 vest. He learned that these are the best type of vests to have and that he learned that from watching the Military Channel. And from watching that, he got all the specs of these level-3 vests." He also mentioned, without being asked, that he had purchased ten such vests—at a price of $1,600 apiece—from Dave's Surplus in New Westminster.

And that wasn't all he had coming. Jamie bragged to the young cop that he had ordered a fully armored Ford SUV and also pointed out that he would have been driving it that night, but a CN Rail strike had delayed its arrival from Ontario.

While Jamie was being examined and talking with Donovan and his partner, other cops who had returned with a warrant were investigating the crime scene, the house and even the Bacons' cellphones and computers. They quickly found Jamie's Glock in a hidden gun compartment in the Corvette and determined the gun inside had been fired four times that night. That was backed up by the presence of four matching Smith & Wesson shell casings found near the Corvette. Interestingly, Jarrod Bacon's DNA was later found on the Glock's magazine. He was not present at the house on the night of the shooting.

The following day, a forensic specialist searched the SUV owned by Karbovanec and shared by the Bacons, and found four other loaded semiautomatic handguns inside their own custom-made, hydraulically operated gun compartments. He and others marveled at the sophistication. All of the guns were unregistered and had their serial numbers altered or removed. One of the guns inside, a Sig Sauer .45, was found to have Jamie's fingerprints on the handle, and Jarrod's fingerprints were found on the device that activated the gun compartment.

Jamie was arrested the night of the attack, and Jarrod was also arrested after his fingerprints were discovered.

News of the incident spread quickly. Most interpreted it as, if not the opening salvo in a UN war against the Bacon Brothers/Red Scorpions alliance, at least a warning shot to intimidate the Bacon Brothers back into the fold.

● ● ●

Fears of an all-out war on the streets of the Lower Mainland intensified about two weeks after the Bacon shooting.

Vancouver police received an anonymous call at 4:02 a.m. on the night of April 26, 2007, about someone walking into apartment 2101 at 1128 Quebec Street with a gun. Police quickly arrived at the luxurious high-rise and knocked on the door. When they entered, they were literally shocked at the immense amount of weaponry openly on display. They immediately arrested the only person in the unit, a nerdy-looking guy named Jong Ca "John" Lee and applied for a search warrant.

When they searched the apartment, they found a treasure trove of illegality. "When I stepped into the room, it was like immediately—wow, what is going on here. It was actually somewhat awesome," said Inspector Dean Robinson said. "It didn't matter where you looked, you saw something that was related to firearms, whether it was a firearm itself, ammunition, gun cases—then there was the swastika flag on the wall in the bedroom along with the military ordnance that we were concerned with that was on a desk. So it really quickly shifted from odd to being really disturbing."

As for weapons, police found fully automatic assault rifles, several handguns, an automatic machine pistol, a silencer, prohibited extra-capacity magazines, rifle scopes, a laser scope, telescoping stocks, ammunition, a homemade electric stun gun and weapons instruction manuals. But Lee didn't just sell weapons and their accessories; he also sold drugs. Police also found a vat containing 3.5 kilograms of MDMA in liquid form. Enough, police estimated, to make 41,800 ecstasy pills. In addition, police also discovered five bags of marijuana—one of 466 grams, one of 99 grams, one of 282.8 grams, one of 25.1 grams, and one of 2.65 grams. There was also a highly accurate digital scale, the type often associated with the drug trade.

As if gun running and drug trafficking were not enough, police found even more evidence that Lee was far from an upstanding citizen. The search of the apartment revealed a number of Canadian passports in other people's names, including at least three passports that had been reported stolen after a violent home invasion in Burnaby on February 13, 2007. On his large number of cellphones and digital cameras, they found photographs of handguns, assault rifles and other firearms displayed as though for sale. He also had a commemorative photo album that featured shots of Lee vacationing in Vietnam with three known senior members of the UN and of him posing in a prominent setting with the entire gang at the March 2005 funeral of UN founding member Evan Appell. To top it all off, Lee's tax returns stated he had made between $6,048 and $20,930 in the years he had inhabited the apartment with his unemployed wife, even though the rent was $21,600 per year. Because Lee had no criminal record, his brother—a successful real estate developer named Brett—was allowed to post $50,000 bail for his release.

Tensions flared again shortly thereafter when a Vancouver police officer conducting a routine traffic stop on May 3, 2007, noticed that the front-seat passenger had a handgun stuck in the waistband of his pants. The man, UN member Greg Allen, was arrested for carrying an unregistered Glock handgun and a silencer. The gun was traced back to Lee's arsenal.

It looked to many like war was imminent. There were two distinct sides (and other, smaller players) intent on dominating the drug trade in the Lower Mainland. All parties could count on legions of heavily armed young men who had little regard for their own safety or that of others.

As had happened several times before in the Vancouver area's history, an intense competition to cash in on a natural bounty—it had previously been timber, coal, gold and a pathway to the Pacific, but this time it was the world's best marijuana—had combined with bitter rivalries and hatreds, although slightly less racially tinged this time, to set the fuse for widespread violence.

CHAPTER 7

GOING PUBLIC: 2007–2008

While the people involved with the drug trade were growing increasingly tense, many people in the Vancouver area were blissfully unaware of the impending violence in their midst. Of course, the police forces in the area knew who the players were and were keeping a quiet eye on them. In fact, many people remarked—even in the mainstream media—that they were grateful to see an increased police presence in problem areas because it kept the "hookers" and "druggies" away. But what they didn't realize was that hookers and druggies weren't the ones they should really have been worried about.

One local businessman who was observant of the changes in the Mount Pleasant neighborhood was Mohamad Ahmed, who owns Shapla Grocery & Halal Meat. At about four in the morning of August 9, 2007, he had just closed his store and popped into a Mac's convenience store for a few things before heading home. Then he heard a tremendous noise and ran outside to see what was happening. "It sounded like a building collapsing or something," he told reporters. But it wasn't. The

buildings were all standing, but a throng of panicked people—
some screaming, some covered in blood—were struggling to get
out of the Fortune Happiness Restaurant two doors away from
Ahmed's own shop. "A lot of people were coming to the door
and were screaming," he said. "Some were sitting down on the
curb, like five or six men and women. The victims were crying."

Ahmed always thought there was something fishy going
on at the Fortune Happiness, although he considered the
newest owner to be "friendly." It had gone through three
owners in the five years he'd been keeping track. In that
same period, the restaurant had been closed down twice,
once for serving alcohol without a license and later for cutting
fish on plywood instead of approved cutting boards. It was
open every night from 5:00 p.m. to 5:00 a.m. and attracted a
lot of young nightclubbers. Most of its clientele were under 30,
and the bulk of them arrived after midnight. Someone had
recently put a cardboard sign in the front window warning
would-be troublemakers that the management had installed
security cameras. Seedy perhaps, but the Fortune Happiness
was hardly an established gang hangout. Police would later
say, "it wasn't on our radar."

On the night of the tragedy, nine men and women were
sitting at a table enjoying a family-style meal when two masked
men broke in and showered them with bullets. Two men died at
the scene—19-year-old Prince Rupert native Zachary Ferland
and an unidentified 26-year-old. Both were "known to police"
and had a history related to drug trafficking. Of the remaining
seven, one was uninjured.

One of those shot was a more notorious gangster, Hung
Van "Scarface" (or "Sonny") Bui, who was shot six times but
survived. Well known as a trafficker and enforcer for hire,
Bui was a veteran gangster who specialized in robbing rival
drug dealers.

All of the victims of the shooting were of Chinese or
Vietnamese descent, and all of the men at the table had been

linked to the drug trade. Law enforcement called the incident "gang related." Word on the street was that the Independent Soldiers were reestablishing their dominance in the area. No arrests were ever made.

Vancouver police called the Fortune Happiness massacre "the worst shooting in the city's history." They'd see worse.

• • •

As with most wars, the conflict on the streets of the Lower Mainland simmered slowly before intensifying, with the period after the dramatic Fortune Happiness shoot-up characterized by individual tit-for-tat shootings and assaults as the sides felt each other out.

A couple of such early incidents were shocking, not just because of the targets, but also because of the blatant disregard the assailants had for putting innocent bystanders, in this case innocent children, in deadly harm's way.

The first came at a bustling restaurant full of people. Quattro on Fourth in Kitsilano is posh and always busy. It was particularly crowded the night of September 8, 2007, as 26 people were at one table celebrating a birthday party. At a little after eleven, two men wearing dark clothes and masks walked up to the plate glass window and fired through the glass at two people inside.

"What we can tell you now is that the 29-year-old man, we believe, was a target of the shooting, that he is well-known to police," said a police spokesman. "It's a very shocking occurrence. Here we have a very popular, busy restaurant in town." The 29-year-old was Gurmit Singh Dhak. Also injured in the attack was his 21-year-old girlfriend.

Both were badly hurt, though neither suffered life-threatening injuries. Still, Dhak refused to cooperate with police. But they weren't too surprised. Dhak had a long history of gang-related trouble. He'd gone to prison for helping an associate shoot a 19-year-old who was in the front passenger seat of his car in 1999. During that investigation, they found him to be in possession of weapons linked to another gang-related shooting in 1998. More recently, he was stopped by police after his Lexus SUV was shot full of holes in front of a seedy strip joint called the Uranus Lounge a few blocks down East Broadway from the Happiness Fortune restaurant. He didn't cooperate then either, and was even arrested for uttering death threats at an officer who attempted to question him.

And the violence was hardly limited to the city. If you drive down 248th Street in the Otter district of Langley, B.C., you'll see typical wooden semi-rural houses, some better than the others, but mostly nothing special. Until you get to 3153. Hidden from public view by a high, thick hedge and protected by a huge gate on its private laneway, the $2.6-million-dollar property has a large in-ground pool and a massive stable. It's called Laughing Stock Ranch, and it operates as a site for kids' parties with pony rides and bouncy castles. The owners, Leonard and Cynthia Pelletier, also hire out their ponies and dogs for film, television and advertising. Leonard also likes to restore old muscle cars.

But police knew him as a close associate of several full-patch Hells Angels. In fact, he was first cousins—and what appeared to best friends—with Nomad full-patch Bob Green. Some media reports claimed Pelletier himself was a full-patch. There's no proof of that, but there are several published photos of him in familiar poses with Hells Angels, including a set of him arm in arm with Green, while they both pose with UFC star Chuck Liddell. Cynthia laughed at the idea her husband was a gangster when confronted by reporters. "We're farmers," she said. "Everybody loves Lenny." Still, between 1997 and 2006, he was arrested several times on charges related to trafficking, possessing stolen goods and dangerous driving.

They also had two teenaged sons at the time. In early September 2007, the older one, 16, was involved in a confrontation between a group he was part of and a rival group of boys the same age. Len put an end to the standoff by severely beating the other group's leader. As these things always seem to end, the losing side skulked away shouting threats.

A few days later, on September 11, 2007, Len Pelletier was driving his younger, 14-year-old son to D.W. Poppy Secondary School in his massive Hummer SUV when he felt like he was being followed by another car. As he drove closer to the school, he slowed down, and the car that he thought had been following him pulled up alongside. When he saw who was inside the car (and perhaps that they were armed), he stomped on the accelerator. Later, he would claim it was to ensure the safety of throngs of innocent high school kids around him.

With his son still in the front seat, Pelletier sped eastward on 47th Avenue and turned left on 236th Street. The other car pursued. Panicked, Pelletier turned right on 52nd Avenue. But the Hummer took the turn wide, slammed into a parked car and careened into a ditch, finally coming to a stop after colliding with a tree. The other car pulled up beside the crashed Hummer and—despite the fact that Pelletier had driven to, and crashed in front of, Peterson Road Elementary School— opened fire.

Neither Len nor his son was shot, but Len did suffer some minor injuries from the crash. Both schools went into lockdown mode.

Later that day, the Pelletiers' older son fell into a confrontation with police. Although they required a taser shot to subdue the boy, he was released without charge. His mother attributed the incident to him being upset over the shooting.

Two weeks later, a joint agreement between the Pelletiers, the RCMP and the Langley school board led to the 14-year-old being removed from D.W. Poppy for "alternative schooling."

The police did not agree with Cynthia that the shooting was the result of a teenage brawl gone out of control. In fact, they seemed to be of the opinion that the incident was part of a bigger conflict that was far-reaching and in danger of escalation. "We are confident that this incident has to do with far greater issues than a group of teenagers that were in a dispute that chose to beat on one another," said Langley RCMP spokesman Peter Thiessen. "This issue that occurred yesterday is linked to something far greater and far more criminal than that. I will leave it to the community to form an opinion and make a decision as to where the credible information may be coming from."

• • •

On October 19, 2007, the Lower Mainland learned that the cops were right. The news was everywhere. Six people had been shot and killed at Balmoral Tower in Surrey: four alleged gangsters and two clearly innocent bystanders. The amount of bloodshed, the cold-blooded planning and premeditation, and the absolute disregard for public safety made the Fortune Happiness shootings look like a birthday party.

When news of the Surrey Six murders broke, all of British Columbia went into a state of shock. Newspapers and radio were alive with news of the murders. Grief-stricken Eileen Mohan's image was everywhere, putting a human face on the horror everyone felt. Police were largely tight-lipped but admitted that the killings were "gang related." Still, it didn't take rocket science for the public to put two and two together.

The common opinion in the area that the drug trade could be nonviolent was dashed. While local media understandably concentrated on the innocent victims, the fact that members of one gang essentially exterminated another was more historically significant. Mohan and Schellenberg were tragic victims of being in the wrong place at the wrong time, but the execution of the Lal gang set a deadly precedent. It had been made abundantly clear that with so much money involved, with so many disparate (and desperate) players involved, there was no way the drug trade could remain peaceful. The Lals and their allies had betrayed the Red Scorpions, and they were given a death sentence. What had been unthinkable now was standard operating procedure. Anyone who stood in the way of a gang's income could expect to die.

It was no longer business as usual. After the Surrey Six massacre, the lines were more distinctly drawn. Everyone in the underworld knew the rules. Mess with the other side, and you would be shot. Yet there were those who couldn't resist messing. The potential danger was rising, but the drug trafficking gangs were still intent on cashing in on the bonanza. While the Hells Angels' flunkies—the Renegades and the Independent Soldiers—dominated the drug trade in Prince George, there was actually enough business there that a new, independent gang emerged.

The name was always a problem. They called themselves the Game Tight Soldiers. The "game" referred to underworld business and "tight" reflected its slang meaning, in some circles, hip and well put together. But when it was all put together, it became a name other gangsters found hilarious, and launched several creative nicknames, pretty much all of which put the members' sexual orientation into question.

When the existence of the Game Tight Soldiers came to light, they were paid a visit by the Renegades. It's customary in Hells Angels–dominated communities for their representatives to offer any rivals a standard ultimatum: work for us or get out of town.

In most such cases, the members of the threatened gang simply capitulate. But there was a real rift in the Game Tight Soldiers—and an opportunity. A series of mass arrests in Winnipeg had left the Hells Angels chapter there in an absolute shambles. That power vacuum led to a group of rival bikers—including a few former Bandidos and some disillusioned Hells Angels associates—to form a new gang.

And, in a move calculated to enrage the Hells Angels, they called it the Rock Machine, after the notorious Montreal-based gang who went to war with the Hells Angels.

So, when the Game Tight Soldiers were confronted by the Renegades, some of them—led by the gang's founder and president, Steven King, born in Barrie, Ontario—accepted the offer and started working for the Renegades. Others, however, packed up and took their talents to Winnipeg, where they hooked up with the Rock Machine.

• • •

But a new player emerged in the game. Apart from the established gangs, their hangers-on and the police, the public—in particular, the families of victims—began to make a difference. Public outrage was mounting, and the Surrey Six killings had given them a powerful, persistent and persuasive advocate—Eileen Mohan. The mother of Chris Mohan, who was among the dead at the Balmoral, Eileen Mohan was interviewed shortly after the murders on CBC Radio and announced that she was launching a campaign for judicial reform. She was sure that even if her son's killers were ever caught, their sentences would hardly fit the crime. That immediately made her someone reporters called when they needed a quotation for their story about how a victim felt or how light sentences were a problem. But as things went along, Mohan, others like her and people who just wanted to see an end to the violence banded together and rallied to quell the increased violence in the Lower Mainland.

The first public display of Mohan's activism came after details of Ronnie Lising's trafficking trial became public in the middle of November 2007. A security-camera video tape showed Lising and fellow full-patch Hells Angel knocking bouncer Randall Bowles to the ground then kicking him outside a popular downtown nightclub in 2005. Lising, who had already been convicted of cocaine trafficking in 2001, was given a $600 fine (which did not go to the victim) and a two-year gun ban, although no firearms were involved. Alvarez was given a year's probation and 50 hours of community service.

The CBC asked Mohan to comment. "I think the public at large will be appalled to see the amount of sentences that were given that were so lenient," she told them. "In this case, we should have put these people away for a longer time."

Eileen Mohan and the family of Surrey Six victim Ed Schellenberg held a Public Safety Rally at Bear Creek Park in Surrey on February 3, 2008. About 200 people attended the event, which began with the release of white doves to symbolize the innocent victims. Several people spoke, including the mayor and the local member of Parliament. But the most compelling, the one people came to see, was Mohan. She delivered. There was something about her honest, heartfelt words that moved people. Of all the speeches, hers drew the most applause and the most tears.

All of the speakers talked about staying involved in children's lives to help keep them away from drugs and gangs, but they all knew that prevention could only go so far. A much larger part of the rally focused on a call for stiffer penalties for violent offenders. Surrey Mayor Diane Watts pointed out that a life sentence in Canada usually results in about ten years of actual prison time, sometimes as little as six, and that Canada does not allow for consecutive life sentences. "We must have consecutive sentences for multiple homicides. When someone is caught for these murders—and they will be caught—they will be sentenced to one life sentence," she said. "That's 10 years—for six murders. That's definitely unacceptable."

Mohan also called for a website dedicated to identifying and making public who the Lower Mainland's gangsters were. She got her wish. Soon after the rally ended, a website called "Gangstersout" was created that included a directory of known and suspected gang members, as well as a blog keeping its readers up to date on organized crime. It is operated anonymously by an administrator who goes by the name of Agent K. It is an invaluable resource for anyone who wants to know anything about crime in the Lower Mainland and is meticulously and courageously kept up to date and accurate.

• • •

The first shot fired in the public's war against organized crime was a dud. Glen "Kingpin" Hehn, the full-patch Hells Angel who, along with his friend Ewan Lilford, was caught with $1.5 million worth of cocaine in 2003, was acquitted on April 30, 2008. Lilford was not charged.

Justice Peter Leask praised Hehn as a witness on his own behalf. When Crown Attorney Ernie Froess pointed out that the cocaine was probably not Lilford's because it would have been foolhardy and dangerous for a person to secretly store cocaine in a locker rented by a Hells Angel, Leask acknowledged that fact, but gave a bizarre interpretation of his own. "On the one hand, he can minimize his risk of detection and apprehension by just aborting the whole fucking thing, right?" he said, no doubt delighting the grade school children attending the trial that day as part of a field trip. "And saying, I thought I was going to do these things, but I'm not going to do them, it's just this morning is not working out for me, or he can try and make the best of things."

And when Froess tried to claim the cocaine was owned by Hehn, Leask rejected that idea entirely. "But to be really clear, he'd have had to have been out of his fuckin' mind to store it in his own locker, all right?" he said. "I mean, that's for sure he wouldn't do that. Let's not spend any time on that theory."

So in Leask's world, when a full-patch Hells Angel and his friend are caught with 52 kilograms of cocaine in a locker leased by the Hells Angel and admittedly used by the friend, it is obvious that the cocaine belongs to an unknown third party because the friend would be too intimidated by the Hells Angel to be the owner and the Hells Angel would be too smart to be the owner.

• • •

Kipling Street is an appealing, if largely treeless, suburban Abbotsford street that ends in a cul-de-sac. Since the houses there are quite large with spacious yards, most of the owners have children. Since the kids all play or at least hang out with one another and go to the same schools, it's a social and friendly block on which pretty well everyone knows everyone else.

But in 2008, there was a couple without kids who lived at the big white siding-and-brick house at 1432 and didn't mix with anyone else in the neighborhood. "They made it clear they had their own set of friends," a neighbor told me. "And wanted to keep it that way."

On the night of Friday, May 8, 2008, there were two strange cars on the street, a giant, customized Ford F-350 pickup and a large silver Mercedes-Benz M-Class SUV. At about 10:40 p.m., the quiet of the evening was shaken by a series of gunshots and the sound of squealing tires. Curious neighbors came to their windows just in time to see the SUV's taillights glowing in the darkness and getting smaller as it sped away.

The victim, a 40-year-old white man, was hit several times while walking across the front yard to his truck in the house's driveway. He managed to crawl back to the porch but collapsed there, dying before authorities—who had been alerted by several 9-1-1 calls—arrived.

The dead man was Duane Harvey Meyer, a former Hells Angels prospect who had risen to a high leadership post in the UN. His importance in that organization was made obvious by his funeral, which looked from its size and scope like a well-known hero had died. Except for who was in attendance.

The entire membership of the UN was on hand—including luminaries like Roueche and Chan—and all but a couple of them were wearing ludicrous "gangster" suits with black shirts and white ties. Many of them, including Roueche, arrived in custom-made black hoodies emblazoned with the message "In memory D.M." Also on hand were a significant number of Hells Angels and Abbotsford police with metal detectors. Pictures from the event would later be used to prove gang connections in dozens of subsequent criminal trials.

• • •

It was an increasingly violent time. Shootings, often in places full of innocent bystanders, were becoming commonplace. The police appeared powerless to stop them. Even when they did arrest somebody, it always seemed as though the courts would absolve the person charged, despite obvious circumstances, or hand out ridiculously small sentences which would then be reduced to merely symbolic punishments.

Frustrated by knowing who the bad guys were but being unable to do anything concrete about it, the Abbotsford police came up with an idea that they hoped would help promote public awareness of the situation, if not actually remove the problem. They issued a public warning on May 31, 2008, stating that any person doing business with or associating in any way with Jonathan Bacon was putting his or her life in grave danger. In truth, the cops could have said that about any of the Bacon Brothers or any of a number of other regional gang members. But the police chose Jonathan not only because they knew he was knee-deep in the drug trade, but also because he was easily identifiable and recognizable. Too often, cops tell me, the public will ignore warnings about members of visible minorities or the kind of person who simply looks like a criminal. To most people, Jonathan looked more like the kind of guy you'd buy a used car from than a gangster. He was, simply put, the boy next door for most Canadians. That made him stand out, and it also reminded the people of the region that anyone could be a gangster.

Unable to put the bad guy away, the best authorities could do was to tell people who he was. That way, if there were more victims, they could at least say they had warned them.

• • •

Jonathan Barber was no gangster, and his fate demonstrated how fatal even the most tenuous link to the Bacons could be. He was just a hardworking guy. He worked a few jobs, but the one he was best at was installing stereo equipment into high-end vehicles. It was a great job, not only because he could use his skills and get paid, but because he could drive around Vancouver in some of the hottest cars available.

On May 9, 2008, Barber was excited to be working on a black Porsche Cayenne, a luxurious SUV made by a sports car manufacturer that delighted drug dealers the world around as much as it horrified Porsche purists. As he drove it from the owner's place in Abbotsford to his Vancouver shop, he had his 17-year-old girlfriend drive his own, lesser SUV close behind.

He didn't know who the owner was; he was just happy to be driving the Cayenne. But others were well aware of exactly whose car it was. In fact, an armed group of UN members were surprised to see Jonathan Bacon's car cruising down the Kingsway.

Barber had no gang connections. But because the gangster look was in fashion, his short dark hair and gold chain gave him a passing resemblance to Jonathan Bacon.

The UN members—Barzan Tilli-Choli, Dan Russell, Dilun Heng, Karwan Saed, Yong Lee and Ion Croitoru (better known as "Johnny K-9," a Hamilton, Ontario–born former professional wrestler and member of Satan's Choice)—took their shot. Oblivious to the other vehicles and pedestrians on one of the busiest streets in Canada, at ten in the evening, they sprayed the luxurious SUV with gunfire. Barber slumped down, dead. The weight of his right foot pressed on the accelerator, and the Cayenne's powerful engine vaulted the big vehicle over the sidewalk and into a nearby furniture store, knocking a big hole in the wall. Panicked by the gunshots and seeing the Cayenne veer off the street, Barber's 17-year-old girlfriend driving the man's own SUV accelerated and collided with several other cars. She was hurt but survived.

Three gang-related murders in less than 48 hours proved to even the most cynical observer that there was a war on. And it was more widespread than simply the UN against the Bacon Brothers. The UN, of course, had a tenuous relationship with the Hells Angels and, by extension, many other gangs, including the Independent Soldiers. And the Bacon Brothers had become synonymous with the Red Scorpions. In fact, once Kabovanec was back out of jail, he shared a car lease with Jamie Bacon and gave the Bacon family home as his address.

• • •

From information they learned during Project Frozen Timber, police in both Canada and the United States knew that Roueche was a major player in drug trafficking from Canada to the United States. And the evidence they collected allowed them to tap his phone.

One of the first things they learned was that Clayton Roueche, like many Canadians involved in the drug trade, was afraid to travel to the United States, where sentences are much stiffer. On April 2, 2008, just before noon, he received a call from a friend named Pam Lee, who asked him if he knew anyone who could give her a ride to the airport in Bellingham,

Washington. She pointed out that she knew it wouldn't be him. "Yeah," he said with a snicker. "I'll never come back." When she pressed him on it, he told her, "I wouldn't even get down there; they'd throw me in jail."

But Roueche did go to Mexico. Not only was it essential to his business, but he also had friends there. And when he was invited to a wedding in May 2008, he did not hesitate to go. On May 19, Roueche landed in Mexico. When he handed over his passport—which had stamps from Vietnam, Japan, Macao, Hong Kong, the Netherlands, the United Arab Emirates, Lebanon and Thailand, but not the United States—he was asked to wait in a separate room. Two officers met with him and told him that American authorities asked them not to allow him into the country. Roueche said he understood and told them he'd get on the next flight back to Vancouver.

He did. But shortly after the plane he was on was in American airspace, the pilot made an announcement: the plane was being rerouted to Dallas/Fort Worth International Airport. He did not give a reason why. "Once on the plane and in his seat," said U.S. prosecutors, "Roueche quickly began sending BlackBerry messages, indicating he was concerned about flying through the United States, saying that perhaps he was being paranoid but he was worried about being arrested. He also BlackBerried information about bank accounts and access codes before he had to turn off the device." Once on the tarmac, the plane was entered by U.S. Customs agents, who arrested Roueche.

Roueche was charged with conspiracy to import cocaine and marijuana into the United States and money laundering. Emily Langlie, spokesman for the federal attorney's office, told media that Roueche was wearing a significant amount of UN-related jewelry at the time of his arrest.

At a federal lockup in Oklahoma, Roueche immediately started making calls, while the feds listened in. When they determined he had been speaking in code (he had actually left a codebook in his holding cell), his phone privileges were lifted.

Langlie also said that he would be flown to Seattle to stand trial. He requested bail, but prosecutors pointed out that the last UN member they granted bail to, Joe Curry, had fled. To emphasize that point, they showed the judge a photo of Roueche and Curry arm in arm at Duane Meyer's funeral. Bail was not granted.

The founder and brightest star of the UN was behind bars. It wasn't a hugely crippling blow, as most members of the gang had their own connections and suppliers, or could easily get in touch with Roueche's. But it was a terrible hit to the gang's morale. The big guy, the founder, the face of the UN, grinning from behind designer sunglasses while cruising around in his Maserati, was off the streets.

• • •

But it wasn't just the UN who was being forcibly reordered. Cedric Michael Smith was one of the founding B.C. Hells Angels and generally considered a heavy player. He was arrested for trafficking a number of times, but the most recent was a big one. In January 2005, nine Hells Angels and Renegades were arrested, including Smith and Norman Krogstad, who had been selling one-kilogram bags of coke— many delivered to a Wendy's fast food location—to an informant who was building a case. The pair were charged, tried, and sentenced and served time, and both were granted parole in March 2007.

Many other Hells Angels blamed Smith for the 2005 arrests, including his own, because he had introduced them to the informant. Of course, he didn't know the man was an informant, but it was still considered a huge faux pas in the industry. So huge, in fact, that there was a price to pay. Smith's old partner from the Renegades, William "Billy" Moore, had been killed shortly after the arrests, and his house had been set on fire in a similar situation.

So when Smith missed a June 17, 2008, meeting with his parole officer, the RCMP sent a pair of officers to his house in Langley. He wasn't there and has not been seen since. There are lots of rumors that explain his absence and fate, but nothing concrete has emerged.

And gang members did not have to be in the Lower Mainland to be in danger. Ahmet "Lou" Kaawach looked like a gangster. A 26-year-old, he shaved his head, had a pencil-thin beard and moustache, had prominent tattoos on his pumped-up biceps and always wore a big gold chain. He also liked to show off his wealth with his vehicle—a red Cadillac EXT pickup truck tricked out with six TV screens and doors modified to open vertically.

That kind of truck and lifestyle do not come cheaply. But money was no problem for Kaawach. He owned a car customization business and law enforcement agencies also say he was the UN's chief contact with the Mexican drug cartels, arranging for shipments of cocaine to be traded for BC Bud. Roueche himself described Kaawach as a wannabe "ladies' man" and spoke about his earnest, if not entirely productive, efforts to rap about his gangster lifestyle.

Things were working out well for him until he was deported after a weapons conviction. Unlike Omid Bayani, who was ordered deported but just never left, Kaawach did actually leave Canada for his native Lebanon. Roueche is known to have visited him there. He also had a residence in Guadalajara, Mexico, where he continued to work as a go-between, between the Sinaloa Cartel and the UN.

His contact in Canada, according to police in both countries, was his good friend Elliott "Taco" Castañeda, a Guatemala-born Canadian citizen who worked as a realtor but seemed to have a lifestyle and set of possessions—like three houses with a value of $1.1 million and a top-of-the-line

BMW—that far outstripped his sales commissions. When a joint law enforcement/Canada Revenue Agency operation looked into his earnings and those of other UN members, and then a revenue agent and 10 cops paid a late-night visit to his house, Castañeda quit HomeLife Glenayre Realty and relinquished his license.

Castañeda went to visit Kaawach in Mexico, probably to iron out their new situation and to meet some people. On a sunny July 12, 2008, the pair went for a bite to eat at the open-air Tacos de Barbacoa El Cuellos restaurant on Calle Pedro Buzeta in the Santa Teresita neighborhood of Guadalajara. They were both mid-taco when a group of heavily armed men burst from a minivan and showered the restaurant with automatic weapons fire. Both died on the scene.

Perhaps, like many Canadian tough guys who go to Mexico, they were in way over their heads. Any of the cartels or sub-cartels could easily have known who they were and killed them in an increasingly commonplace way of doing business in Mexico. Or UN members, afraid Castañeda was going to spill information about them now that he was under severe legal pressure, had him eliminated. Although there was a wake for him at the Rain Bar and Grill in Abbotsford (police seized two handguns from the crowd), it's unlikely too many in the UN would miss Castañeda.

• • •

Jonathan Bacon, his girlfriend Rayleene Burton and his business associate Godwin Cheng had been in and out of court, fighting against the charges that arose after the police found them with drugs, weapons and cash in 2005. Their defense team based their argument on the thesis that since the police did not have an active search warrant, the decision to arrest Bacon and Cheng was illegal. Since the police only saw them exchange bags for cash, they did not have reasonable evidence to believe that what was inside the bags were drugs or that there were weapons in the car.

Despite the fact that Bacon and Cheng were caught red-handed, the judge agreed that the police had no right to arrest or search them or the car. And, of course, since Burton was only stopped on the basis of the earlier arrest, her arrest was unlawful, as well.

On July 16, 2008, Bacon, Burton and Cheng walked out of court free. It was just another in a growing list of law-enforcement attempts to stop the Bacon Brothers that had failed. Caught with drugs and weapons? No problem for the Bacons, just a matter of showing up in court a few times. They were beginning to appear untouchable, even invincible.

• • •

But it wasn't just the Bacons. In Prince George, tensions were rising as competition in the lucrative drug market had caused friction between the existing gangs. Few in these hastily put-together organizations had the feelings of "brotherhood" that bikers claim is the reason their clubs exist. Instead, individuals within the gangs began to undercut one another in an attempt to get increased market share. Traditionally, the penalty for such a crime in Hells Angels–controlled gangs has been execution.

Police were dealing with a series of shootings and beatings in which neither victims nor independent witnesses would cooperate with them. But on August 6, 2008, they caught something of a break. They received 9-1-1 calls about a red SUV being driven erratically with a gun protruding from a window. A few minutes later, while police were searching for the truck, a series of calls came in reporting shots fired on Upland Street.

Police rushed to the scene, a known crack shack, and found a 19-year-old man severely injured with several gunshot wounds. The victim had been in the backseat of a Lincoln Navigator parked in front of the house when it was sprayed with gunfire. The two people in the front seats—Garrett McComb and his girlfriend Brittany Giese—were unharmed. The victim was sent to a nearby hospital and survived. Of the several people in the house at the time, police managed to convince one of them, an admitted crack addict and alcoholic, to cooperate with them. His eyewitness account led them to arrest three members of the Independent Soldiers—Fabian Charlie, Jesse Bird and Eric West—and charge them with attempted murder, causing bodily harm with a firearm, aggravated assault and a number of firearms charges. Police also found a red Ford Explorer with a license plate that matched the original 9-1-1 calls outside the house. Its engine was still warm. A search of the house revealed a shotgun wrapped in a T-shirt and three shotgun shells.

Actually, they arrested three other Independent Soldiers but did not press charges against them. It did not go unnoticed in the community that while the three men who had charges laid against them were of aboriginal origin, the three released were all white.

But things did not go well for the police. The victim, known as W.B., refused to testify. After police were alerted by an anonymous tip, McComb and Giese, who'd been in the car with W.B., were found murdered in their home, shot multiple times, on October 7, 2008. Their Lincoln Navigator SUV, still bearing bullet holes from the night W.B. was shot, was parked outside. Nobody was arrested for their murders.

When the case against Charlie, Bird and West finally came to trial in October 2009, Justice Karen Walker determined that the sole witness who came forward was not credible enough, and the trio walked.

In Prince George, as in the Lower Mainland, it appeared not only that gangs could sell drugs with impunity from the law, but they could also settle their scores with gunfire with little or nothing to fear from the courts.

• • •

The UN's reorganization continued in the Lower Mainland. Mike Gordon was a 33-year-old realtor who lived in Chilliwack with his wife and 4-year-old son. He was very good at what he did, making some big, high-commission deals, mostly in the Fraser Valley. At least a few of them were for his close friend, Clayton Roueche. In fact, Rupert Roueche, Clayton's dad, let Gordon put up a billboard at his scrapyard.

At 8:30 p.m. on August 20, 2008, there were a number of 9-1-1 calls reporting gunfire on Promontory Road in Chilliwack. When responders arrived, they found Gordon dead, slumped behind the wheel of his BMW in the parking lot of the Teskey Market grocery store.

It's been widely reported that Gordon was killed because he had been "hanging out with" one of Roueche's enemies, but with Roueche behind bars awaiting trial in the U.S., he had bigger fish to fry than to order the killing of an old friend over a personal matter. Besides, ordering such a hit while in custody when he knew the authorities were listening to everything he said (and most of what his friends and associates said) would put him at a ridiculous level of risk. It's also been postulated that Gordon was part of the Canadian Revenue Agency/RCMP investigation and was a risk to incriminate others. No matter what the absolute truth is, it's clear that somebody—almost certainly associated with the UN—wanted Gordon dead.

And the violence kept going. James O'Toole was born in Dublin, Ireland, and was raised in Vancouver. Music was his passion. While most of his peers and friends were performing rap and hip hop, O'Toole preferred schmaltzy slow rock. After living in Australia for a while, touring with a band called

Napoleon, he returned to Vancouver and performed under the name Jed Cruz.

His music career was still fledgling, but O'Toole appeared to live very well, with all the affectations of youthful success of the time and place. Police say he was involved with several Asian-dominated crime organizations and may well have been a trafficker himself. His sole conviction, though, came from a 2001 incident in which he pulled a handgun and threatened some kids who were throwing vegetables and eggs at him and some friends as they exited the Luv-A-Fair nightclub one evening.

He'd been arrested for assault in 2008 after a fight in a Whistler nightclub but would never go before a judge. At 1:00 a.m. on August 30, 2008, O'Toole was leaving yet another Vancouver nightclub. The yellow Toyota Prius taxi he was in stopped at a red light. Then suddenly, the silver Mazda MPV minivan that had been behind him went into the oncoming lane beside the Prius. Once in position, the men inside slid open the van's door and opened fire on the Prius.

The driver was seriously shaken, but unhurt. O'Toole was dead.

• • •

Jack Woodruff was a bad dude. And he looked like it. He had a fleshy face with a thick, protruding eyebrow ridge, and the look in his eyes, even in happy times, was threatening. And he has admitted to killing three people. But he wasn't really a gangster, just a bad dude.

But somehow, he found a woman who loved him. Karen Batke came from Cape Breton Island in Nova Scotia. After moving from Canada's poorest region to its richest, she became involved with Woodruff and eventually moved into his basement apartment in Surrey.

It wasn't blissful. I've been told that he was very abusive. In fact, his abuse may have led to her death. Years after she went missing, Woodruff would admit that he'd killed her. He claimed that she came at him with a baseball bat, but "fell" into a plate-glass table that managed to open an artery in her leg so that she began losing a remarkable amount of blood. In his story, the bleeding-out woman who was less than half his weight charged at him again. He was so afraid for his own life that he somehow managed to put his two meaty paws around her neck and squeezed until she went limp and, when he released his grip, fell to the ground dead. Woodruff then said he took her body to an undisclosed waste management facility where he threw it among the trash. Her body has never been recovered, and Woodruff was acquitted of her murder.

He'd not only managed to get away with killing Batke, but he'd put it behind him. And perhaps put it on his resume. Whether it was known that he'd already killed and gotten away with it, he was hired (he won't say by whom) to carry out an assassination.

Lisa Dudley had a lot of experience running marijuana grow ops, and she had one in the large and secluded house she shared with her boyfriend, Guthrie McKay, in a wooded section of Mission.

Woodruff had been instructed to kill Dudley and, "if necessary," McKay. He didn't ask why; he just assumed it was a drug debt. And his plan was not complicated. He arrived in their backyard at 10:41 p.m. on September 22, 2008, and stood on the deck. He could see them inside, sitting on a couch and watching television. He fired six shots. The first shattered the glass door, the other five hit McKay in the face, back and chest, and Dudley in the face and neck. He then fled.

A neighbor called 9-1-1, and the Mission RCMP sent out a car with Constable Mike White and Auxilliary Constable Danielle Girard, a volunteer with limited training, to investigate. When they arrived, White drove around the area and talked with the person who called 9-1-1, but did not inspect Dudley's house specifically. In fact, neither officer got out of the car.

Four days later, a curious neighbor dropped by Dudley's house. When nobody answered, he went around back. Seeing the shattered back door, he went up on the deck to take a look. Spotting both Dudley and McKay on the ground, he called 9-1-1.

Responders were shocked to see that Dudley was alive, though paralyzed from the neck down. Somehow, she had survived for four days, without food or water, or the ability to move away from her boyfriend's dead body. They quickly got her into an ambulance, in which she finally expired on the way to a hospital.

It took years, but Woodruff eventually confessed to the murders in March 2012. At the time, he said it was his conscience, but others have claimed he was presented with the Crown's evidence and realized he could not win a court battle. In any case, he never said on whose behalf he killed Dudley and McKay. And while he did cop to killing Batke and throwing her body in the trash, he still maintained it was self-defense and did not tell her grieving children where they could find her body—if it still existed.

But Woodruff was the exception. After four years, he finally broke down—and nobody would have called him a pillar of intellect or resolve—and admitted far more than the cops ended up charging him for.

But at the time he killed Dudley and McKay, nobody knew that the perpetrator would get caught or go to prison, and to tell the truth, few even had the optimism to hope for it. Law enforcement had failed to catch people so many times, and those few they did catch seemed to get a free ride from the court system. And after the ridiculously bad job the police had done with the Robert Pickton case—he had once confessed to 49 murders and a myriad of other crimes, but was found guilty only of six counts of second-degree murder—there was simply no faith in the authorities' ability to stop or even slow violent crime.

There seemed to be nothing that could stop gangs from meting out their own justice, however they felt like it. It was all about money. If a grower, importer or dealer didn't want to work with the gang exactly the way the gang wanted, there would be big trouble, even a death penalty. But what made it worse for the Lower Mainland was that there wasn't just one gang. Growers, importers and dealers who worked with the UN were immediately enemies of the Red Scorpions and vice versa. In the ever-changing shady underworld of alliances, alienations and pettiness, people involved in the drug trade were exposed to danger all the time and from just about anyone. And, as the senseless murders of Jonathan Barber, Chris Mohan and Ed Schellenberg proved, you didn't even have to be part of the drug trade. You just had to live close by.

PART III

BREAKING THE BACONS

I've written a number of true-crime books, and they are generally well-received by critics and readers alike. But I have had some complaints. Some people—including notable motorcycle gang members like Donnie Peterson and Mario Parente—have complained that I don't speak to enough bikers or others who are alleged to be in the drug trade. They have told me that I only get the opinions of "cops, snitches and lawyers."

But that's not entirely true. I do talk to bikers and others who are said to be in the drug trade, and it always works at as some variation of the following conversation:

Biker: I'm an outlaw.
Me: Okay, what laws do you break?
Biker: None of them. You can't prove anything.

Things are slightly different for this book. Since so many people were killed, I spoke with a number of the friends and families of victims of the violence, and they, almost to a person, took a different tack. I'm not talking about innocent victims like Mohan and Schellenberg here, but the people who had adopted the gangster lifestyle and paid the ultimate price.

They invariably told me that their deceased friend or family member was a good person who had simply fallen into danger either for being in a gang or having friends that were. They all seemed to think that joining the gangster life was inevitable, that economic and social conditions in the area made it impossible for a large sector of the population to do anything else. You may recall the kid from Prince George who told cops he got involved in the drug trade because his only other option was minimum wage. He's a definitive example of how many young people were thinking at the time: that the drug trade was the quickest, easiest and perhaps only way to earn any real money. The camaraderie, the women and even the violence (itself a draw for many young men) were all bonuses.

It's an old story, one we've heard a million times. Just like the crack wars that began in Manhattan's Washington Heights neighborhood in the 80s and spread around the world—and it could be argued that the troubles in the Lower Mainland are a terrible vestige of that first spark—it all began with some kid, bored in math class, idolizing the drug dealer in his Cadillac full of girls.

And just as the generations before them in other places created distinct looks and cultures, the drug dealers in the Lower Mainland (and the countless others who emulated them) had clearly defined habits, rituals and modes of dress. Shaved heads were de rigueur, and the few that kept their hair tended to care for it and style it slicked back with an almost obsessive passion. Tattoos were a necessity and indicated not just affiliations, but personality traits and philosophical and religious beliefs. Working out and having a hard body bulging with muscles was desirable. Professing belief, or at least strong interest, in eastern religions was standard, as was the practice of martial arts, especially mixed martial arts, the type of fighting made popular by the UFC.

Despite my years of research and writing, and the fact that I grew up in a poorer, more violent time in a city as drug-addled and full of crime, they all told me the same thing: "You just wouldn't understand."

They're right, I don't understand. And hardest of all to understand is how, even as the gangs of the Lower Mainland careened toward all-out war and citizens like Eileen Mohan led public campaigns to end the lenient treatment of convicted thugs, gang culture continued to hold sway over the hearts and minds of so many while the justice system seemed as ineffectual as ever.

CHAPTER 8

PARALYSIS: 2008–2009

One of those people I wouldn't understand was Joe "J Money" Krantz, even though I've actually been called by that same nickname. He looked the part, with tats, pumped-up muscles, lots of jewelry and a habit of wearing his hair in cornrows. Adopted, Krantz had a hard time fitting into mainstream society, and what his friends called "feelings of inadequacy" drove him to work out obsessively. Though never truly big, he was very strong and served as manager of the World Extreme Fighting Fight Team and a mixed martial arts trainer to some pretty big names at his World Extreme Fighting Club. He even fought a few times.

On April 15, 2008, police raided his home. In it, they found 4.5 ounces of cocaine, 8.7 ounces of crack, 2 ounces of heroin, a 9mm handgun, a .380-calibre handgun, two sets of brass knuckles, body armor, schedules and a ledger for his runners (both day and night shifts), and product inventory sheets with codes for cocaine and heroin. And, so that there was no con-fusion as to who his friends were, the police found clothing and paraphernalia with logos from the Independent Soldiers' Kelowna chapter and the Hells Angels' Nomads chapter. The drugs were all divided into single-use packages, and the handguns—both loaded—were found out in the open on the kitchen counter.

They also found Krantz's 8-year-old daughter, who was not in the house at the time. After his arrest, she was interviewed by a social worker, whom she told, "Dad is always selling little white rocks." She described how Krantz broke a large rock into smaller pieces and put the "rocks" and the "dust" into little bags. She also described backpacks full of cash and a machine her dad "used to grind the green moss" that was put in rolling papers and smoked. She did, however, point out that she had never seen guns or ammunition around the house.

The girl assumed her dad had been arrested for the little white rocks and told them he often talked about hockey equipment (his records indicated that various drugs were given code names like "helmets" and "shoulder pads").

She also described a strange existence at her dad's house (at which she lived only on weekends), in which she was subject to great wealth—including a big-screen plasma TV and a queen-sized bed in her room—but also great secrecy. Her dad and his girlfriend had forbidden her to talk about money. She recalled one time in which she innocently mentioned that she was glad they were "rich," and her father hit her, confined her to her room and took away her Nintendo DS as punishment. She also talked of traveling with her father while he took what were almost certainly drugs to various people to "sell for him" and how she had seen him share a smoke with a lady whose "house st[ank]."

Six months later, on October 20, 2008, Krantz was just closing up his strip-mall gym, the World Extreme Fighting Club, at about nine in the evening when he was killed by a spray of gunfire.

It's not uncommon for the death of a gangster to be memorialized, but after Krantz was shot, the community came alive in a festival of mourning. Facebook pages popped up extolling him as a great guy and, invariably, a great father. Most of the people who posted on them used pseudonyms. A couple I spoke with via e-mail extolled his sense of humor, his style, his kindness and generosity and, always and above all, his attentiveness as a father. When I brought up the fact that I don't think a good father, much less a great one, hits a child for an innocuous remark, takes her on drug runs, and has her live part-time in a house full of dangerous drugs and loaded weapons, they all said the same thing: "You just don't understand."

So hard did his community take Krantz's death that a number of videos memorializing him showed up on YouTube, at least two of which showed pictures of his daughter. And then something truly surprising happened. A few days after his death, a mural in his honor appeared on a wall at R.E. Mountain Secondary School in nearby Langley. It depicted a red heart wrapped in a gold ribbon surrounded by 11 huge diamonds. Along with his name, its three bits of text read: "Rest in peace," "Tragically gunned down October 20th 2008" and "Always missed but never forgotten one love always."

Many of those same people were surprised and even saddened to see the mural painted over, despite the fact that it was a tribute on a public high school to a man facing drug and weapons charges who was gunned down by fellow gangsters.

Later, when his girlfriend, Nicole Cooper, reported on Facebook that "social services" would not pay the $1,050 she requested for a gravestone for the man who drove a tricked-out Cadillac Escalade with 22-inch spinners and a vanity license plate that read "JMONEY," it was met with outrage and dismay from her supporters.

• • •

Everyone involved in the drug trade in Canada knows American cops are not like Canadian cops and, more important, American judges are not like Canadian judges. If you get caught down there, you're very likely to spend a long time behind bars, God knows where, with God knows whom.

Smart traffickers, like Clayton Roueche and many Hells Angels, do their best to stay out of the United States, doing their business in Canada and vacationing in Mexico or places like the Dominican Republic.

But the United States is where the money is, so somebody has to go there, despite the obvious risks. And, due to a three-year investigation, the American authorities knew who it was. Robert Shannon was a Maple Ridge truck driver, and his friend, Abbotsford's Devron Quast, managed a car dealership. But American authorities also alleged that they had higher-paying jobs running a drug exporting business for the B.C. Hells Angels and that Shannon had even once paid to have a rival murdered.

In June 2008, an undercover officer lured Shannon, Quast and some associates to Ferndale, Washington, with the lure of a big haul. (Ferndale is a humdrum town not far from the Canadian border whose claim to fame comes from the fact that every time town authorities paint over the Metallica logo on its main bridge it reappears, as if by magic, soon thereafter.) At the house, authorities arrested Shannon, Quast and some of their American contacts—Todd Gabriel, Chance Gerrior and Korinne Doggett. Arrested later were Phillip Stone of Abbotsford, Richard Jansen of Chilliwack, Tomohisa Kawabata of Vancouver (whom they said paid $3.3 million for a load of marijuana to be delivered to New York City) and Jesse Holmes of Blaine, Washington, who they alleged rented a warehouse in Bellingham for the weed.

What was shocking about the Shannon arrest was the magnitude of it. Not only did the Americans seize 1,300 pounds of cocaine, 7,000 pounds of BC Bud and $3.5 million in cash, they learned of a sophisticated operation run on behalf of the Hells Angels, who were fortunate to escape indictment, although it came out in court that full-patch Hal Porteous once stepped in to intimidate a debtor on Shannon's behalf. Shannon, attempting to look much more youthful than he really was, can also be seen in a self-aggrandizing (and unintentionally funny) rap video Porteous made about his gangster lifestyle. The investigation revealed that Shannon was the leader of a group who transported weed over the border primarily in hollowed-out logs on timber trucks, but also in RVs and even in a church van. Their business was so developed, they offered insurance to their suppliers, giving them a $425 payout for every pound of weed confiscated by law enforcement. It was also learned that Shannon ordered the killing of Independent Soldier Jody York, who owed the organization $70,000. Shannon let York off the hook after the would-be assassin shot and missed.

And, as is the fear among Canadian drug traffickers, the American courts came down hard. Shannon was sentenced to 20 years (which in the United States really means 20 years). Quast, seeing which way the trial was heading, cut a deal with prosecutors in which he totally gave up everything on Shannon and received a lighter, 75-month term. Before he turned, Quast received letters from Shannon at first imploring him not to cooperate with prosecutors, then threatening him if he did. In a truly pathetic move, Shannon even threatened Quast's grandmother, who was in a nursing home.

• • •

While it looked like the Americans were doing a pretty good job of putting Canadian gangsters behind bars, some disturbing facts about how known gangsters are treated north of the border came to light.

At 10:30 p.m. on New Year's Eve 2008, a man walked into the Mission Memorial Hospital's emergency room. He'd been shot. He was bloodied and in poor shape, but not in immediate danger of losing his life. As is always the case in Canada, the emergency room staff called the police because a firearm was involved; but they quickly realized that they might have been involved in something larger when they were undressing him and saw he was wearing a bulletproof vest.

The man was Dennis Karbovanec, admitted killer, long-time Red Scorpions member and extra-close associate of the Bacon Brothers. Police arrived to question him and begin an investigation. It's not a crime to get shot, and Karbovanec refused to talk about who shot him or why, but he was actually already in trouble.

With a warrant already out for his arrest, on October 23, 2008, Karbovanec had been stopped by police. They found he was wearing a bulletproof vest and had a loaded handgun with a silencer in a hidden compartment in his leased GMC Yukon Denali. He was charged with 11 counts of weapons possession and other infractions. The officers who had the Denali stopped claim Jonathan Bacon drove up in a black Mercedes-Benz and motioned for Karbovanec to come with him. He only left, without Karbovanec, after the cops had drawn their weapons.

Knowing who was really in charge, Abbotsford police negotiated with the Bacon Brothers to facilitate a deal for Karbovanec. They promised to drop all but one small charge on the condition that the Bacons surrendered their friend's entire cache of weapons. On Karbovanec's behalf, Jonathan Bacon brought Abbotsford Detective Lyle Simpson 114 sticks of dynamite, a hand grenade, 7 handguns, 2 shotguns, a hunting rifle and an Uzi submachine gun. Karbovanec was then released on $15,000 bail.

When news of that deal and of vacation pictures of Kabovanec and the Bacon Brothers, among others, enjoying great times at Mexican resorts while facing tons of charges in Canada emerged, people became outraged. Social media and the comment areas of mainstream media were alive with people complaining about the fact that accused murderers could be gallivanting around the tropics. It appeared as though their own law enforcement and courts were doing nothing to keep the bad guys off the streets. The police knew who the criminals were; there just didn't seem to be anything they could do about it. What made it more galling was that the same kids committing the same crimes just a few miles to the south were being put away for long stretches.

. . .

And the rough justice of the gangs continued unabated. Joshua Hedrick was a tough guy who worked as an enforcer with the Crew, the Prince George crack dealers and enforcers. He'd been arrested several times for aggravated assault and other violent crimes. He was a friend of Scott Payne, the leader of the Renegades. But he had been, according to police, reducing his involvement with the gang and living at his mother's house in Maple Ridge.

On January 11, 2009, he received a phone call at his mother's house at about 8:30 p.m. He took the phone out to the back patio to talk and never returned. His family found the phone on the patio table and were immediately suspicious.

They reported him missing on January 13, and police became more suspicious of his whereabouts when he didn't show up to appointments with his parole officer.

In August, a boater on the Fraser River near Douglas Island in Port Coquitlam discovered a badly decomposed body in the water. Tattoos and other factors led the coroner to identify it as Hedrick's.

. . .

January 16, 2009, was an ordinary day for Abbotsford police until they received a number of calls from people claiming they had seen a man with a gun at Sevenoaks Shopping Centre. When police arrived, witnesses pointed out the group of men they had seen with the firearm. The cops were not surprised to see that the men in question were all three Bacon Brothers. They were searched and questioned, but no gun was found. Jonathan was wearing a bulletproof vest, but since it wasn't stolen, there was no basis to charge them and they were released.

The fact that he was wearing a bulletproof vest in a mall in broad daylight was a testament to how dangerous the Bacon Brothers perceived their lives to have gotten, especially after the Karbovanec shooting. And they were right.

Four days after the Sevenoaks incident, Jamie was driving his black Mercedes-Benz SL55 convertible northwest on South Fraser Way when he pulled up beside an SUV stopped at a red light at the intersection of Sumas Way. It was about 10 minutes before four in the afternoon. As he was waiting for the light to change, the back window on the right side of the SUV slid down and someone inside the truck fired at Bacon. Six shots went into the Mercedes (another blew out the back window of a nearby pickup truck, but the driver was unhurt). Jamie floored it, speeding through the intersection, down South Fraser, before merging onto West Railway Street, where he hit the median and crashed into the front entrance of a Keg restaurant. Police, alerted to the area after the first shots were fired, found Jamie a few hundred yards away from the wrecked Mercedes. He was wearing a bulletproof vest under his trademark hoodie. It probably saved his life.

• • •

People I've talked to who knew many of the people killed in Vancouver's gang wars invariably tell me that the person who was killed was a good person, not just a gangster. They were kind or generous or good with children. They had a quality or number of qualities that transcended gangster life.

Of course they did. The drug trade, at least at the top end, is extremely lucrative and is one of the increasingly rare career choices for those who are not educated or bright enough to establish a legitimate career. Or, for those who can, the drug trade offers a very lucrative, even glamorous, option. In the Lower Mainland, with spiraling prices and declining employment, the drug trade attracted thousands. Many of them were otherwise ordinary people lured by the easy money, camaraderie and glamorous lifestyle.

One of them was Andrew "Dru" Cilliers. He had received minor acclaim in February 2004 when he and two friends, Simon Prodromidis and Andrew Henderson, pulled an unconscious man from a burning car. What the papers did not say was that Cilliers was out on bail awaiting trial for a drug trafficking charge in 2002. Found guilty shortly after the heroic incident, he received a six-month conditional sentence (which meant no jail time if he made weekly visits to a parole officer), nine months probation and, for reasons not made clear at the time, a ten-year firearms ban.

Some years later, Cilliers, who had a job at an auction house, moved into 6267 131A Street, a nice reddish brown house at the corner of 62B Avenue. He had originally moved in with his girlfriend, but after many arguments loud enough for the neighbors to be aware of, she left in the summer of 2008. Dru was not alone long, though. Soon after the girlfriend left, Dru's brother moved in.

Friends and neighbors considered Dru affable and hardworking. But he had revenue streams aside from the auction house, and he had friends who might have been operating on the far side of the law. Len Pelletier—best known as the Hells Angels associate who'd been shot at while dropping his son off at school and the cousin of notorious Nomad Bob Green—just happened to have cosigned on the lease of a Harley-Davidson for Cilliers.

Neighbors—who generally had positive feelings toward Cilliers, at least, after his girlfriend left—were shocked to hear gunshots at his house just after midnight on January 27, 2009.

When police arrived, they saw Cilliers, shot in the head, still alive but unconscious in the driveway beside the house. Paramedics put him in an ambulance and he died in a nearby hospital at 3:30 a.m.

Who killed him and why are still mysteries. Pelletier's wife Cynthia appeared to be sincerely broken up about his death, calling him an "excellent, excellent guy" and claiming he was just like family to them. "It is too sad. It is too fucking sad," she said. "All I can say is he was a great kid. The young people today don't realize once you're gone, it's gone."

There was an outpouring of public sympathy on social media that dwarfed the one for "J Money" Krantz. A Facebook page dedicated to his memory (since deleted) had several hundred followers and thousands of views. Cilliers might have been the great guy his friends say he was, but he was definitely in a risky business.

As if to underline exactly who ran things in the Lower Mainland, Cilliers' friends threw him a memorial party at T-Barz, the notorious strip joint frequented by Hells Angels.

• • •

With the number of drug-related shootings at an astounding level—but arrests rare and convictions rarer—police were frustrated, and their options were running out. After finding out that Jonathan Bacon had moved into a condo at 651 Nootka Way in their city, the authorities in Port Moody reacted in what they thought was the best way to maintain public safety. On February 3, 2009, the day after Erickson was murdered, the City of Port Moody and the Port Moody Police Department issued the following warning:

> As part of the response to gang violence which has gripped
> many communities throughout B.C., the Port Moody Police
> Department is taking steps to warn the public, friends, and

associates of the BACON brothers, that there are significant threats to their safety.

The Port Moody Police Department through its investigation and information received from other police agencies, have learned there are plans to murder Jarrod, Jamie and Jonathan BACON. The BACON brothers are well known to the police and have been linked to violence and weapons in the past. The BACON brothers have been approached by police and advised of these threats, but appear to be unconcerned for their safety or that of their friends, associates and, particularly the public. Due to the seriousness of the threats made against the BACON brothers, those associated to them in any way are being advised to discontinue their association or interaction immediately.

The Port Moody Police Department has been aware of a BACON presence in Port Moody for some time, and specifically one BACON brother is currently residing in Port Moody. Highly–trained and specialized officers are routinely patrolling areas of concern within our community and monitoring any suspicious activities related to the BACON brothers. The recent escalation in indiscriminate public violence has caused us sufficient concern to issue this public warning.

The safety of the public is paramount; the Port Moody Police Department in partnership with other police agencies, in particular the Abbotsford Police Department and the Integrated Gang Task Force are working vigilantly to ensure that the safety of the public is uncompromised.

Particulars for the BACON brothers are:

Jonathan David BACON, DOB 1981-01-31, age 28
  Description: Caucasian male, 5'-11" 201 lbs, black hair blue eyes
  Marks/Scars: scar left wrist
Jarrod Wayne BACON, DOB 1983-03-14, age 25
  Description: Caucasian male, 5'-9" 190 lbs, brown hair and brown eyes
  Marks/Scars: "Sleeve" tattoo left arm, scar on forehead

James Kyle BACON, DOB 1985-08-01, age 23
   Description: Caucasian male, 5'-10" 236 lbs, brown hair
   and brown eyes
   Marks/Scars: "Sleeve" tattoos both left and right arms.

The warning about Karbovanec hadn't worked. But the authorities in Port Moody hoped the warning about the Bacon Brothers would.

CHAPTER 9

WAR: FEBRUARY–MAY, 2009

Not surprisingly, the Port Moody warning didn't work. If anything, it only made the gangsta-wannabe kids in the Lower Mainland admire the Bacon Brothers even more. The boys had proven they were not just untouchable by law enforcement, but also by their enemies. They were wearing fancy clothes, driving the best cars with pretty girls and doing whatever they felt like, and nobody could stop them. Their lives were like the twisted fantasies of a bored 12-year-old. The warning only put an official stamp on it.

It's not that the police were not investigating. The killers had more chutzpah and ego than they had any technical knowledge of how best to go about assassination. They left behind a huge mess of DNA and other evidence. But real investigations are not at all like the magic they show on TV and in movies. To build a compelling case from even the sloppiest murder scene takes lots of hours of hard work and no small amount of luck.

And though the killings sparked outrage in the community, among those in organized crime, it drew respect. The Red

Scorpions, who many in the know blamed for the murders, made a loud and clear statement. By publicly executing those who would not play by their rules, the Red Scorpions established themselves as a force to be reckoned with. Sadly, the murder of eight people raised their credibility on the streets.

One of the Bacon Brothers' closest friends, Raphael Baldini, did not heed the warning. Baldini, of course, was well known as the tenant who had leased the apartment in which the Surrey Six murders had taken place. He was not there at the time, of course, and was not considered a serious suspect, but many—including Eileen Mohan—believed that he had information that could lead to an arrest or arrests. And he was still allegedly in the game, out on bail facing a trafficking and weapons charge with co-accused Jaspreet "Justin" Chahil from an October 2008 raid. Chahil, who was also charged with assault and uttering death threats, would later plea bargain down to one charge of trafficking and be sentenced to one year. Baldini was also facing charges from November 2007—one month after the Surrey Six murders—after a search of his vehicle yielded two loaded, unregistered handguns.

Hours after the warning about the Bacon Brothers was issued, Baldini was sitting in the driver's seat of a friend's white Range Rover SUV, talking on the phone. The car was parked in the lot of the Guildford Town Centre, a large and busy mall in Surrey. At about 5:20 p.m., rush hour, the unidentified person on the other end of the call heard Baldini's final words: "Oh my God."

What had shocked Baldini was the sight of armed thugs piling out of an SUV that had screeched to a halt right in front of him. They opened fire on the Range Rover, hitting Baldini several times before laying rubber for a quick exit.

Police and an ambulance arrived after a flood of 9-1-1 calls. A desperate attempt was made to save Baldini's life, but he expired in the parking lot, although further attempts to revive him took place in the ambulance and at a nearby hospital. "It certainly appears as though it's a targeted event, and has all the earmarks. There were multiple shots heard and all of them entered the deceased," said Corporal Dale Carr of the Integrated Homicide Investigation Team. "We've got a lot of witnesses to deal with, and we're speaking to each one of those as the night goes on." He added that the parking lot was very busy at the time and that it was surprising nobody else got hurt.

Baldini's was no ordinary hit. And it set tongues wagging all over the Lower Mainland. His closeness to both the Bacon Brothers and the Surrey Six murders could not be denied. His murder could well have been from the usual circumstances, but it could also have been a targeted assassination aimed at weakening the Bacon Brothers' organization, or it could also have been someone who wanted to make sure he kept his mouth shut about the Surrey Six, even though police claimed he was not cooperating with them. No matter what the intent, both missions were accomplished.

In spite of all the evidence to the contrary, Baldini's mother, Cindy, maintained her son had no gang connections. "It's easy for police to say that because he's gone," she told the CBC. "He's gone, but I'm here to defend my son's name."

As was becoming increasingly popular, social media sites were flooded with tributes, ranging from people who barely knew Baldini to his mom. One of the more interesting ones came from Jourdane Lal, younger sister of the two Lal brothers killed in the Surrey Six massacre. She wrote,

> no words can explain how our family will miss your smilin face, you are one of the few who truly cared, who cried tears not for us but with us, i can only hope to show the same love to your family as you always showed for us, thank you for being there, they'll take care of you up there...rest peacefully my friend.

She, at least, believed that Baldini had nothing to do with the murders of her brothers.

As if to further mock (or reinforce) the police warning, an hour and a half later, another body was found. At seven o'clock that evening, a man walking down a residential street in Port Coquitlam noticed a red pickup truck with the driver's-side window broken. He looked inside to see a blonde-haired woman slumped over the wheel. The corpse belonged to 21-year-old Brianna Kinnear, who had been shot several times while in a friend's truck.

She was five weeks into an eight-month conditional sentence she received for trafficking Oxycontin, cocaine and weed. She operated the phones at a dial-a-dope organization with her boyfriend, Jesse Margison, and their mutual friend Tiffany Bryan. Margison and three other members of their organization had been shot at and survived.

The Lower Mainland was clearly at war. And it was clearly more complicated than the UN against the Red Scorpions. The Bacon Brothers had thrown their lot in on the Red Scorpions' side, and since both sides were actually supplied by the Hells Angels and their allies, neither could count on support or allegiance from them or any of their related gangs like the Independent Soldiers. Even if they had wanted to stop any confrontation, the Hells Angels did not have the manpower (or reputation anymore) to impose their will upon what were now established, powerful gangs. That meant that the war in Vancouver was less a conventional side-against-side confrontation than it was a guerrilla war in which nobody really knew whom they could trust, and who was their enemy. The solution for many was to trust nobody, pack a weapon and, if you could, wear a bulletproof vest everywhere you went.

But business had to go on, so the movers and shakers had to extend their trust to those close to them. And one of the Bacon Brothers' closest confidantes was Kevin LeClair. A Port Moody native, LeClair was a mixed martial arts fighter and trainer. He even had a professional win under his belt—against Lethbridge, Alberta's Brenden Anderson—to go with losses to an American and a Brazilian. He also had a number of arrests on his record, dating back to 2001, including an assault in May 2008.

A couple of days after the warning, on February 5, 2009, Port Moody police watched as LeClair drove his silver Lincoln pickup truck to Jonathan Bacon's building on Nootka Way a little after noon. Jonathan got into the truck, and the two headed downtown. They had only driven a block when they were stopped and questioned by the cops. Jonathan "nonchalantly" told them they were headed out for coffee at the Starbucks in the NewPort Village shopping complex. The cops had no reason to detain them further.

On the following day, February 6, 2009, LeClair drove the same vehicle to the Thunderbird Centre mall in nearby Langley. As he was parking his truck in front of the Marketplace IGA grocery store at about four in the afternoon, he was approached by two men. Within a few feet of the Lincoln, they pulled guns from under their coats and sprayed the big truck with bullets. Dozens of witnesses claimed to have seen them running toward the mall's movie theater, where they were picked up by a vehicle and spirited away. "I was washing a front table, heard what sounded like firecrackers, looked up and there was a guy holding a handgun shooting at a truck over in front of the IGA," said a witness who did not want to be named. "The whole parking lot was full of smoke. All of a sudden, the truck started revving constantly. A young man jumped into a van and pulled out of here with two cars following behind."

Because of the extent of his injuries, first responders summoned a helicopter to airlift LeClair to a nearby hospital. He lingered overnight and died the following morning.

Later that week, on February 12, 2009, the Port Moody police issued another public warning, this one about Dennis Karbovanec. I doubt anyone felt the least bit safer.

But Nicole Marie Alemy probably felt safe driving down 148th Street in Surrey with Green Timbers Urban Forest by her side and her 4-year-old son in the backseat of her husband's snazzy pearl white Cadillac CTS coupe. It was 10:30 a.m. on a bright Monday morning. Her mind might well have been on her birthday—which had just happened to fall on Valentine's Day two days earlier—and the gift that was still waiting for her at her mom's house in White Rock. But as she stopped at the light at the corner of 96th Avenue, the passenger windows in the car beside her slid down and men with guns sent a volley of shots at Alemy's head.

Nicole was killed immediately. As the perpetrators sped off, her foot no longer supplied pressure on the brake pedal and the Cadillac rolled into the ditch and came to a stop after colliding with one of the Green Timbers trees. Two witnesses ran to the car, rescuing the 4-year-old.

Nicole had never been in trouble with the law before—just a few tickets—but her husband had. Alleged to be a high-ranking member of the UN, Koshan Alemy had been arrested on May 12, 2007, after a search of his car (not the Cadillac Nicole was driving) uncovered a loaded Ruger P39 semiautomatic pistol with the serial number filed off.

Nicole's murder was no case of mistaken identity. Nicole looked nothing like Koshan. And, although she had been ticketed for excessively tinted windows in the past, the windows of the Cadillac were perfectly clear.

After Nicole's murder, social media came alive. Facebook, Twitter and the message boards on media outlets were inundated with comments. They took two sides: one maintained that if Nicole was engaged in the drug trade, her murder was the product of a risk she had taken for herself and that she had put her son in extreme danger because of it; the opposing view suggested that there was little if any evidence that Nicole was engaged in drug trafficking and that, even if she was, it did not make her responsible for what happened to her. Many theories were floated online as to why she was assassinated, but the one that kept coming up over and over again focused on her close friendship with Raphael Baldini.

But something else happened that surprised many. The people of the Lower Mainland, who had been almost unanimously reluctant to speak out against crime, started to talk. In fact, the tip lines set up by police received so many calls that they were swamped. For the first time in the area's history, potential tipsters actually had to be put on hold because traffic was so intense. "We're starting to see a bit of a groundswell, if you will, of people just saying, 'Enough is enough, we're fed up, we're going to give a call,'" said RCMP Corporal Dale Carr of the Integrated Homicide Investigation Team. Two calls in particular stood out—both by men who admitted to being longtime gang members, but were also disgusted by the brutal murder of a mom in front of her horrified 4-year-old.

There was far less moral outrage over another violent event that day. Tyler Willock had worked closely with the Independent Soldiers and the UN, but of late had become a close associate of the Red Scorpions and the Bacon Brothers. Because of a shooting incident from the previous December, Willock was out on bail awaiting trial on five weapons charges when he and his friend, Fraser Sutherland, and two unidentified women were riding in Sutherland's Range Rover during a night on the town on May 9, 2008. They were stopped in front of the T-Barz parking lot when they were met with gunfire from another SUV that pulled up alongside.

As soon as he realized what was going on, Sutherland sped away towards his home in Langley. Willock, in the back seat, was unharmed, but Sutherland had been hit in the left shoulder. Losing blood and unable to maintain a grip on the wheel, Sutherland made it as far as 216th Street and the Fraser Highway before giving up. Willock called an ambulance. Sutherland survived. The two women were unhurt.

Earlier in the same day, two ambitious Surrey youth—Paul Hillsdon, who ran for city council at age 18, and Trevor Loke, another 18-year-old who was the Green Party candidate for Surrey-Newton—announced they were holding an anti-gang rally in Surrey's Central City Plaza on February 22, 2009. Several hundred people attended, and several speakers, including Eileen Mohan, made speeches.

One person who had no plans to attend such a rally was Red Scorpions tough guy Shane Messent, who also went by the name Randy Jones. He had a long criminal record. Between July 30, 2005, and June 1, 2006, alone, he faced no fewer than 11 charges for trafficking, assault and assault with a weapon from seven separate incidents. The night after the Alemy murder and Willocks-Sutherland shooting (and the anti-gang rally announcement), Messent went to practice his profession. The Red Scorpions had told him there was a grow op in a house on Fraser Street that was not cooperating and needed to be taught a lesson.

On February 17, 2009, Messent and 19-year-old associate Travis Chartrand arrived at the house and knocked on the door. For what happens next, we have to rely on the claims made by Nazreen Dean, the woman who answered the door. She says she was greeted by two armed men she did not recognize asking for someone she did not know. When her brother Aleem Mohammed came to see what was going on, Messent shot him in the chest and both visitors then fled. At that point, her other brother, Amir Mohammed, chased Messent down, tackled him, wrestled the gun away from him and shot him in the chest, killing him immediately. Aleem Mohammed survived, and charges against Amir Mohammed were stayed. It was all, according to Dean, a case of mistaken identity. Her mother, Mabel Mohammed, agreed, pointing out that the intruders were looking for someone named "Azim," and her boys were named Aleem and Amir.

As the weather grew warmer, there were a number of violent deaths that could well have been related to the gang war. Cory Konkin was not known to police and appeared to have had no gang-related activities, so it was a big surprise when his body was taken from an overturned SUV in a rural Maple Ridge ditch on February 26, 2009. He had been shot in the head. It could well have also been a case of mistaken identity.

At 6:40 p.m. on March 2, 2009, police in Delta, a community just west of Surrey, answered a couple of 9-1-1 calls reporting what they later called "suspicious activity" at the entrance to the Watershed Park and Delta Golf Course on Highway 10. When they arrived, they found a man—Sukhwinder "DB" Dhaliwal of Abbotsford—dead with several gunshot wounds, including at least one in his head. His body was beside his gray Cadillac.

Dhalilwal was, like most victims, well known to police. He had been arrested the previous May in a raid and faced seven charges, including possession for the purpose of trafficking, possession of a prohibited firearm with ammunition and careless use of a gun. Seized at the time were 7.5 ounces of crack, 36 grams of heroin and two loaded handguns. He was out on bail awaiting trial when he was shot. He had a previous conviction for an incident in which he threatened a man's life and for which he paid a $500 fine. Friends and coworkers described him as a great guy and expressed surprise at the concept that he was a drug dealer. No arrests were made in his murder.

The next day saw even more violence. Xing Li operated a brothel in a 25th-floor luxury apartment on Madison Avenue in Burnaby. What appeared to be a client entered the apartment at about eight in the evening, walked right past Xing Li and entered the next room. He reemerged with Ping Li, a prostitute who was also pursuing her MBA. The assailant, 17 at the time, had a gun up to her temple. He told Xing Li (no relation to Ping Li) to buzz in his associate, who was waiting in the lobby. Xing Li refused to do so, explaining that any robbery wouldn't be worth their while because he had almost no cash in the apartment.

Angered, the assailant (who was also of East Asian descent) pointed the gun at Xing Li and asked him if thought the gun was fake. Without waiting for an answer, the young man fired two shots. One missed, while the other went through Xing Li's arm and embedded itself in his abdomen. Xing Li immediately went down, losing blood and unable to see what was going on, but he could hear Ping Li begging for her life. She offered the young assailant money to spare her. Then Xing Li heard two shots, and Ping Li's voice stopped. Barely conscious, he managed to dial 9-1-1.

Xing Li's wife, who was in another room, came running to the scene, just as the young man was escaping. Xing Li survived. Ping Li, who showed no vital signs when first responders arrived, was rushed to Vancouver General Hospital but could not be revived. Police said the botched robbery had the signs of a gang operation.

A couple of hours after the brothel invasion, police in East Vancouver answered a 9-1-1 call at the corner of East 3rd Avenue and Kalso Street. They found a man, Abbotsford's Sunil Mall, slumped over the wheel of his car, dead. Mall was well known to police, with a record dating back to 2001. He was said to have been close friends with Clayton Roueche, but had switched allegiances to the Bacon Brothers after Roueche was arrested.

As other people were murdered—like small-time dealer Laura Lynn Lamoureux, prostitute Kimberley Hallgarth and real estate developer Marc Bontkes—the media and public openly wondered if the authorities could do anything to stop gangsters from murdering with impunity.

In response to the incredible amount of violence, Vancouver mayor Gregor Robertson called for the formation of a metropolitan police force, to remove the communication and logistical barriers that separated the current police forces in the Lower Mainland. Warning that there was an unacceptable level of violence—other shootings that week, including at a crack shack and a gas station, were less well known because there were no fatalities—and that the 2010 Winter Olympics were on their way, he pleaded for the public to come forward and help fight crime. He said they were "losing the battle" and needed something to "turn the tide."

Speaking on behalf of the RCMP and the multi-force homicide team IHIT, Corporal Peter Thiessen was noncommittal on whether or not he thought that would help and pointed out that he thought the number of police was not the problem; the lack of public involvement was. "I wouldn't say the area is under-policed, but certainly we could use additional resources," he said. "We're trying to engage the public because we cannot do this ourselves. This is not about more police on the street necessarily, this is also about the public becoming engaged in a problem that they need to help us solve."

And, like many other commentators at the time, he pointed out that parents had to be more observant and take responsibility for their children if they wanted them to make it home. "When you have a young 20-something living under your roof that doesn't get up in the morning, but is driving a $100,000 car and wearing a $1,000 suit and has a pocketful of cash, you have to question where that money is coming from," he said.

So after Thiessen pointed out that the cops were essentially powerless without community involvement—and we had seen how effective public outrage was in catching the killer of Nicole Alemy—many in the Lower Mainland were surprised when arrests related to the Willock-Sutherland shooting and other offenses were announced early in March. The suspects in the Willock-Sutherland shooting were familiar names to anyone who was following the news of the gangs in the Lower Mainland. The best known was the notorious Barzan Tilli-Choli, who many believed had taken over the leadership of the UN when Clayton Roueche landed behind bars in the United States. Also in the SUV from which the shots were fired were UN member Aram Ali, Tilli-Choli's associate Nicola Cotrell and Sarah Trebble, who had been the girlfriend of Hells Angel Larry Amero (they still shared the lease of a Cadillac Escalade) and had been a character witness for

Sasan Ansari, who was convicted of the 2008 murder and mutilation of Joshua Goos.

Tilli-Choli, Ali and Cotrell were charged with first-degree murder, and Trebble was charged with being in a car in which she knew there was an illegal firearm. All were released on bail, even though Tilli-Choli had already been ordered deported.

Although he had escaped from the targeted assassination attempt (and the alleged perpetrators had been caught), Willock was not out of the woods. While the UN had made it abundantly clear they would like to see him dead, they were not the only thing he had to fear. Willock had a habit of running his mouth, and it had occasionally got him into trouble. He had the particularly bad taste to joke about the death of LeClair, laughing while saying that now that LeClair was dead, he could keep the $40,000 he owed him. Few found it funny, and one Red Scorpion—Albert Jackman, who was so close to LeClair that he had a tattoo of his face—found it worthy of punishment.

On the night of May 8, 2009, Jackman and his 20-year-old associate Wesley Kelemen arranged to meet Willock at his house in Langley. When they arrived, Jackman told Willock they had private business to discuss, so they went into Willock's bedroom, leaving Kelemen and the roommate in the living room.

Once the door was closed, Jackman ordered Willock to the ground. He then secured his hands and feet with plastic cable ties and put strips of duct tape over his mouth and eyes. And that's when he took the sledgehammer out of the hockey bag. He pounded Willock so badly that he put dents in the cement floor. The floor, walls, furniture and even the ceiling were spattered with blood. But Jackman was careful. None of the twenty hits threatened Willock's life. He hadn't meant to kill him, just to make him hurt. And that he did, smashing joints and damaging various organs.

When he was satisfied that Willock had paid sufficiently for his little joke, Jackman then put his hammer back in the bag and walked in the living room. He collected Kelemen and left, telling Willock's roommate to call 9-1-1.

Jackman was not shy about the assault afterward. He was heard discussing it on an unrelated wiretap in which he said, "I wish the fuck I had beat him until he was dead." And he later told an undercover officer that he would "clip every member of his family if he squealed." Willock did not cooperate with police.

On the evening of May 28, 2009, Kyle Barber and his girl-friend, Hayley Lloyd, were relaxing in bed watching TV in their home at 24421 Fraser Highway in Langley when she heard a truck park in their driveway. Lloyd recognized the truck as belonging to her neighbors but did not know the two men who got out of it. When the two men approached the door, Lloyd asked what they wanted with the door still shut. They told her that they lived next door and that their barn had been broken into. Lloyd had seen a ladder up against the building leading to an open window the day before, but didn't know what had happened there. Still, she wanted to help so she opened the door a few inches to talk with them. When she said she couldn't help them, the two visi-tors pushed past her and stormed into the house. The shorter of the two, Albert Jackman, started shouting questions, asked them what they knew about the $50,000 stolen from the grow op next door. When Barber told him he didn't know anything, Jackman tried to intimidate him by telling him he was in the Red Scorpions, showing tattoos (including one on his neck) to back up his claim. "You took my shit, my $50,000 worth of shit," he bellowed. Barber said he didn't know what they were talking about but offered them a half pound of weed, some LSD and magic mushrooms, and the few thousand dollars they had. Jackman said it wasn't enough, so Barber told him they had more downstairs. Indeed they did. In fact, as revealed at trial, Barber and Lloyd had a grow op with about 200 plants in the basement.

Once downstairs, the taller, younger intruder—Gregory Barrett—held onto Lloyd, immobilizing her. Jackman forced Barber to kneel, grabbed a pair of scissors and started punching him with the blade between his fingers. He took a moment to wash the blood from his hands, then forced them to go back upstairs. Jackman ordered Barber to lie on the floor. Instead, Barber threw a small space heater at him. Jackman grabbed a knife off the top of a dresser and chased Barber, stabbing or slashing him whenever he got close enough. In a final bid for freedom, Barber crashed through a window.

The invaders left, taking a shotgun Lloyd had under the bed, but not the drugs or cash. Lloyd then called 9-1-1, and used an old T-shirt to try to stop the blood that was pumping out of Barber's throat. She later identified Jackman and Barret from photographs the police had of known gang members.

It's likely that among the pictures she saw both Sean "Smurf" Murphy and Ryan "Whitey" Richards. Old friends and small-time drug dealers, Murphy and Richards were both heavily involved with the Red Scorpions. That association proved fatal. Early in the morning of March 31, 2009, police came across a car stopped beside Bateman Park in Abbotsford. Its driver's-side window was missing, its front bumper had been torn off and its owner, Murphy, was found dead slumped over the wheel. A few hours later, passersby found Richards's body behind the Yellow Barn Country Produce vegetable market in Abbotsford, a few feet from the Chilliwack line. "We don't believe these homicides were random and there is a strong possibility that the victims' own criminal lifestyles led to their deaths," said police spokesman Casey Vinet. "It's unknown at this time if the two cases are in any way connected, but it is something investigators are carefully considering."

In spite of a few high-profile arrests, including that of Tilli-Choli, it appeared as though the gangsters still ruled the streets of the Lower Mainland. Bodies were piling up at a horrendous rate, and the few people actually getting arrested seemed to be literally getting away with murder.

That belief changed for many people on April 3, 2009, when police arrested Dennis Karbovanec and charged him with three counts of murder for the killings of Christopher Mohan, Ryan Bartolomeo and Michael Lal. Even more shocking was the fact that he had agreed to confess to all three charges, despite knowing that would guarantee him the most severe punishment Canada has to offer—life in prison with no chance at parole for 25 years.

The next day's news was even more shocking. Police arrested a veritable who's who of the Red Scorpions gang: Cody Ray Haevischer, Matthew James Johnson and the previously untouchable Jamie Bacon. All three were charged with first-degree murder, and Haevischer and Johnson were charged with first-degree murder and conspiracy.

A neighbor who saw Bacon's arrest told me that it was a huge spectacle. "It was like a movie, a war movie," he said. "The cops looked like soldiers, all dressed in black with body armor and heavy weapons." Bacon was led from the house—in a hoodie, track pants and handcuffs—and taken away.

Later, Red Scorpions founder Michael Le and someone identified by police as "Person X" were also arrested.

About a year and a half after the Surrey Six murders, Jamie Bacon and two of his Red Scorpions buddies were going down for it. Although nobody thought it would make a dent in the drug trade, many wanted to believe that if one of the previously untouchable Bacon Brothers could be held accountable, maybe there was hope the violence would at least slow down.

But not everybody believed it would. History had shown that high-profile arrests tended to make places more violent as opportunists fought for the business arrested individuals left behind. "What they do is they disturb the balance in the industry, and that creates opportunities for new and less-disciplined groups to come in," said Rob Gordon, director of criminology at Simon Fraser University. "The same kind of thing happened when they had sessions with the Hells Angels a little while ago. There is a colossal drug industry operating behind these kinds of individuals who, to my mind, are actually fairly low down on the pecking order."

CHAPTER 10

THE YEAR OF THE RAT: 2009–2010

It's easy to think that Jamie Bacon and his pals could have gotten away with the Surrey Six murders. With no definitive eyewitness statements and no real physical evidence to connect them to the incident, it's very unlikely police could have built a strong enough case to bring them to trial, and even if they had, charges would likely have been stayed due to a lack of significant evidence.

Not that they didn't know who did it or why. Sources close to police have told me that they knew that Michael Lal and his allies had long been involved with the Red Scorpions, but there had been a bitter dispute over how much "tax" they were kicking upstairs to the Red Scorpions' brass (which probably included the Bacons). The Lals and their friends then decided to break out on their own, which, of course, the Red Scorpions could not tolerate. In the Lower Mainland's drug trafficking circles, breaking such rules meant capital punishment.

But, as with many cases in which the cops knew who did it, there was very little the authorities could do about it—until one of the killers had a remarkable change of heart. Ever since police put out a warning about Dennis Karbovanec and the Bacon Brothers, they had been tailing them, watching their every move. Of course, the gangsters and police officers spoke with one another as they got more familiar. And it was on April 1, 2009, that Karbovanec told one of them he wanted to "come clean."

It wasn't an April Fool's Day prank. Karbovanec told the cop he wanted to confess, to admit the whole thing. The cop told him to get a lawyer and then turn himself in. He did.

It may be easy to think that the anti-crime rallies and other activist actions did little but preach to the converted, that the real criminals ignored them or even laughed at them. But in this case, they actually worked. After he confessed, Karbovanec granted an interview to *Vancouver Sun* reporter Kim Bolan. She had been covering the Lower Mainland's underworld for years and probably knew more about organized crime than law enforcement or most of its participants. He told her that it was Eileen Mohan that made him do it. While many gangsters lack the basic empathy—or at least pretend they do—to be moved by the suffering of others, Karbovanec clearly was.

And while experts normally say front-page arrests actually increase violence by opening up the market to competition, there was something different about this one. Many Lower Mainland youth idolized the gangsters, especially the Bacon Brothers. Until the Surrey Six arrest, they appeared untouchable. Until that point, they were like the mythical gangsters of movies and popular music. They lived above the law, drove fancy cars, wore the latest styles and had the prettiest girls. They made millions selling drugs, and they got away with murder.

But if a Bacon Brother was sent away for a long time, it could well take the luster off their image. Kids would be a lot less likely to idolize them.

• • •

But the drug- and gang-related violence did not stop, or even slow down, right away. In Kamloops, Damien Marks's dad, Robert, had qualms about his son's new best friend and roommate, Ken Yaretz. Yaretz, just 24 years old, seemed like he could be trouble. Marks wanted to press the issue with his son; he kept meaning to, but never really got around to it. He should have.

Indeed, Yaretz had been in trouble. He'd been sentenced to nine months for trafficking and, in August 2008, had been in a car that was stopped by police that also contained Jayme Russell, president of the Kamloops chapter of the Independent Soldiers.

Marks and Yaretz were moving to a bigger basement apartment, also in Kamloops, on April 17, 2009, when both men went missing. They were, Marks's dad said, heading up to nearby Knouff Lake to pick up some of Yaretz's stuff.

Up in Knouff Lake there was an associate of theirs who was deeply involved in trafficking. In fact, Roy Fraser had been arrested with $120,000 worth of marijuana and hashish in his native Saskatchewan in 1999 and had since relocated to a trailer on a remote property. Neighbors told the media that it was "common knowledge" that the property contained a grow op owned by the Hells Angels.

About a month after Marks and Yaretz went missing, police executed a search warrant on Fraser's property during an investigation about some stolen goods. While searching Fraser's property, they came across the bodies of Marks and Yaretz in a shallow grave.

Fraser was charged with murder and, to the dismay of many, granted bail. He fled and eventually turned himself in to Burnaby RCMP in October 2010.

• • •

On September 11, 2009, a motion came through the B.C. courts that raised many eyebrows. Jamie Bacon sued Debbie Hawboldt, the warden of Surrey Pretrial Services Centre. In it, he claimed he was mistreated by having his mail, telephone and visitation access unfairly limited. He also claimed that he was held in solitary confinement without justification.

After his arrest, Jamie was given a standard mental-health screening, which indicated he was not a risk to harm himself or other inmates. Despite that, he was taken to a segregation wing and put in a small, windowless cell, in which he was kept 23 hours per day, with the other hour allowing him into another small room. Then, his petition said:

> He was subsequently moved to another cell (210) which he said was filthy and smeared with 'blood, feces and mucus.' The bed was a concrete slab with a vinyl-covered foam mat. He had one sheet and a thin blanket, but was not allowed a pillow. He said that there was no change of bedding in the five weeks he was there. The petitioner said that he was not allowed a pen until May 4, 2009. He said the lights in his cell were on 24 hours per day. He said that they could be dimmed to some degree at night, but that happened only at the discretion of the guards. Cell 210 had a video camera mounted in a corner above the door. It was positioned such that the petitioner could be monitored while using the toilet in his cell. When he attempted to cover the lens, he was advised he could not do so and threatened with an unspecified disciplinary infraction.

He complained to authorities at the time and was told that the video camera had nothing to do with him or what he had done, but was simply because the facility wanted to "make best use of available cells."

The hour he had outside that cell, he said, was the only time he was allowed to shower or make contact with counsel. He was not allowed to call anyone else and was denied nail clippers, use of the laundry and the remand center's gym. Bacon said he was also denied his right to vote in the federal election.

His petition also said he was subsequently moved to cell 227, a medical isolation unit, because 210 was needed for co-defendant Cody Haevischer, who was being sent there for disciplinary reasons. Bacon noted that he, having done nothing to merit it, was already being held in the cell used to punish other inmates.

Cell 227, he stated, was a marked improvement (he had better shower access, wasn't—as far as he knew—under video surveillance and had some time in common areas). But it was still not up to the legal standards Corrections Canada is supposed to enforce, and when amenities like a television and a microwave were repaired (after his complaints, he said), they were quickly destroyed again by "mentally ill" inmates.

More than a year later, his claims were upheld, and he was granted damages.

• • •

It was the B.C. gangs' reliance on cocaine supplies from Mexico—where a massive military crackdown on the drug cartels had turned much of the country into a war zone—that gave law enforcement the upper hand.

Beginning on January 19, 2009, the Combined Forces Special Enforcement Unit (CFSEU), started to receive calls from a man known as GL, offering to become an informant on high-profile drug cases.

A Canadian, GL pled guilty in California to a charge of conspiracy to traffic cocaine from Mexico. That led to a light sentence by American standards—46 months. After 30 months, he was transferred to a Canadian prison, at which he served a little more than two months before he was granted full parole.

Back on the street, he made a point of running into an old friend from a truck-driving job he had in the 1980s, Wayne Scott. GL was well aware that Scott's daughter Carly was Jarrod Bacon's girlfriend and that the two had a toddler together. He spoke with Scott about getting back into the drug trade and asked if he could arrange a meeting with him and Jarrod specifically to discuss trafficking. "You and the kid have a lot in common," Scott said to him. "You should get together."

Scott set up a meeting with GL and Jarrod at his own house in Abbotsford in late February 2009. Over a kitchen table, they spoke about the shortage of cocaine in the Lower Mainland and how the quality had gone way downhill. GL then told Jarrod that he could get his hands on a great deal of high-quality cocaine from friends in Mexico. But, he maintained, they would not be interested in any small-time deals. The minimum order would be at least 100 kilos. Jarrod said he was very interested and wanted to know what sort of time frame he would be looking at. GL assured him that he could complete such a deal in two to three months. Jarrod said that he was impressed and would like to discuss the matter further at a later date. Although Scott split his time during the meeting between the house's kitchen and living room, he did not participate in the discussion about the deal.

A couple of days later, they met again in Scott's kitchen. Jarrod said he had assembled a team of backers. One he identified as a wealthy Indian Canadian berry farmer who lived on 0 Avenue. That one backer alone, he said, was prepared to float $3 million in cash. Then Jarrod told GL that he wanted to start with 10 kilos per week, and if it was high enough quality, he would increase the order to 30 or even 40 kilos per week.

The following day, GL left for a six-week contract position as a camp manager for a diamond mine in a remote part of northern B.C. Without either cell or landline service, GL stayed in contact with Scott via satellite phone.

The day after GL returned to Abbotsford, May 2, 2009, he met Scott at a local restaurant for breakfast. Scott told him that Jarrod had been awaiting his return and that his backers were eager to get the ball rolling but needed a taste test before they'd invest any real money. GL told him that was entirely possible and that he would need a deposit of $3,000 per kilogram they ordered.

With Jarrod and Scott (and their backers) well into the plan, GL approached police again. He signed a contract to become an agent source and agreed to allow police to record any and all conversations between him and Jarrod or Scott. They then rented a warehouse on his behalf to store his truck and the propane canisters the cocaine would be transported in.

GL then told Scott he was flying to Mexico in June 2009 and that he would bring back a five-kilo sample. He also told him to make sure that Jarrod was aware of what was going on. Acting now under police direction, GL didn't actually go to Mexico, and the police, who had some understandable trust issues as far as he was concerned, refused to give him five kilos of cocaine to use as a sample.

But he soldiered on. At the end of July 2009, police recorded GL arranging meetings with Scott with the purpose of getting him or Jarrod to visit the warehouse to see how his operation worked. When asked about the sample, he said that it was still sealed in a propane canister and that if the backers wanted it, they would have to come and get it. The official transcript shows that GL told Scott that he didn't want to risk being caught with it in his truck:

GL: I am not fuckin' driving around with the thing. I am not asking you to drive around with the fuckin' thing. These guys are gonna have to clean themselves, however they fuckin' do it. I don't care if they drive around for six fuckin' hours and then we'll all get together and have a little show and tell and after I give them the show and tell and show them all my vehicles, explain the deal, explain how it's gonna go down, what it's gonna cost to get into this thing. If they're still interested, then I'll open it up for 'em. They can take their fuckin' sample and pss-ee-you.
Scott: Yeah.

GL: It's too serious, because I know when we were sittin' in here, he says, okay. This is when we were—before.

Scott: Yeah.

GL: He says, yeah. Well, you know what? I'm...I'm gonna get Wayne to come down and get it, and do this, and do this, and do this. You know what? There ain't enough money in it to be the fuckin' taxi for this shit. You're gonna get looked after. You're gonna get looked after 'cause I...I...I ground some good numbers down there. You're gonna get looked after. Actually, I'm probably gonna tell him I'm gonna look after you 'cause this way, if this asshole gets in trouble, I'll still look after you because he'll have the fuckin' Hindus behind him to finish off the deal and it'll be between him and the Hindus...

After that, GL made repeated calls in hopes of arranging a meeting at the warehouse, stressing that he wanted Jarrod and "the fucking Hindus" to come. Scott stalled:

See, I think like Jarrod said and I...I...I haven't seen him there for quite a while since Carly moved out, he used to come to the house [indiscernible]. He's a big fucking Hindu.

He also assured GL in the same conversation that he'd talk to Jarrod. Scott said he'd let Jarrod know, but that he might have a hard time getting together with him because he had "so much heat on him."

After a few abortive attempts, GL arranged a meeting between Jarrod, Scott and himself at Scott's house. Scott pointed out that Carly had been the avenue through which he spoke with Jarrod.

In Scott's kitchen, at about 2:30 p.m. on August 8, 2009, Jarrod greeted GL and pulled a large green erasable note board out of a bag, telling him "this is how we do it." It's an old but effective trick, one pioneered by former Hells Angels national president Walter Stadnick. If a house is bugged, traffickers write their conversations on the board and then quickly erase them. That way, there's no hard evidence because no verbal communication is exchanged. And since the board is constantly erased, nothing written on it can ever be recovered. Many in law enforcement are aware of the practice and take measures against it because it is so crudely effective. But the Crown made a crucial mistake with Jarrod. One of the conditions of his bail (Jarrod was facing weapons charges and due for a court date in December) was that he was not allowed to own a "whiteboard," which is what all erasable note boards are commonly called because they are usually white. Jarrod cleverly circumvented that restriction by simply buying a green one.

But unlike Stadnick, he sometimes deviated from the discipline required to communicate solely by the board. Police were able to record snippets of their conversation. When asked if the buyer would be happy with decent enough quality cocaine that it could make excellent crack, Jarrod said, "He'll just be happy, like . . . he'd be jumping up and down." GL took that to understand he'd be celebrating. He then asked Jarrod if the buyer could come up with the deposit he had asked for. Jarrod answered, "I'm pretty sure I can convince him." And when GL asked him if his curfew or police surveillance would pose any problems, Jarrod told him, "Once I know they're all good, it'll be easy each time . . . less than a few hours. You know we have cars here and we . . . it's like we have a truck [inaudible] special compartment [indiscernible] so I'm not like just gonna throw them over my shoulder and drive them some place. It's gonna be a lot smarter than that."

Jarrod then told GL his foolproof methods for testing cocaine and offered $30,000 per kilo, higher than the $27,000 GL had expected. GL found that suspicious. Jarrod also pointed out that since he was on $175,000 bail, he wanted to keep the number of people who knew about the deal as small and discreet as possible. He said he wanted knowledge of the transaction limited to himself, GL, Scott and Carly. He finished the conversation by telling GL he had $3 million on hand and could come up with $2 million more, if necessary.

GL called Scott a couple of times and arranged a meeting at a Tim Hortons on August 10, 2009. Scott, who spoke freely at the meeting, said Jarrod "felt better after the meeting with GL." Then he asked GL if Jarrod told him what his commission would be. GL told him that Jarrod would pay him $30,000 per kilo and $5,000 per kilo to Scott for arranging the deal.

Then they dealt with logistics. When Scott asked where the money drop should take place, GL suggested Scott's house. "While I'm going to assume that he's going to leave it and I'll just pick it up at your house," he told him. "What you don't want is you don't want money and dope in the same place. I'll tell you what happens then—guns come out." Scott agreed that his house was ideal, saying his basement was full of empty boxes and that there was plenty of room to "hide a frigging duffel bag of fucking cash."

After that meeting, GL was anxious to speak to Jarrod, but Scott had some difficulty getting an answer from him, even though he had spoken directly with Carly and given her a note to give to Jarrod. Finally, at 2:17 p.m. on August 13, 2009, Scott called GL and told him to meet with him and Jarrod at his house at 5:00 p.m. With police watching, GL arrived at Scott's house at 5:08 p.m., and Jarrod—driven by an unidentified friend who did not leave the vehicle—showed up at 5:15 p.m., while Scott got there three minutes later.

Police saw the three men talking in Scott's garage. Jarrod did not bring his green board this time but, as a precaution, made both men deposit their cellphones with his in the garage. But GL was wearing a wire and recorded the conversation as they discussed details of the exchange:

Jarrod: Yeah, so I talked to, um, like I said, um, I'm on bail so I can't do it myself.

GL: Oh, like I know your hands are tied, buddy.

Jarrod: Yeah, so I talked to, um, he's a broker. This is what he does for a living.

GL: Yeah.

Jarrod: And what he does is he knows every guy in the game, and they all go to him to get the shit, right? So basically, my friend can get rid of all of 'em no problem. He can dump them no problem. Um, like I said, I'm not even going to profit from this, I'm just going to give, uh, the Wayne his cut and make sure maybe...

GL: Get some love down the road for whatever, yeah.

Jarrod: He gets some shit and whatever, maybe you know, like I said. Once I'm off my bail, I can go near it, but, but right now, like I can't even go near it. But I have a friend that's no heat, no nothing. So basically he wants a hundred. And he says he can, he can do the deposit, he can give you the money, no problem. He says he wants to do it in tens. Ten at a time. So he'll leave you 30,000 deposit and then, um, within, you know, five, six hours he's gonna go get it and bring your money back.

GL: And I can bring it here and...

Jarrod: Yeah.

GL: Boom, boom, and away we go.

Jarrod: And he wants to do it in tens.

GL: That's fine.

Jarrod: So in that way, he says it's just less money to deal with.

GL: Well, in 10 days and it's done.

Jarrod: And he said basically, yeah. Boom, boom, boom, he can do it 10 in every day. He said, in fact, like he can do this all the time. He knows every major guy around and they all come to him. So basically, my friend's like fucking like hugging me, he's so happy with me.

They then discussed the dearth of high-quality drugs in the area and moved on to prices. When Jarrod complained about paying a deposit up front before the drugs had even arrived, GL began to explain how complicated his process was. Jarrod interrupted him, saying: "We're not interested in how you do because the more you tell me, the more I get worried that this is a setup." He then further distanced himself from the deal, claiming that he wasn't the dealer, just "an enforcer."

But he did want to know how things would work once the big shipment of drugs had arrived from Mexico. As they worked out the details, Jarrod told GL, "Come by, I'll get a kid to come by, I'll leave the thirty grand with Wayne, you get my kid to bring the shit, I'll have the money dropped off. Boom, that's it." He closed the meeting by making sure everyone was on the same page and told GL that he had faith he was not part of a "setup" because he had used Scott, whom he trusted, as a middleman. At 5:28 p.m., Jarrod left in the same truck he came in.

Two weeks later, GL phoned Scott to make sure everything was still going as planned. They spoke in code, referring to the drugs as "pickup trucks" and the amounts as "miles." Scott complained that he had an argument with Carly. Apparently, she thought it was her deal and that the commission should go to her, not her dad. GL laughed and came up with a solution— Jarrod should pay him the entire amount, and then GL would kick the commission back to Scott.

After a few more calls in which Scott asked GL to run down the prices, amounts and commissions again, on August 26, 2009, GL told Scott that the drugs had arrived, and that he had 72 kilos in the warehouse. After some delays because Scott had to get his motorcycle serviced and Jarrod had decided to go to the PNE, they agreed to meet in a cemetery, at which GL aired his worries about Bacon's sincerity. Because Bacon had not shown him any money and was hoping to get $300,000 worth of coke basically on spec, GL told Scott he would be just as happy to find another buyer. He recorded the following conversation:

GL: You know what, and, and I actually almost got a feelin' this is over his fuckin' head, just the whole concept of—you know what, we got a deal goin', I have fuckin' done 110 percent of what I'm gonna do, he hasn't shown me 10 fuckin' cents and he wants 300,000 dollars worth of credit in 20 minutes for two hours, you know, so I'm just about deck. I'm ready to take a fuckin' walk, you know, this all too good to be true thing, well, you know what, it ain't that good, buddy, because it's fuckin' time to show up with some fuckin' cash and and show up when you're supposed to show up, where you're supposed to show up...

Scott: Yeah.

GL: ...But anyways, what are his concerns I'm done a...so I'm...

Scott: No, no concerns.

GL: Yeah.

Scott: No, my concerns is wha...okay, like, is, ah, I mean, I'm all new to this, this is something that I've never done before.

GL: I've done it three times today I got...

Scott: 'kay so...

GL: ...it pretty much down...

Scott: ...So he, if he brings me 30 grand, what's, what's the process after that?

GL: Okay, well ah, he'll get 10...

Scott: ...Well, he's supposed to, he's supposed to give me 30 grand, like, he's bringin' that money, like he's [indiscernible].

GL: Yeah. Then come meet me at the warehouse, bring a duffel bag, somethin'...

Scott: Yeah.

GL: ...and fuckin' wheel ya inside, have, we'll pick 10 out, he, he does whatever the fuck he wants with them, he checks them out, I ain't gonna fuckin' spend his money, his money ain't gonna leave the warehouse, but I'm not deliverin' 10 when I got 70 or 80 there, I got a little bit too much on my plate and that's not...

They then discussed who would pick up the drugs and the identity of a "partner" Jarrod had mentioned. GL threw out a name, but Scott believed it was his daughter. Scott then suggested Jarrod come to the warehouse to pick up the drugs, but GL said there was no way he'd do it while he was on bail and under constant surveillance. He then suggested they put it in Scott's house. Scott didn't like that idea and told GL that there was no way the drugs would be in his house overnight. GL said that was okay with him, they could just use his house as the money drop. But he also warned that if he did not get paid within 24 hours, he would sell the drugs himself. Scott assured him he would get paid, and then he went home.

Less than an hour later, at 6:18 p.m., an SUV registered to Susan Bacon and driven by David Bacon pulled up at Scott's house. Jarrod exited the vehicle and walked into Scott's house through the garage. At 7:09 p.m., he emerged with Scott. Police say they caught him on video motioning "ten o'clock" to Scott.

Jarrod left with his dad, and Scott kept walking down the street. A distance away from the house, Scott called GL. Scott told GL he had met with Jarrod, who told Scott that he'd drop the cash off at Scott's house at ten that evening. He also said that it wasn't determined who'd pick up the drugs yet.

GL got angry. "You know what ten o'clock says to me?" he asked. "Pitch black and guns." Scott assured him that Jarrod wasn't planning to rip him off and that the kid dropping off the money was one who lived in his house and had worked for Jarrod for a while.

Scott appeared to have a little trouble with the arithmetic involved, so GL took out a sheet of paper and calculated that the deposit and commission on the 72 kilos would be a total of $456,000.

They then discussed Jarrod's curfew (which was nine o'clock), and GL then attempted to have Scott convince Jarrod to make the drop himself, while it was still light out. "I'm just trying to figure out if this is real. Gonna... I mean obviously this makes sense," GL said. "So he's home at nine o'clock and can't fucking move." Scott then assured GL his money would be delivered at 10:00 p.m. GL was not satisfied with that. He told Scott to text Jarrod and tell him that GL refused to work in the dark and "it's daylight, he's still mobile or can be mobile, he's got an hour or two to do his thing."

At eight that evening, David Bacon drove Jarrod to Scott's house just as Scott was arriving. Police surveillance teams videotaped Jarrod and Scott having a very "animated" discussion. As soon as Jarrod and his dad (who did not get out of the SUV) left, at 8:07 p.m., Scott called GL and told him, "I just had a fucking little talk with that little boy here just a second ago." They then agreed to meet in 15 minutes at the warehouse.

A few minutes later, GL called him back. "Before I come tearing back, and before you get all excited," he asked, "are we talking, or is he going to buy the truck, or what are we doing?"

Scott stalled. "I'll let you know when I see ya," he said. "I'll tell ya this, I'll tell ya the scoop. Yeah, the money's en route, it's en route, and I tell you ya what I need to tell ya when I see ya."

Mollified, GL then told Scott he'd rather meet at the cemetery instead of the warehouse. Scott was surprised; he said he had just about arrived at the warehouse with the understanding the deal would go down there.

The police, listening to all of the phone conversations, had already infiltrated the warehouse, and an emergency response team was waiting both inside and out.

Just as they were deploying, Scott arrived at the warehouse and, after seeing a couple of what he thought might have been cop cars, drove on past.

Just after nine, Scott received another call from GL. He said that he'd seen a Cadillac that "was skulking through the parking lot there, and within about five minutes, it was showtime." Scott agreed with GL's opinion that the warehouse was a bad place to meet at the moment and said he was headed home. Scott then said he planned to "erase everyone's phones, that stuff out of my phone," and continued, "And, and I'm not fuckin' you, like it's like I was supposed to text junior back there on yes or no [indiscernible noise], I can't fuckin' do that either."

GL did his best to calm Scott down and told him they would speak again the next day.

At about two in the afternoon, GL called Scott and heard some interesting news. That morning, Scott had been called to a job site at—of all places—the building next door to the warehouse. A friend of his there told him that he had been approached by the police the night before and they told him they were "staking the place out." Scott then told GL that he believed that "somewhere, all the way, somebody knew something was going on." He then went on to tell GL that other men at the job site had reported seeing and even talking to cops at the warehouse the night before. He even went on to tell GL that if the cops questioned him about driving by the warehouse the night before, he'd tell them that he had just gone "to scope out the job [next door] to see where he needed to park in the morning."

That would be the last time GL and Scott would speak on the telephone. CFSEU officers arrested Jarrod Bacon and Wayne Scott at their homes without incident on November 26, 2009. No actual drugs had ever been involved, but the police felt they had damning enough evidence from the conversations GL had recorded. In their investigative report, the CFSEU said that they believed Jarrod had no intention of paying GL and was instead going to steal the drugs. They also believed that Scott was not aware of Jarrod's plan and that he genuinely thought he was negotiating a huge drug deal. Carly was not charged.

Unbeknownst to Jarrod and Scott was the fact that on the same day, CFSEU officers also arrested Doug Vanalstine— who'd taken over as boss of the UN after Barzan Tilli-Choli went down—and his fellow UN members Daryl Johnson and Nicholas Wester.

Interestingly, just as Jarrod was on bail for weapons charges, Vanalstine was on bail from a charge for trafficking in the

United States that stemmed from Clayton Roueche's arrest, and Johnson was also on bail, waiting for a court date regarding a trafficking charge in the Okanagan district. Scott had no previous record, but Wester had served time in the U.S. for trafficking. After his arrest, Jarrod admitted to using Oxycontin and cocaine, smoking marijuana daily and regularly taking steroids.

Neither of the two groups had realized they were caught in the same operation until the jail-yard rumor mill at the remand center informed them the following day. But it was something the police obviously felt some pride in. "These types of arrests definitely show the community we are targeting the right people," said Superintendent Dan Malo of the CFSEU. "We're targeting the people who are the highest risk to public safety."

On that very same day, the IHIT announced the arrest of Sophon Sek on manslaughter, and break and enter, in connection with the Surrey Six murders. Sek was something of a celebrity in the Lower Mainland; his gap-toothed grin and thumbs-up pose were plastered over much of the area after he beat 678 other players to win the 2009 B.C. Poker Championship at the River Rock Casino in Richmond just days before. In fact, he had yet to collect his $364,364 in prize money. Police made motions to seize the money, which Sek's lawyer, Alan Ip, fought. It was Eileen Mohan, though, who seemed to have the best handle on the winnings. "I don't think he'll be able to enjoy his money for a long time," she said.

Also on that same day, Kelowna mixed martial arts fighter Geoff Meisner went missing. A heavyweight at 6'1", 275 pounds, Meisner had a 0–1 record after losing to Louisville, Kentucky's Ron "The Monster" Sparks at the Colosseo Championship Fighting event in Edmonton on March 6, 2009.

On November 27, 2009, his wife, Tammy, drove him to the Orchard Park Shopping Centre to retrieve his truck, a brand new white Ford F-350 pickup, that he had left in the parking lot overnight. That was the last she ever saw of him. The truck was found later that evening in the lot of a Starbucks less than five minutes' drive away. There was no sign of struggle.

In her public appeal for his return, Tammy Meisner claimed his profession was as "a mixed martial arts fighter and protein salesman." Later, when she was petitioning the court to have him ruled deceased so she and their four young daughters could gain access to his assets, she admitted that his primary sources of income came from "the Hells Angels Motorcycle Club and another criminal gang known as the King Pin Crew."

The King Pin Crew was a Kelowna-based Hells Angels puppet gang allegedly run by Dale Habib, a bar owner whose patrons numbered a few full-patch Hells Angels. The King Pin Crew's logo consisted of three conjoined skulls, the middle one of which was crowned. Their official Facebook page lists them as a professional sports team and bears the slogan "we love kick'n peopl's head's in!!!"

And events from around the country would also affect the Lower Mainland gangs. In Winnipeg, police had managed to turn Michael Satsatin, the secretary-treasurer of the Zig Zag Crew (perhaps the most powerful Hells Angels puppet gang since the heyday of the Rockers in Laval) to turn informant. In exchange for $450,000 and personal immunity, Satsatin recorded 37 official Zig Zag Crew meetings over 13 months. The evidence he collected led to 31 arrests, including every full-patch member of the Zig Zag Crew, a cousin of an NHL player and a former RCMP officer on December 1, 2009.

A less likely seeming arrest that came from Satsatin's evidence was that of Eric Sandberg, a well-educated, middle-class Surrey man with no arrest record. In fact, he was also undergoing treatment for rectal cancer, a type with a far less than 50/50 survival rate.

But the tapes didn't lie. Sandberg was recorded during trips to Winnipeg, where he had grown up, dealing ecstasy, trafficking weapons and collecting debts. He was recorded telling the Winnipeggers that he could get them "any kind of" firearm they wanted and bragging that the Hells Angels and their allies in the Lower Mainland could "wipe out" any opposition. Many took that as a confirmation of the widespread belief that the Hells Angels were not just cozying up to the Red Scorpions and Bacon Brothers, but also distancing themselves from the UN.

He was also recorded managing an operation in which Satsatin deposited $1,000 per month in a CIBC account to repay a $20,000 debt he had incurred with another, unnamed, Lower Mainland trafficker.

The Winnipeg media portrayed Sandberg as the "independent drug dealer" his defense team made him out to be. But that seems unlikely, even ridiculous. If he was an independent drug dealer (which, in the Lower Mainland, was almost impossible to be at anything but a subsistence level because of the Hells Angels' attempts to monopolize the trade), it would be unlikely he would also be able to traffic heavy weapons. It's also very unlikely he would be welcome at official Zig Zag Crew meetings or that he would be bragging about the Hells Angels strategic power in the Lower Mainland. And it's even harder to believe an independent drug dealer would go all the way to Winnipeg to make sure that a high-ranking Zig Zag Crew member was paying his debt to another drug dealer in an orderly and timely manner.

A more plausible explanation is that although Sandberg was not a member of the Hells Angels or a related club, he was held in high enough esteem by them to be their ambassador to their friends in Winnipeg. He was, in all likelihood, there selling Hells Angels' supplied drugs and weapons, and ensuring the locals' accounts were all up to date. And unless he was caught red-handed or on tape, he never would have been suspected of a thing.

• • •

While Canadian law enforcement was concentrating on getting inside the gangs, the Americans were doing their best to establish a deterrent. Clayton Roueche's trial in the United States had been stacked against him from the start.

Despite the Maseratis and the condos, Roueche claimed he could not afford an attorney and asked the court to appoint him one. It was a bold move, part of a strategy to discredit prosecution claims that he made millions from the drug trade.

Canadian investigators raided his home and discovered what they called "a kit for kidnapping or murder." It consisted of a gun, handcuffs, full-face masks, night-vision goggles and bulletproof vests. Then authorities on both sides of the border started offering deals to UN members and associates who were charged with various offenses if they could provide any information on Roueche. Plenty did.

On December 15, 2009, the court in Seattle, about two hours' drive south of Abbotsford, handed down a remarkable sentence. Roueche was to serve 30 years in an American prison. If it had been a Canadian court, his crimes probably would have netted him about six years, of which he would likely spend only four behind bars. But in the United States, 30 years generally means 30 years.

He emerged in the news about a year later when images from his Facebook page were made public. Some of the pictures he posted were of East Asian imagery (dragons and things like that), one was an inspirational poem and another was a drawing celebrating the UN's 13-year anniversary. Most interesting, though, were the pictures of himself. He had slimmed down and hit the weights, and was posing with a number of new friends, most of them Asian. He was soon transferred from Lee penitentiary in Jonesville, Virginia, to the massive Federal Corrections Complex in Lee, Florida. If he serves his entire sentence, he'll be free in 2039, when he's 64.

• • •

There was now little doubt that the long, arduous plan for law enforcement to take down the Bacon Brothers as a criminal organization was working out. Jamie and his friends were behind bars waiting for the Surrey Six murder trial and things did not look good for them. Jarrod and his son's grandfather were also in jail, awaiting their turn before a judge on trafficking charges. With tons of recordings of conversations featuring them dealing with a rather efficient and motivated informant, their chances of getting away with it looked pretty slim, too.

But everyone knew that the brains of the Bacon Brothers, what made them so powerful and so prominent, was Jonathan—the oldest one, the smart one. To get to him would be to really bring down the Bacon Brothers.

Law enforcement's previous attempt—in which he and his friend Godwin Chen were caught with drugs and weapons, and his girlfriend, Rayleene Burton, had been caught trying to escape with cash—resulted in failure when Justice Donald Gardner ruled the evidence inadmissible because the police did not have the authority to search the vehicle the deal went down in or the vehicle Burton had fled in.

It doesn't happen very often, but the Crown actually appealed the Bacon-Cheng-Burton acquittal. And, in an even rarer occurrence, a team of judges found that one of their peers had made a mistake. The B.C. Court of Appeal tribunal agreed unanimously. Gardner had erred in determining that the arrests and subsequent searches were illegal or unwarranted. They ordered a new trial.

Jonathan Bacon was not behind bars, but he was in big trouble. And the Teflon sheen that he had sported for so many years had fallen away. Though they were still far from eliminated, the myth of the Bacon Brothers' invincibility had been extinguished.

CHAPTER 11

THE WOLF PACK: 2010–2011

While two of the Bacon Brothers were behind bars and the other was awaiting trial—and well aware he was under close police surveillance—the rest of the drug scene in British Columbia continued without them, just as it had without Roueche and Tilli-Choli. But the vacancies at the top were being filled by lesser talents.

One person who was involved in the drug trade hardly fit the stereotypical description of a drug user or trafficker. Kelowna's Brittney Irving was a pretty, dark-haired 24-year-old. Although she usually sported a tan, you could always see her trademark freckles on her nose and cheeks. Several people I spoke with recalled her as a delightful personality, full of life with a great sense of humor.

She was also a healthcare professional. Irving served as a care aide, a registered assistant who aids nurses and practitioners in hospitals and other facilities. She was even known to show up at work on her days off, just because she so enjoyed the company of her patients and coworkers. And she saw what drugs could do to people.

But she had a problem. Irving had become addicted to Oxycontin, a highly addictive oral painkiller with clinical similarities to heroin (in fact, it's commonly known as "hillbilly heroin" in the United States). And she didn't fit that description, either. Typically, Canadian Oxycontin users are over 30 and live in the Atlantic provinces or rural Ontario. Few work in the healthcare industry, in which knowledge of what Oxycontin can do is widespread.

But she was an Oxycontin user and paid for her addiction the way many people in B.C. do—by selling weed. In fact, in March 2009, a police raid at a grow op at a luxurious beach house at 387 Brealoch Road uncovered 1,500 pot plants. Two men and one woman in the house were arrested. Irving also lived in the house but was not present when the raid went down and was not charged. Without anywhere else to live, she checked into a motel. Sources have said that the grow op was part of a massive Hells Angels–operated network. She was also known as a heavy drinker and had been known to associate with Hells Angels, Independent Soldiers and members of the King Pin Crew.

On April 6, 2010, she left the Kelowna Days Inn at about one in the afternoon. She told a family member that she was going to a meeting in the Rutland area but didn't give any details. It was the last time any of her family saw her alive.

She did, however, say a lot more to her ex-boyfriend, Shaun O'Neil, who was still a close friend. "She said, 'I'm going to meet someone that is a real bad person, and I'm scared of doing what I'm going to do. But this is the last time; don't convince me not to. I love you and pray for me,'" he said, repeating the words that still haunt him. "That was the last I ever heard from her. For the rest of my life, I'll regret not convincing her not to go."

She was going to trade some weed for Oxycontin. She was reported to have taken 80 pounds of weed and $200,000 with her.

Her empty, locked blue 2001 Ford Explorer was found at seven the following evening in a deeply wooded area by West Kelowna RCMP acting on an anonymous tip. It was parked on a gravel shoulder of Philpott Road where it meets Highway 33. There were no signs of struggle.

Her brother, Neal, claimed that Brittney told him she was going on one last run before she committed herself to rehab.

The man she was going to meet was Joelon "Joey" Verma, an immigrant from Fiji. He did not have a criminal record, but was, as the saying goes, "known to police." Well known.

Verma was known to be good friends with Independent Soldier Donnie "Blaze" McWhirter, who had recently been arrested for sexual assault. Later, Verma would admit to being an Independent Soldier himself. Verma's girlfriend at the time was a pharmacy technician, making access to Oxycontin at least feasible.

Almost two months later, on May 25, 2010, Irving's remains were found not far from where her car was discovered. The RCMP did not release a cause of death, but they did say that the missing person investigation was now a homicide investigation.

Verma was later arrested and charged with both murder and robbery.

The details of the allegations against Verma have yet to come out at his trial, but social media have been alive with rumors and accusations. Some believe that Irving was killed because she was a rat whose information led to the beach house grow op being taken down. But that's a very unlikely scenario. If Irving was participating in the grow op, telling the cops would not be the way to pay for her Oxycontin addiction.

Others maintain that she owed dealers a huge debt and was murdered for it. There is some plausibility to that. Hells Angels and their associates frequently execute recalcitrant debtors, sometimes over relatively minor amounts of cash. Although it's true that dead people can't pay their debts, murders can make an effective deterrent for others. But money didn't seem to be Irving's problem. She revealed little anxiety about her meeting, aside from the fact that she knew Verma was "a bad man," and did not appear to be having money problems before her disappearance.

More likely is the theory that she needed her Oxycontin and took the weed and cash she had on hand to pay for it. But Verma, like so many before him, appears to have thought that he could have the weed and cash and keep the Oxycontin. The only thing that stood in his way was an unarmed 125-pound woman.

If Irving's murder was met with shock, and even outrage, the next major drug-related killing was not. Juel Stanton, a full-patch member of the East Vancouver Hells Angels, had an arrest record dating back to 1988 but first showed up on the radar in October 2001, when it was alleged in court that he, his brother Norman and Damon Bartolomeo robbed a grow op and held its owner, Alexander Goldman, captive, beat him up and stole his 1987 Toyota Camry in front of his friend, Nunzio Mela. Damon Bartolomeo was the older brother of Ryan Bartolomeo, who was one of the Surrey Six victims.

Although he owned a construction company named Juel Forming, it was well-known within the community that Stanton was a debt collector for the Hells Angels and that he was extremely violent and unpredictable. Port Moody Police Department Inspector Andy Richards, a biker expert, said that he was actually surprised the Hells Angels allowed such a "loose cannon" into their membership. Indeed, it is a rare man whose violent tendencies make the Hells Angels and biker cops think twice.

Stanton's trial took forever, with bail hearings, appeals and so forth. It was revealed in other trials that the bar at the Hells Angels' East Vancouver clubhouse sported an old pickle jar that was used to collect funds for Stanton's defense.

He wouldn't get it.

In a very rare occurrence, Stanton was kicked out of the club in May 2010. For a full-patch to be expelled over behavioral issues, it requires a unanimous vote by every other full-patch member of the chapter. "He was certainly very, very volatile and very high-maintenance from a club perspective," said Richards. "He drew a lot of unwanted police attention and a lot of unwanted public attention to the Hells Angels." Vancouver police had previously issued a public warning about Stanton, who liked to flash his Hells Angels tattoos at people he hoped to intimidate, and had reportedly warned the Hells Angels themselves that they would crack down on them if Stanton was not reined in.

On the morning of August 12, 2010, at 6:15 a.m., Vancouver police received 9-1-1 calls reporting a shooting at 202 West 11th, a luxurious red-brick house just a few blocks away from City Hall. It was owned by Stanton and his wife, Akrivoula. Neighbors recalled the red-and-white Hells Angels flag that used to fly there and the video cameras that watched the property. First responders arrived to find the deceased body of Stanton, filled with bullet holes. He was a few hours away from a court appearance in which he was to have given his side of the grow-op rip story.

It's unlikely that Stanton's murder will ever be solved. Many think it was house-cleaning by the Hells Angels, who did not want Stanton to either talk or get in their way. "If it was an in-house thing with the club, it is done, it is over," said Richards. "I don't think anybody is going to retaliate against the club. I don't see much coming from this."

He was right, there wasn't a gang war on anymore. Although both the UN and Red Scorpions continued to exist and do business, they no longer had the manpower, leadership or will to fight it out on the streets. Instead, the Hells Angels and their allies were hard-pressed to keep up with demand. After all the arrests, the manpower needs weighed on the various subgroups like the Independent Soldiers, the Renegades, the King Pin Crew and the Game Tight Soldiers. A lower quality of functionary was recruited, and one of the results was more violence.

For years by this point, Vancouver had been haunted by the missing women of the Downtown Eastside. Over the years, at least 60 women—mostly aboriginal, drug-addicted and involved in the sex trade—had gone missing. The investigation moved at a snail's pace, and what appeared to be police indifference and incompetence enraged many in the area.

Finally, the evidence pointed to something many in the community already knew. The women were dead. And they were killed by Robert "Willie" Pickton. Lucky enough to have inherited a large pig farm in the booming Lower Mainland town of Port Coquitlam, Pickton became a multimillionaire by selling off lots of his farm to residential and commercial developers.

He celebrated his wealth by throwing massive parties on his farm, which now featured a nightclub called Piggy's Palace. The parties, which had as many as 1,700 guests at a time, often featured local political, media and sports personalities and, always, Hells Angels and their buddies.

For entertainment, Pickton would drive around the Downtown Eastside, asking any likely-looking woman if she wanted to go to a party. Dozens, if not hundreds, did. Many did not make it back.

Pickton had been on police radar, mainly for violating fire codes and for not filing the appropriate paperwork for Piggy's Palace. In March 1997, he was arrested for the attempted murder of a guest at one of his parties. She claimed he handcuffed her and stabbed her several times before she managed to disarm him, stab him with his own knife and flee. She did indeed have several stab wounds and, on the night in question, Pickton was treated for a single stab wound, as well. For reasons unknown, police dropped the investigation.

A friend and employee of Pickton's put two and two together after finding purses and other belongings of some of the missing women. He went to the police, but after three searches of the property with no results, they again stopped investigating. And, despite a 1999 tip that Pickton had a freezer full of human flesh on his property, they did not investigate.

In February 2002, police investigating an illegal firearms report on Pickton's property unearthed a prescription inhaler owned by one of the missing women. He was charged with two counts of first-degree murder later that month.

His jury trial, which began in 2006, was shrouded in secrecy because of publication bans. Without any real evidence released to the public, rumors and half-truths were everywhere. Some claimed he had killed hundreds of women; many believed he ground their flesh and sold it as sausage meat in the area.

So when he was found guilty of just six counts of second-degree murder in December 2007, people were mystified. More than that, they were outraged.

Both sides appealed, but the decision was upheld by the Supreme Court on July 30, 2010. The publication ban was lifted a week later. The now-public details of the investigation and trial appalled many. The unwillingness the police showed to pursue Pickton, despite overwhelming evidence, smacked hard of racism, sexism and bias against drug addicts and sex workers. Many felt that police treated crimes against aboriginals, drug addicts, sex workers and, in particular, women as less important than they should have. The police forces of the Vancouver region, already fighting bad reputations decades in the making, looked cold and indifferent to the suffering of the victims because of their own biases. At a time when they were needed most, they came off as unwilling to help.

And it was in that tumultuous, almost paranoid period that disaster struck a young woman named Ashley Machiskinic. On September 15, 2010, her body was found in an alley behind the Downtown Eastside's notorious Regent Hotel. Answering a 9-1-1 call about a woman falling from the hotel's fifth floor, paramedics found Machiskinic's body at 5:27 p.m. and declared her dead at the scene.

Several eyewitnesses were interviewed. Some of them said it looked like she fell, others that she had been pushed. Many reported that she had hit her head on overhead electrical wires on her way down. One witness claimed to have seen her shoes thrown down after her.

Video from cameras in the hotel lobby indicated nothing out of the ordinary. There were no signs of struggle, no indications of weapons and no suicide note. The window in question was quite large and low to the floor. Investigators decided that it would be possible to fall out of it "if sitting or kneeling" in front of it. A chair was found in front of the window, with its back to the outside.

Machiskinic was exactly the kind of person activists believed police considered second-class citizens. She was of aboriginal descent and she had problems not just with alcohol, but also with cocaine, methamphetamine, morphine and heroin. Diagnosed in 2004 with chronic schizophrenia, she had been hospitalized many times, including one 10-month stint, for mental-health issues.

The investigators asked the witnesses if anyone might want to harm Machiskinic. There was no shortage of suggestions. All of the people named were interviewed by police, and all denied involvement with her death. All were also able to provide alibis for the time of her death.

According to the coroner's report, her body revealed severely traumatic injuries to her "anterior surface"—which disagreed with many activists' claims that she landed on her back, which they said was evidence that she was pushed rather than fell—and head injuries consistent with hitting the overhead wires. But there were no injuries that indicated a struggle or altercation.

The autopsy also revealed that Machiskinic's body contained a "potentially lethal" amount of cocaine and an "elevated" level of alcohol.

The coroner did not rule out murder, suicide or misfortune.

Unsatisfied with the investigation and sure the police were not taking the matter seriously, activists—organized and experienced after the Pickton investigation and trial—declared her death a murder. A vigil was held in hopes of drawing attention to Machiskinic's fate on October 4, 2010. Police arrested three of the participants for trespassing.

At a "town hall" meeting on October 6, 2010, Vancouver police chief Jim Chu faced a series of often shouted criticisms of his officers' unwillingness to help the women of the Downtown Eastside. All Chu could do was to repeat that police could only help victims if witnesses come forward. "The Vancouver Police Department has a commitment to provide safety for all," he said. "The police department is greatly enhanced if you help us."

One woman, who said she lived in the nearby Europe Hotel, responded by saying that she had seen a woman abducted by a man and reported it to police, but they refused to take her seriously even though she had a license plate number for the vehicle.

One of the most well-known activists, Angela Marie MacDougall, executive director of Battered Women's Support Services, said she knew what was going on: Machiskinic was murdered over a drug debt. "The rapes and the beatings are standard [punishment]. What is a little bit unusual are women's heads being shaved…and women coming out of windows," she said. "I know of about six in the last two years. They're not deaths all the time, but to injury or deaththey are thrown out of windows. We know this is a way that drug dealers deal with debts."

And she was hardly alone in that opinion. "There's been a few women lately thrown out of windows, at the Balmoral, the Regent," said Gladys Radek, organizer of Walk 4 Justice, an organization in support of missing and murdered women. "Women missing fingers, wearing wigs because their heads have been shaved…"

Sadly, history backs up their opinion. Hells Angels associates all over B.C. had used violence and even murder to punish debtors. Fingers, even hands, had been severed over relatively small debts. While many make the point that the life of an addict like Ashley Machiskinic may not have been of utmost importance to police, it would certainly mean nothing to a dealer unable to get any more money from her.

Whether Machiskinic was murdered or not will never be conclusively determined unless someone, perhaps the perpetrator, comes forward. But what's important to remember is that murders and torture over drug debts were happening and are happening. It's a dispiritingly familiar manifestation of the old cliché about drug addiction and supply. People, often in sad circumstances, turn to stimulant or opiate drugs, which are highly addictive. In order to support their habit, they give everything they have or can get their hands on. When they run out of anything of value, they fall into debt with their dealer, leaving them at the dealer's mercy. The drug dealers in British Columbia are not merciful people.

One of the Hells Angels–affiliated gangs that sold drugs in the Downtown Eastside was the Game Tight Soldiers, who had originated in the neighborhood and were not known as being very merciful. But business had been good, and the gang had expanded to drug-hungry Prince George. A few days after Machiskinic's death, one of the Game Tight Soldiers' founding members, Eric Fiske, and an unnamed female associate went into the woods to retrieve a bag left there for them by another associate. But they did not know that the associate who left the bag there was working with the RCMP.

When Fiske threw the bag into the back of his pickup, the officers pounced. He was charged with possession of two loaded handguns, a MAC-10 submachine gun with ammunition and 228 grams of cocaine. A subsequent search of his home turned up 56 more grams of cocaine, 159 doses of heroin, 1.5 kilograms of marijuana and other related drug-trafficking paraphernalia.

Although Prince George is a 10-hour drive from the Downtown Eastside, Fiske's arrest was a stark reminder of the drugs and violence that linked him, the Game Tight Soldiers, the Hells Angels and the entire trafficking world with victims like Machiskinic and Irving.

In truth, though, victims like Machiskinic and Irving are a lot rarer than dead bodies of the gang members themselves. Fighting for territory with rivals, holding out or not paying on time (even if your stash had been stolen or your grow op robbed) were often punishable by death. Everyone wanted their piece of the pie, and nobody liked to share.

As glamorous and attractive as the gang lifestyle appeared to be, there was also the grim reality that members—from the high-flying, Maserati-driving overlords to the lowest street-corner crack merchants—woke up every day knowing that they faced death. One mistake, one accident, and their next trip could be to the morgue.

One of those gang members was Gurmit Singh Dhak, one of the founders of the increasingly powerful Dhak Gang and the man who'd been in injured in the 2007 Quattro shooting. With the vast reduction in size and scope of both the UN and the Red Scorpions/Bacon Brothers, gangs like the Dhaks were gaining business as drug-hungry users looked for suppliers and quality product.

But Gurmit, who had been shot in a crowded restaurant years before, knew that the gang life was not a good life, despite its obvious rewards. In an effort to dissuade at-risk youth from following the same path he did, Gurmit agreed to speak with the Odd Squad, a group of police who make presentations to the region's youth to inform them about the dangers of the gangster lifestyle in hopes of de-romanticizing it.

In a video of the interview, Gurmit, wearing a Raiders cap, answers their questions politely, calmly and knowledgeably. When asked what he thought his future was, Gurmit replied:

> Oh, I'll either probably wind up dead, or…my future in gangs is…if I could turn back time, I would never do it again. Every day I've got to look over my shoulder; I've got to worry about my family, I've got to worry about, like, if I jump out of my car, am I going to get shot? Or, you know, I could be walking in the mall, and walking out and getting shot. I don't know.

When asked if he wanted to get out of gangs, he told them: "Oh, I want to get out. But it's too late now to get out. I have too many enemies."

He then said he'd "do anything" to keep his own kids out of gangs, that "deep down" all gangsters were scared and that schools should do more to inform kids exactly how dangerous being in a gang is.

That tape was made in June 2010. At 5:50 p.m. on October 16, 2010, Burnaby police responded to 9-1-1 calls about shots fired at the Metrotown Mall. When they arrived, they found the bullet-riddled body of Gurmit Singh Dhak slumped over the wheel of his black BMW SUV. Police referred to it as a targeted hit and pointed out that although the mall was open, there were very few people near the site of the shooting and that nobody else was hurt.

With so much of British Columbia's gang population behind bars or scared to act, more and more veteran gang members were forced to do work they would ordinarily slough off to others. A perfect example of this is what happened to Joseph Bruce Skreptak.

A full-patch member of the Hells Angels East End chapter, Skreptak was one of the founding members of the Kelowna, or K-Town, chapter. In 2005, police busted a huge grow op in a house he owned, but he managed to get off scot-free because he testified that the marijuana in question belonged to his tenants and that he had no knowledge of their activities. His truck was even parked outside the house when the raid went down.

That brings to mind the Hells Angels' recipe for success in Canada: they mastermind the operation and make the big bucks, but when the hammer falls, there's always someone else, someone lower down the proverbial totem pole, to take the blame.

But those people were becoming rarer, and sometimes the Hells Angels had to take on jobs they previously thought were below them.

In October 2010, police saw a luxury SUV speeding and driving erratically in Salmon Arm, a town near Kelowna. Officers stopped the car and, using the smell of marijuana as a validation, affected a search. Inside the vehicle were several firearms (including a sawed-off shotgun), bulletproof vests, a baseball bat, an axe handle, bear spray and a device specifically designed to jam cellphones. A number of Hells Angels opponents who had been killed or had gone missing had their cellphones jammed just about the time they had gone missing or been attacked. Arrested were Skreptak, Carl Ennis, Dennis Miner and Cory Montemurro on numerous charges, but all were eventually acquitted. Since all, according to police, were "sporting" Hells Angels paraphernalia, each must have been at prospect level or higher. The officer who stopped them was not only sure he'd done the right thing, but was also surprised by their audacity. "I think it's fair to say they were up to no good," said RCMP Staff Sergeant Kevin Keane of the Salmon Arm detachment. "It was snowing and the roads were under winter conditions, and these people were going down the road pretty quick."

A couple of weeks later, on November 1, 2010, Skreptak was arrested for breaking into a Kelowna residence and allegedly beating up a father and son. The dad was sent to a hospital, but the son was less badly injured.

A few years earlier, the suggestion of a full-patch, especially one of Skreptak's long standing, beating up a father and son instead of pawning it off on some underling would have been preposterous.

And there was still tension in Prince George, where a number of loose organizations (all answering to the Hells Angels, but not to each other) were experiencing friction. One local gangster who rubbed a lot of people the wrong way was Joey Arrance. The owner of the Twisted Soul Tattoo and Body Piercing Shop downtown, Arrance had also been also a prospect (or striker) for the Renegades. He'd been charged with sexual assault as a result of an incident at the Renegades' clubhouse in July 2010 and, on September 19, 2010, was arrested again after a search of his home revealed a 10mm Glock pistol, spare magazines, a defused hand grenade and a bulletproof vest. Also charged were the two other residents of the house—Arrance's girlfriend, Kirsten Fredin, and her wheelchair-bound mother, Linda Fredin. By that time, Arrance was a member of the Game Tight Soldiers.

While Arrance was behind bars at a Prince George Regional Corrections facility, someone torched his shop. Less than 24 hours later, arsonists set fire to his home. His girlfriend's mother, Linda Fredin, was in the house at the time. She was airlifted to Vancouver to be treated for burns and smoke inhalation, but succumbed to her injuries a few days later on December 3, 2010.

And the Hells Angels in Kelowna were just as sloppy. Dain Phillips was not involved in gangs or the drug trade. But when the former minor-league hockey tough guy heard that a couple of local brothers were giving his own sons a tough time, he went over to their place to see if he could iron things out with their parents.

Instead of a discussion, he was beaten to death with a baseball bat, hammers and other objects on June 11, 2011. Charged were Robert Thomas, Norman Cocks, Robert Cocks, David McRae, Matthew McRae, Anson Schell and Thomas Vaughan.

Interestingly, Thomas and Norman Cocks were full-patch members of the Hells Angels, while Robert Cocks was president of the Throttle Lockers, yet another puppet club, this one based out of 100 Mile House.

Flabby, pig-faced Thomas fled. All the others were taken into custody, and all but Norman Cocks were granted bail. It marked the first time in 28 years that a full-patch B.C. Hells Angel had been charged with murder.

Thomas eventually turned himself in. He too, was denied bail. In a bizarre twist, while they were waiting for trial in North Fraser Pretrial Centre, both of the full-patch Hells Angels were involved in fights, which they lost. Thomas got into an altercation with Matthew Johnston, one of the accused Surrey Six killers and a well-known Red Scorpion. Thomas was knocked cold, while Johnston was uninjured. Cocks had his nose broken by Stephen Matheson, a prisoner charged with robbery who had low-level gang connections.

In previous years (and to this day, in most places), an attack on a Hells Angels full patch in jail or prison generally meant a death sentence. But on the British Columbia scene in 2011, that preferred status had declined so significantly that neither of the men who assaulted Thomas and Cocks saw any significant retaliation behind bars.

But it's not as though the Hells Angels didn't have friends behind bars. And they'd soon get more. With so many arrests in Kamloops, the Independent Soldiers there needed a new leader. They got one in Jeff Oldford, whose résumé included a theft conviction in April 2008, a sexual assault arrest in December 2010 and a trafficking arrest in April 2011.

Steve Bodie was a small-time drug dealer in Kamloops at the time. He was definitely on the Independent Soldiers' radar, as well as the cops'. He was at his North Kamloops home when he answered a knock on the door on August 5, 2011. Five men, armed with baseball bats and guns, burst in. After they blocked his escape, the men proceeded to beat him brutally, breaking many bones in his ribcage, hands and fingers.

They then threw him in a truck and took him to a deserted roadway about 10 miles from town. He was dumped by the side of the road, the truck running over one of his battered hands as they drove off.

Bodie managed to get to a nearby farmhouse. The residents dialed 9-1-1. Police raided Bodie's house without a warrant. They said they were concerned that another resident of the house could be in danger. He wasn't there, but two of the alleged assailants were. Eventually rounded up and arrested were Oldford, Brett Haynes, Adam Colligan, Greg Brotzel and David Byford.

The Independent Soldiers must have been desperate for cash because less than a month after the Bodie attack, on August 21, 2011, almost the exact same crime occurred.

Another, unnamed, drug dealer received a call from a female acquaintance asking him to meet her near the Aberdeen Medical Centre. The woman then took him into an alleyway in which two men—one with a gun, the other with a baseball bat—were waiting. The two thugs threatened the dealer with the weapons and demanded his cash and drugs. They took his cash, wallet, backpack and cellphone.

Although the victim complied, one of the men hit him over the head with the bat anyway. The trio then fled. Police described the hit as "potentially lethal." ·

Left for dead, the dealer managed to crawl to a nearby Tim Hortons, at which he called 9-1-1.

• • •

With all the arrests, assassinations and intimidations, the drug trade was in a state of flux. There was no real shortage of manpower (there never is) but a shortage of leadership. The number of people who are confident enough that they can run a drug-trafficking organization and stay alive and out of jail are few.

And by 2011, jail and the grave had taken quite a few of them from British Columbia.

But one very well-known one remained. Despite having two brothers behind bars, despite being out on bail, despite the police-issued warnings, despite media following him everywhere, despite everyone knowing that many, many people would love to see him dead, Jonathan Bacon was still walking the streets, still taking meetings and still living the life of a gangster.

The old gang structure in British Columbia was falling apart like European alliances in the 1930s. The UN, Red Scorpions, even the mighty Hells Angels were in serious disarray. But as alliances dissolve, new ones are formed, and those still in the upper reaches of the game put aside old differences and got together.

Back when he went to high school in Langley, Larry Amero was a skinny little guy who was frequently bullied. But by the time he was an adult, he had been transformed into a steroid-fueled behemoth. His thigh-like arms were unable to fall naturally at his sides because of his ridiculously pumped-up lats, giving him a wide-armed, ape-like stance.

He also started covering himself with tattoos. His right hand, entire back, left arm and the left side of his chest were extravagantly inked. But the most important tattoo was on his otherwise inkless belly. In an arc, the intricately decorated letters spelled out, in all caps, "Hells Angels."

Indeed he was a full-patch member of the White Rock Chapter of the Hells Angels. And he had a long records of arrests for drug trafficking and manufacture. Over the years, he had been associated with all the players in the Hells Angels sphere of influence: Randy Jones, Bob Green, Villy Lynnerup, Hal Porteous and the like.

But he also had other friends. In fact, over the years, he had become quite close with three men in particular, none of them Hells Angels. They were Jonathan Bacon, Randy Naicker and James Riach. Together they were about to become the Wolf Pack.

CHAPTER 12

BACONS' END: 2011–2012

Randy Naicker was an interesting fellow, to say the least. Fiji born, he admitted that he had helped to found the Independent Soldiers but claimed it was just a company with a clothing line and had nothing at all to do with gangs or drug trafficking. He came to media attention in 2005 when he was arrested for the kidnapping of Harpreet "Happy" Singh. While out on bail for the Singh kidnapping and extortion charges, Naicker found time to attend the notorious Castle Fun Park meeting. Naicker threw his considerable weight around while he was behind bars, instructing two of his men to brutally assault a UN member in their block. He may not have known it at the time, but when word leaked back to the UN, they vowed he would pay with his life. Released on day parole, Naicker spent his nights at a halfway house near Vancouver's trendy Cambie Village. On September 29, 2009, two armed men burst into the halfway house. Checking the sign-in book at the front desk, they saw an entry that said Naicker had just left on his way to a convenience store. They tore out after him. But the book had

confused another resident, Raj Soomel, for Naicker. The gunmen found Soomel and assassinated him in front of horrified
shoppers, then fled.

James Riach, another Independent Soldier who had
attended the Castle Fun Park meeting, was at a lower level than
Naicker, and had been arrested on weapons charges in 2008.

Years later, after their spate of arrests and assassinations,
Riach, Naicker, Amero and Jonathan Bacon had become quite
close. Police, media and even members of the public frequently
reported seeing them together. In fact, several witnesses said
they saw Amero and Jonathan Bacon touring around Burrard
Inlet in Amero's high-powered and gaudily painted speed boat
Steroids & Silicone. Yeah, he named his boat *Steroids & Silicone.*
Eventually, the Port Moody police stopped the boat with Bacon
and Amero on board for a chat.

But what they didn't know at the time was that Bacon,
Amero, Naicker and Riach were doing more than just hanging
out. Looking to cash in on the sudden scarcity of drugs on the
streets, they were forming their own organization.

Known as the Wolf Pack, this new organization would be
a side project for Amero, who would remain a Hells Angel. It's
not unusual for Hells Angels to have moneymaking operations
on the side, as long as their fellow members are made aware of
it and offered a chance to be involved. The notorious Montreal
chapter had set up a corporation of sorts called the Table that
was dedicated to the sale of drugs and included non-members,
as well as a number of full patches.

While the Castle Fun Park meeting, at the time, appeared
to be a summit meeting between the Independent Soldiers and
the UN, as represented by the Bacon Brothers, in the clearer
light of 2011, it appeared more as though it was a recruiting
meeting, with the Independent Soldiers (acting, as they always
did, as the Hells Angels' proxy) luring the Bacon Brothers away
from the increasingly independent and unreliable UN to the
more docile and malleable Red Scorpions.

It also looked very much like a planning meeting to wipe out the upstart Lal brothers. A plan that later resulted in the Surrey Six massacre.

It's almost a year later, and Jason (not his real name) is still scared. Not only will he not let me publish his name, he also doesn't want his workplace or any description of his physical appearance to make it into print. All I can tell you is that he was working in "the area" when the big hit happened, and that he's in his early 20s. Still, he'll talk, and so few will.

"I was on my way to work, and I heard gunshots," he told me. "It wasn't like bang-bang; it was more like buh-buh buh-buh buh-buh." That makes sense: several witnesses reported that the assassins used AK-47s, and Jason's description is not inconsistent with their signature sound. I had been skeptical on this point because mainstream media have a habit of reporting almost any gun capable of automatic fire as AK-47s.

"Then I heard people screaming and brakes screeching," he said. Again, this makes sense as there was a good deal of traffic going by, and when one sees an assassination, one tends to panic.

Jason says he ran outside and saw people running in every direction. He saw one old man trip on the curb and land on his face. Cars, he said, were going everywhere. A few moments later, he doesn't know how long, the sirens started, tons of them. Once the cops started rounding people up, reality set in. Something serious had happened, but Jason was still confused as to what exactly it was.

Then he saw the white Porsche full of bullet holes, and he had a pretty good idea.

What actually did happen can be pieced together from eyewitness reports and surveillance camera footage.

It was August 14, 2011, about 2:45 p.m. A white Porsche Cayenne with six people crammed into its five seats was leaving the Grand Bay Cafe at the Delta Grand Okanagan Resort & Conference Centre. Just as the vehicle was exiting the parking lot, it was approached by two masked men in black pants and black hoodies carrying AK-47s. Despite the masks, eyewitnesses said they could tell the masked men were white. To the left of the truck, the gunmen opened fire, shattering the driver's side windows and sending 7.62mm shells into the passenger compartment. One witness said that his military experience told him exactly what it was—automatic weapons fire. Another witness, who refused to be named but claimed he'd seen a heavily tattooed man and two women enter the Porsche, described what he saw to the *Vancouver Sun:*

> I pretty much seen some guy with a mask unload a clip, ran back out here to the sidewalk, ran back in unloading a clip, jumped in a silver Explorer and hoofed it that way. At least 30 shots, at least a full clip. I went back to look and those guys in the vehicle had blood all over. Everything about the shooter was black: the ski mask, his clothes and the gun.

Once they finished shooting, the men then jumped into a silver SUV that had pulled up and sped away. They were followed by another, smaller vehicle. At exactly the same time, a speedboat took off from the resort's dock at a very high rate of speed, headed across Okanagan Lake.

Surveillance cameras captured the moment when the Porsche's rear door was forced open from the inside. A man, white with dark hair, managed to extract himself from the wreckage. He was obviously hurt, but not severely so. After quickly surveying the scene, he ran, blending into the chaos as witnesses and others fled.

That's when police and paramedics began to arrive. The first two ambulances took care of the two men taken from the front seat—they appeared to be more seriously hurt. The next two took the two women who were still in the back.

A police helicopter zoomed in to survey the scene. Just as aerial officers reported seeing the suspect SUV speeding south near Gyro Beach, the paramedics pronounced that one of the men (the one in the front passenger seat) was dead on the scene. Eyewitness reports and video showed that paramedics worked frantically on a large, young white man with short dark hair. His clothes were taken off to help find the wounds, and his chest and arms had a number of tattoos, none of which would be seen if he were wearing a shirt.

The escaping SUV—now described by police as a Ford, perhaps an Expedition—was reported to have stopped on Gordon Drive, south of the city. The occupants fled. At that moment, 9-1-1 received a series of frantic calls reporting shots fired on the same block. It was later discovered that the "shots" were actually loud pops from a propane cannon, a device some farmers use to scare away birds.

Back at the scene of the crime, many eyewitnesses expressed grave concern for one of the victims. A slim young woman with long blond hair, she had been removed from the back seat but was not moving. She was alive, but things did not look good for her.

Rumors started to fly on social media. It was obviously a gang hit. Nothing was taken, automatic weapons were used, it was clearly well-planned in advance and the victims appeared to be young people with large amounts of disposable income.

And since the Hells Angels were in charge of every gang in town, the overwhelming majority of accusatory fingers pointed directly at them. The only dissenters were those who thought outsiders were attempting to make a significant crack in the Hells Angels' hegemony.

Fueling the fire was the fact that 80 Hells Angels and their friends had shown up for a golf tournament at nearby Michaelbrook Ranch Golf Club, despite the local chapter having only about a dozen members.

While social media were going wild with speculation, mainstream media caught a break. Jesse Johnston, crime reporter for News1130 in Vancouver, received a text that the dead man was Jonathan Bacon. He reported it immediately.

Suddenly things were coming together. Jonathan had been seen partying with his close friend and Hells Angels full patch Larry Amero in the same part of town the night before. Stills and video of the scene were showing up on mainstream media, as well as the Internet. Many claimed to recognize the badly injured man (shown still sitting in the driver's seat, his face turned toward the camera) as Amero. Many then speculated that the blond woman who had been shot was his longtime girlfriend Sarah Trebble.

Police found the suspect vehicle, a Ford Explorer, burned out from the inside.

A hastily put-together press conference informed the media that one person was dead and others were injured in a shooting. But the media had already run with the story, reporting that the dead man was Jonathan Bacon and that Amero was the badly injured one.

They were right. Well, mostly. Jonathan Bacon, the front-seat passenger, was indeed dead. Amero, the driver, was in critical condition. But the blond woman who had been so badly hurt was not Trebble. In fact, it was Leah Hadden-Watts. The 21-year-old waitress also happened to be the niece of Michael "Spike" Hadden, owner of Haney Hawgs, a Harley-Davidson customization shop. He was also a full-patch member of the Haney chapter of the Hells Angels and allegedly their president. His son, Jesse (Leah's cousin), was also a full patch.

Hadden-Watts had taken a direct hit in the neck. Surgeons removed two of her shattered vertebrae, but she was left a quadriplegic, unable to move anything but her head again for the rest of her life.

Also shot while inside the Cayenne but far less severely hurt was Hadden-Watts' roommate, Lyndsey Black. She made a full recovery.

The mystery man who emerged from the car after the shooting and fled the scene was James Riach, Independent Soldier and newly minted member of the Wolf Pack.

• • •

The Kelowna shooting was a sobering moment for the people of British Columbia. It made them well aware that masked gunmen with automatic weapons could strike with absolute impunity. It was like Mexico, where the cartels had the cops outgunned and outsmarted, and killed whom they pleased when and where they pleased. There was no way these guys were ever going to get caught unless they were overcome by feelings of guilt or bragged about what they had done in front of an informant. Nobody in their right mind would take that bet.

But, perhaps more important, it showed one sector of the population, those who could be swayed by the gangster lifestyle, that nobody in it was safe. The Bacon Brothers, whose arrogance and visibility were synonymous in the area with the concept of the gangster who lived above the law, had effectively ceased to exist.

Jonathan—the oldest, the smartest, the boss—was dead. The other two brothers—both of whom were looking at long prison sentences—were lost without him. Neither had the intellect, charisma or connections to do what their big brother had. Without him, they were just another pair of thugs.

It also meant the end of the Wolf Pack, such as it was. Before it had even gotten off the ground, one of its members was dead, another was in critical condition and another had abandoned his critically wounded friends at the scene of the shooting.

The only other member—Randy Naicker, who was not in Kelowna at the time of the shooting—was well known to have a price on his head. Naicker was eventually gunned down outside a Port Moody Starbucks at about 5:30 p.m. on June 25, 2012. Many of his friends were quick to back up his claim that he had left the gangster lifestyle after the Kelowna shooting (scared straight, as it were). But those old debts don't just go away.

And one other effect of the shooting was that it removed any of the last lingering notions that full-patch Hells Angels could still operate by proxy and avoid punishments, both legal and extra-legal.

At the time of the hit, many observers of organized crime in the area speculated that the Hells Angels were to blame. Jealous of Amero's success on his side project, they said, they thought they'd eliminate him, or at least take him down a peg or two.

But that proved to be a ridiculous assumption. Amero was a quick healer who proved little worse for wear shortly afterward. He was welcomed with open arms back into the Hells Angels' fold. Indeed, the next time he made the news was in July 2012. At the corner of Viger and Saint-Hubert in Montreal, Amero ran a red light and crashed his large, black SUV into a car driven by a 21-year-old woman. Despite severe damage to his own vehicle and dozens of eyewitnesses, Amero kept on driving, and was finally pulled over by Montreal cops at Saint-Hubert and René Lévesque. Amero then failed two Breathalyzer tests and was charged with impaired driving, impaired driving causing bodily harm and hit and run.

Police at the time considered his presence in Montreal to be more than just tourism. With drug and vice markets far outstripping Vancouver's, Montreal had been the epicenter of Canada's Hells Angels since they arrived in 1977. But a recent police raid, Operation SharQc, put 111 full-patch members behind bars. In the past, the Canadian Hells Angels have been known to move members to chapters with their membership reduced by arrest, just to keep them alive and to keep the cash coming in.

The Kelowna shooting did not do much to affect the drug trade in British Columbia physically, but it probably did psychologically. For years, many at-risk youths had idolized the gangsters they saw on the news. The talked like them, dressed like them and—with disturbing frequency—wanted to grow up like them.

But there was a big difference now. All their idols had fallen. Bindy Johal? Dead. Clayton Roueche? Serving 30 years in the United States Jonathan Bacon? Dead. Suddenly, the gangster lifestyle was not looking as attractive as it had a few years earlier.

Of course, drugs were still sold after that, but the violence took a huge downturn. The war was over. The Bacon Brothers were among the losers.

• • •

The two surviving brothers had little to be hopeful about. Both were facing trials in which the Crown's cases were overwhelmingly strong.

Jarrod Bacon's trial along with his girlfriend's father, Wayne Scott, was a media sensation and, at times, absurd.

Early on, he lashed out at his enemies. He said that members of the media should "lose their licenses" for printing lies about him and his brothers and for implying his parents were involved in drug trafficking or at least aware of their sons' activities. "You want to talk bad about me or my brother, that's all good because I signed up for that," he said. "But they are good, hardworking normal people. They had nothing to do with this whatsoever."

He accused the RCMP of playing dirty by using Scott, who had no criminal record, to get to him. "It's pretty gross that the police targeted a working guy to get at me," he said. "I feel bad for Wayne. He is a victim in this."

And he pointed out that GL, a lifelong trafficker, had gotten rich on the taxpayers' dime just to bring him down. "They paid this guy an obscene amount of money so he could retire on a beach somewhere."

Jarrod admitted that he turned to crime after being expelled from school for fighting. In fact, he said, he had made violence his career. When asked what his role in organized crime was, he responded that he was a "professional street fighter."

Realizing that a trafficking conviction would almost certainly net him a longer prison sentence than a robbery conviction, he argued in court that his intent was not to purchase the drugs, but to steal them. When Crown Attorney Peter LaPrairie asked him, "You and Wayne Scott agreed to obtain 100 kilograms of cocaine from GL so you could profit from it, right?" Jarrod snapped back, "No, this case is an attempted robbery. There never was any money at any point in time. My intention the whole time was to rob him. You should save that little speech."

LaPrairie called him a liar and pointed out that Jarrod had admitted to lying in court back in 2008 to get out of solitary confinement.

Jarrod went into more detail about his robbery plan. He said he did not have to bring any weapons because he could easily overpower GL, who was older and smaller than he was. In fact, he claimed that GL would "turtle" (fall into a defensive ball) after a single slap. Then he boasted, "I could take GL with one hand tied behind my back."

He claimed that neither Wayne nor Carly Scott had any idea of the robbery plan. "Wayne had no clue what was going to happen," he testified, adding, "I do not discuss my business with girls. Period." Perhaps he didn't realize that his statements exposed both of them to the idea that they were sincerely attempting to broker a huge drug deal.

When a recording appeared in which Scott told GL that Bacon's parents were involved in the deal, Jarrod vehemently disagreed. "Wayne wasn't being truthful with what he said," he testified. "All he said was that he came over for a dinner and I was off to the side and writing, and he said they must have known. But they didn't know. How can you hear what was written on a board?"

He also denied a Crown assertion that his friend Brian "Shrek" Dhaliwal was involved, putting up cash for a potential deal. "I don't know how you can slander a person who has no role in this whatsoever," he said.

Finally, Jarrod blamed the whole thing on his own drug addiction, claiming to be a regular user of Oxycontin, cocaine, steroids and marijuana. "I would crush and snort between two and four Oxys a day," he said. "I did blow on the weekends."

The drugs, he said, made him paranoid, desperate and indifferent. When he was high, he said, he would breach his bail conditions to annoy the police and because he just didn't care "When I was on drugs, I would breach the conditions whenever I wanted," he said in court. "When you are injecting steroids and you are snorting Oxycontins, you don't care about anyone's feelings. You just care about doing more pills, and that's it."

When asked how he acquired the drugs under heavy police surveillance, he admitted that he would have them delivered to Scott's house (even when Carly and their toddler son were there), which contradicted his earlier testimony that neither of the Scotts were involved with or even aware of his part of the drug trade. "I was on drugs but I was also trying to maintain a normal life," he said. "I was wired to Oxys really badly in August. I was a slave to the pills. It's a disgusting habit."

It was while he was high, Jarrod said, that he decided to rob GL. "When he was pressing, saying, 'I'm going to be in Abbotsford, I can get you drugs and show them to you,'" he testified, "I was like, 'Okay, perfect, this guy is getting robbed.'"

But while Jarrod and his defense team were concentrating on robbery as their motive, they seemed to have forgotten that no matter how Jarrod came by the drugs, the simple possession of 10 kilos of cocaine was tantamount to a confession of trafficking. No matter how he acquired the drugs, he was—in the court's eyes, at least—a trafficker.

As the trial drew to a close, there was little to debate but the sentencing. The Crown, citing Jarrod's long record, family history and admission of a violent past, asked for 21 years. The defense, acknowledging all that but pointing out that he was the father of a young son and that his decision-making ability was hampered by drugs, asked for eight.

On May 4, 2012, Justice Austin Cullen laid down the sentence. Pointing out that there was no evidence that Jarrod had ever held a job, and drawing attention to his previous run-ins with the law, his family's criminal past and that "the circumstances of his life and experience to this point do not permit much optimism for his rehabilitation or inclination towards leading a law-abiding life," he sentenced Jarrod Bacon to 12 years.

But, of course, it was more complicated than that. Cullen gave Jarrod almost five years' credit for the time he had already spent behind bars, leaving just seven years and two months on his sentence. Barring complications, that meant the latest he would be released would be July 2019, when he would be 36 years old. Since he would be eligible for parole after half his sentence, that means he could apply as early as July 2013.

The Crown quickly appealed. They claimed that Cullen had "failed to give due consideration to the principles of denunciation and deterrence" and that he had also neglected his duty to make an order of delayed parole eligibility for the client. It's unlikely the appeal will get far since the sentence was much longer than is normal in such cases, and since there was no actual cocaine involved, the sentence was on thin ice to begin with.

Scott's sentencing was adjourned until September 2012.

• • •

The case against Jamie Bacon and the other alleged Surrey Six conspirators seemed secure after their old friend Dennis Karbovanec admitted his involvement. After pleading guilty to three counts of second-degree murder and one count of conspiracy, Karbovanec was sentenced to life with no chance at parole for 15 years. In the overwhelmingly likely case that the others are found guilty, they should expect harsher sentences (depending on their involvement, of course) because they did not confess.

As always, though, there were complications. Surrey RCMP Sergeant Derek Brassington appeared to be a real cop's cop. He had worked 14 years in major crimes, the last seven in homicide. He had even married a fellow Surrey RCMP officer. As one might expect, he was a key investigator in the Surrey Six investigation.

But before the trial, he was reassigned and then later suspended when information surfaced that he allegedly had an affair with a key witness. Not only was the unnamed aspiring model in question an old girlfriend of Karbovanec's, but she had also had an affair with another of the accused, none other than Jamie Bacon. Oh, and she was pregnant, allegedly with Brassington's child. Brassington faced serious charges of obstruction. His lawyer blamed his "inappropriate relationship" with the young woman in question on the stress of working homicide for seven years. Also charged were Brassington's boss, Inspector Dave Attew, and Constables Paul Johnson and Danny Michaud, who allegedly knew of the affair and did nothing about it.

Of course, a witness who was romantically involved with both an investigator and an accused murderer on the same case was a major complication. Her testimony could be swayed in either direction. But it was unlikely to allow the accused conspirators get off—at least that's what the person who knew most about the case had to say. Nor would the controversy about lawyers overcharging the government that emerged during the trial. The case was simply too important to be derailed by relatively inconsequential matters. "Obviously, it will raise serious questions about witness tampering, [and] overtime being charged when it shouldn't have been. The defense lawyers will try to make this case even more complicated,'" said Eileen Mohan, mother of the murdered Chris Mohan. "They [the accused] cannot be let go just on a technical ground."

. . .

The Bacon Brothers are gone. One's dead, the other two in prison. The surviving ones will be released some day, probably sooner than the public would prefer, but they won't reassume their old positions of power—not without their dead brother Jonathan, who was clearly their leader.

The cynical opinion would say that the demise of the Bacon Brothers operation had very little impact on the drug trade in British Columbia. And there is something to be said for that opinion. The Bacons were players to be sure, but the amount of drugs they moved was hardly a big proportion of the total. And in situations like this, there is always someone else who takes their place. The Bacons certainly never moved anywhere near as much product as Roueche, and while there was a noticeable dip in the amount of drugs moved after he went down, it was short-lived. As long as there is a ridiculous amount of money to be made trafficking drugs, there will be no shortage of people volunteering to try their hand at it.

Despite that basic truth, things have changed for the better in British Columbia. No longer are daytime shootings commonplace. Drive-by assassinations now seem like a thing of the past. It's still a very dangerous game, but one could say that the war is over.

The very public collapse of the Bacon dynasty had something to do with that. People, when they join the drug trafficking world, often are intellectually aware of the dangers involved but do not have the visceral fear of death or imprisonment that perhaps they should.

But there was something different about the Bacons. They were middle-class boys next door, kids with a comfortable past and an enviable future. But when it was all said and done, they went three up, three down after they decided to pursue careers in trafficking. The fact that they were so easy for many people to identify with made the reality of their fates sink in for many. Suddenly, the twin specters of long imprisonment and murder seemed very real and had to be factored into any decision to enter the game or not.

And there was also their involvement in the Surrey Six murders, which caused revulsion among the public. It was one thing for gangsters to kill gangsters (and that happened at a sickening rate for a while), but to see two innocent people die like that for no reason was sobering. And there was no way to escape it. A massive public outcry galvanized around grieving mother Eileen Mohan made sure that anyone who was involved in trafficking had to be constantly reminded of the innocent victims of the world they were in. It was enough to break the spirit of Dennis Karbovanec, as hardened a criminal as any.

The lasting effect of the dramatic and very public saga of the Bacon Brothers was not to reduce the amount of drugs trafficked in and out of the province, but rather to put a definite cap on the violence which had, up until then, been escalating out of control.

Just a few years earlier, there were legions of high school kids in the area who idolized the Bacons and wanted to be just like them. The fancy cars, fancy clothes and legions of girlfriends seemed like they were pulled directly from a schoolboy fantasy. But now that the area's most prominent drug traffickers were rotting behind bars or six feet underground, the gangster lifestyle didn't seem so attractive after all.

Without realizing it, and certainly without trying, the Bacon Brothers actually made British Columbia a safer place.

INDEX

A

Abbotsford, British Columbia, 4, 9, 40, 54, 62, 63, 64, 68, 69, 70, 81, 101, 104, 105, 106, 112, 114, 122, 126, 128, 145, 146, 147, 152, 168, 170, 171, 175, 185, 186, 190, 198, 212, 243

Aburto, Marlin "Marlo," 82

Ahmed, Mohamad, 135, 136

Ahuja, Rabinder, 107

Alemy, Koshan, 182

Alemy, Nicole Marie, 182

Alexander, Christina, 104

Alkhalil, Khalil, 12, 86

Alkhalil, Mahmoud, 12, 86

Allen, Greg, 133

Alekseev, Aleksandr, 32, 33

Alekseev, Eugeniy, 32, 33

Alvarez, Rob, 84, 143

Amero, Larry, 187–88, 231, 234, 238, 240

Amoretto, Frank, 125

Anderson, Brenden, 180–81

Ansari, Sasan, 187–88

Arrance, Joey, 228

Attew, Dave, 245

B

Bacon, James Kyle "Jamie," 68, 70–71, 91–92, 121, 122, 123, 124, 129, 130–31, 148, 172, 175, 191, 193, 195, 196, 213, 244, 245

Bacon, Jarrod, 68, 70, 71, 91, 92, 129, 131, 175, 197, 198, 199, 200, 201, 202–04, 206, 207, 208, 209, 213, 241–44

Bacon, Jonathan David, 68, 70, 130, 175, 206, 207, 228

Bacon, Susan, 68, 130, 206

Bahman, Merhdad "Juicy," 126

Baldini, Raphael, 10, 13, 178, 183

Balmoral Tower, 7–9, 12, 14–16, 19, 140

Barber, Jonathan, 147–48, 159
Barber, Kyle, 189–90
Barger, Sonny, 29
Barrett, Gregory, 189–90
Bartolomeo, Damon, 12, 218
Bartolomeo, Norman, 218
Bartolomeo, Ryan, 12, 190–91, 218
Bath, Gurwinder Singh, 87
Batke, Karen, 156, 157, 158
Bayani, Omid, 126, 127, 151
Benji, Kulwinder "Jassy," 44, 45
Benji, Rajinder "Little Raj," 44, 45
Big Circle Boys, 22, 23, 24, 41
Binhamad, Haddi, 49–50
Bird, Jesse, 154
Black, Lyndsey, 238
Bodie, Steve, 229, 230
Bolan, Kim, 194
Bontkes, Marc, 186
Boucher, Maurice "Mom," 57
Bowles, Randall, 142
Brassington, Derek, 245
Brienza, Romano, 84, 96
Brienza, Vincenzo "Vinnie," 84
Brotzel, Greg, 230
Brown, Steve, 9–10, 16
Brown, Zachary, 9–10
Bryan, Tiffany, 180
Budai, Michael Kim, 46, 47
Bui, Hung Van "Scarface" (or "Sonny"), 136
Bui, Winston Thieu Anh, 83
Burnaby, British Columbia, 7–9
Burton, Rayleene, 106, 152, 213

Buteau, Yves "Le Boss," 30
Buttar, Bal, 47, 48, 49, 50
Buzeta, Calle Pedro, 152
Byford, David, 230

C

Cali Cartel, 39, 40
Campbell, Thomas J., 24, 25
Carr, Dale, 179, 183
Castañeda, Elliot "Taco," 151, 152
Chahil, Jaspreet "Justin," 178
Chan, Jing Bon, 83, 128
Chan, Randy, 47, 48
Chana, Parminder, 44, 45, 49
Chand, Vikash, 49
Charlie, Fabian, 154
Chartrand, Travis, 184
Chee, Peter, 36, 37
Cheng, Godwin, 106–07, 152–53, 213
Chilliwack, British Columbia, 4, 40, 54, 55, 105, 112, 155, 168, 190
Chu, Jim, 26, 42, 223
Ciancio, Roberto Salvatore, 35, 36, 37, 40
Ciarnello, Rick, 84
Cilliers, Andrew "Dru," 173–74
Clark Park gang, 27, 28
Cocks, Norman, 228–29
Cocks, Robert, 228–29
Colligan, Adam, 230
Combined Forces Special Enforcement Unit (CFSEU), 197, 208, 209

Cooper, Nicole, 167
Corrections Canada, 54, 197
Cotrell, Nicola, 187–88
Coulter, James, 53, 54, 55, 56, 59, 60, 61, 62, 63, 75, 77, 105
Crew, the, 93, 94, 95, 171
Criminal Intelligence Service of Canada (CSIS), 23
Croitoru, Ion "Johnny K-9," 147
Cruz, Jed, 156
Cullen, Austin, 244
Curry, Joe, 150

D

Daggitt, Roger, 31, 32, 33–34
Daval, Naveen Shiv, 87
Davis, Ken, 110
Davis, Rachel, 88
Dean, Faisel Ali, 44
Dean, Nazreen, 184
Desjardins, Daryl, 105
Dhak, Gurmit Singh, 137, 225, 226
Dhaliwal, Brian "Shrek," 242–43
Dhaliwal, Sukhwinder "DB," 185
Dheil, Amarjit Singh, 48
Dhillon, Bakhar Singh, 46
Doern, Ken, 27
Doggett, Korinne, 168
Donovan, Byron, 168
Dosanjh, Gerpal Singh "Paul," 86
Dosanjh, Jimsher "Jimmy" Singh, 44
Dosanjh, Ranjit "Ron," 46

drugs,
  cocaine, 3, 5, 25, 32, 33, 34, 39, 40, 44, 45, 47, 79, 80, 84, 85, 89, 97, 101, 107, 109, 112, 114–15, 123, 125, 143, 144–45, 149, 151, 165, 168, 180, 197, 198, 199, 201, 209, 222, 224–25, 243
  ecstasy, 56, 60, 61, 79, 101, 107, 111, 113, 123, 132, 210
  GHB, 84, 126, 127
  heroin, 23, 25, 35, 41, 54, 80, 89, 123, 165, 185, 216, 222, 224–25
  marijuana, 4, 12, 24, 25, 54, 60, 75, 79, 83, 84, 88, 89, 90, 101, 107, 109, 110, 111, 113, 123, 132, 133, 149, 157, 168, 195, 209, 225, 227, 243
  methamphetamine, 3, 5, 25, 60, 98–99, 101, 114, 222
  morphine, 222
  opium, 20
  Oxycontin, 5, 80, 180, 209, 216, 217, 218, 243
  Percocet, 80
Dudley, Lisa, 157–58
Duhr, Paul Singh, 108

E

Elshamy, Dean, 108
Ennis, Carl, 122, 123, 129, 170, 181, 190, 194, 227, 244, 247
Enright, Jeremy, 100
Espadilla, Barry, 123
extortion, 20, 47, 123, 127, 233

F

Fanning, Tim, 109
Ferland, Zachary, 136
Fews, Brian, 110
Fielding, Greg, 111
Filonov, Sergey, 32
Filonov, Taras, 32
Fiske, Eric, 224, 225
Forster, John, 106, 107
Fraser, Roy, 195
Fredin, Kirsten, 228
Fredin, Linda, 228
Froess, Ernie, 144

G

Gabriel, Todd, 168
Game Tight Soldiers, 141, 142, 219, 224, 225, 228
Gardner, Donald, 213
Gastown Riots, 25
Gault, Stephen "Hannibal," 126
Gerrior, Chance, 168
Gerth, Jane, 103
Ghavami, Nima, 99
Giesbrecht, Shawn, 94, 95
Giese, Brittany, 154
Giles, David, 127
Gill, Preet "Peter" Sarbjit, 46, 47
Ginnetti, John "Ray," 31–33
Girard, Danielle, 157–58
Goldman, Alexander, 12, 218
Goos, Joshua, 188
Gordon, Mike, 112, 155
Gordon, Rob, 191
Graves, Ray, 40
Graves, Sonto, 40

Green, Bob, 97, 125, 138, 173, 231
Guess, Gillian, 47

H

Habib, Dale, 210
Hadden, Michael "Spike," 238
Hadden-Watts, Leah, 238
Haevischer, Cody Ray, 191, 197
Hallgarth, Kimberley, 186
Hang, Hy, 21
Hanna, Terry, 125
Hanson, Audey, 97, 98
Harley-Davidson, 25, 32, 98, 173, 238
Haugen, Dustin "Princess," 104, 105
Haughton, Kevin, 111
Harvey, Jeff, 123
Hawboldt, Debbie, 195–96
Hayer, Tara Singh, 43
Haynes, Brett, 230
Hehn, Glen "Kingpin," 84, 85, 144
Hells Angels, 4, 12, 23, 25, 29–32, 34, 35, 38, 41, 50, 56, 57, 58, 59–60, 61, 62, 63, 67, 83–84, 85, 86, 87, 89, 90, 92, 93–94, 96, 97, 98–99, 100, 107, 113, 115, 116, 117, 123, 124–25, 126, 127, 128, 138, 141–42, 145, 146, 148, 153, 166, 168, 173, 174, 180, 191, 195, 200, 210, 211, 216, 217, 218, 219, 220, 224, 225, 226, 227, 228, 229, 231, 234, 237, 238, 240
    Nomads, the, 124, 125, 166

Henderson, Andrew, 173
Hendrick, Joshua, 95
Heng, Dilun, 147
Hillsdon, Paul, 183–84
Hogan, P.V., 116
Holmes, Jesse, 168
Holtz, Alphonse, 95
Hong Kong, China, 21, 22, 149
Hooites-Meursing, Anton
   Brad Kornelius, 77, 78, 79,
   80–83, 123
Huang, Hong Chao
   "Raymond," 23–24
Hui, Richard, 88
Hung Ying (Red Eagles),
   21–22

I
Independent Soldiers, the, 12,
   68, 85, 86, 87, 90, 96, 98,
   107, 123, 124, 137, 141, 148,
   154, 166, 180, 183, 195, 216,
   219, 229, 230, 233, 234
Irving, Brittney, 215, 216,
   217, 225

J
Jackman, Albert, 188–90
Jai, Ling Yue (David So), 21
Jansen, Richard, 168
Johal, Bhupinder "Bindy"
   Singh, 42, 47, 50, 68, 89,
   108, 241
Johal, Sarpreet, 123
Johl, Karmen Singh, 87
Johnson, Daryl, 208
Johnson, John "JJ," 86

Johnson, Matthew James, 191
Johnson, Paul, 245
Johnston, Jesse, 238
Johnston, Matthew, 229
Jones, Randy, 11, 184, 231
Jung, Richard, 66

K
Kaawach, Ahmet "Lou," 151,
   152
Karbovanec, Dennis, 122,
   123, 129, 131, 170, 172,
   176, 181, 190, 194, 244,
   245, 247
Kawabata, Tomohisa, 168
Keane, Kevin, 227
Kelemen, Wesley, 188–89
Kelowna, British Columbia, 95,
   99, 115, 166, 209, 210, 215,
   218, 217, 226, 227, 239–40
Keung, Law Kin (Allan Law),
   21
Khun Khun, Gorinder Singh,
   48
Kim, Ho-Sik "Phil," 46
King Pin Crew, the, 210, 216,
   219
Kinnear, Brianna, 180
Kitsilano, British Columbia,
   4, 137
Klassen, Daryl, 41
Kocoski, Nicholas "Nick," 112
Konkin, Cory, 184–85
Krantz, Joe "J Money," 165–67,
   174
Krogstad, Norman, 115, 150
Kumar, Sharmila, 111, 112

L

Lahn, John (Laurent Jean-Guy
　Rahal), 82
Lal, Corey Jason Michael, 11–12
Lal, Michael Justin, 11–12,
　190–91, 193
Lamoureux, Laura Lynn, 186
Langlie, Emily, 149–50
Lanot, Mao Jomar, 87
LaPrairie, Peter, 242
Le, Quang Vhin Thang
　"Michael," 10–11, 19, 66, 191
LeClair, Kevin, 180, 181, 188
Leask, Peter, 144
Leclerc, Daniel, 112
Lee, Jong Ca "John," 132
Lee, Pam, 148–49
Lee, Yong, 147–48
Li, Ping, 185, 186
Li, Xing, 185–86
Lilford, Ewan, 84–85, 144
Lising, Ronaldo "Ronnie," 84,
　98–99, 113, 114, 142–43
Lloyd, Hayley, 189
Loke, Trevor, 183–84
Los Diablos, 21, 43, 44
Lotus Gang (Lotus Brothers),
　21, 22, 44, 48
Low, Park Shing, 21
Lynnerup, Villy, 116, 117,
　127, 231

M

MacDougall, Angela Marie,
　223
Machiskinic, Ashley, 221, 222,
　223, 224, 225

Mafia,
　Chinese, 20
　Indo-Canadian, 12, 43, 44, 45,
　　47, 50–51, 68, 86, 108, 117
　Italian, 34
　Punjabi, 43
Malo, Dan, 209
Mann, Roman "Danny," 47–48,
　49, 50, 54, 69, 70, 211
Margison, Jesse, 180
Marks, Damien, 195
Matheson, Stephen, 229
McComb, Garrett, 154
McKay, Guthrie, 157, 158
McLeod, Randy, 80–81
McRae, Matthew, 228
McWhirter, Donnie "Blaze,"
　217
Meisner, Geoff, 209, 210
Meisner, Tammy, 209, 210
Mela, Nunzio, 218
Messent, Shane, 184
Meyer, Duane, 111, 150
Michaud, Danny, 245
Mickle, Michael "Zeke," 34
Miner, Dennis, 227
Miraback, Braydon, 110–11
Miraback, Zachary, 110–11
Mohammed, Aleem, 184
Mohammed, Amir, 184
Mohammed, Mabel, 184
Mohan, Christopher, 7–8,
　14–15, 19, 142, 159, 161–62,
　191, 245
Mohan, Eileen, 7–8, 13, 14–15,
　16, 140, 142–43, 163, 178,
　184, 194, 209, 245, 247

Molsberry, Robert, 83, 84
Montemurro, Cory, 227
Moore, William "Billy," 96,
    150–51
Moyes, Bobby, 35–41
Murphy, Sean "Smurf," 190
Myles, Douglas, 127

N
Naicker, Randy, 123, 231,
    233–34, 239
Narain, Sanjay, 45
Narong, Edward "Eddie"
    Sousakhone, 10–12, 19,
    66, 67
Narwal, Harpreet, 123, 233
Narwal, Roman, 123
Naud, Michael, 12
Neal, John, 127, 217

O
Okanagan Valley, 25, 29
Oldford, Jeff, 229, 230
Olson, Greg, 33, 46, 48
O'Neil, Shaun, 216
Operation E-Pandora,
    98, 113
Operation Frozen Timber,
    105, 109
O'Toole, James, 155–56
outlaw motorcycle gangs, 25,
    28, 29–30, 31, 74

P
Padley, Robert "PDog," 82
Parente, Mario, 161
Park Gangs, the, 26, 27, 28

Patriquin, Patrick, 94
Payne, Scott, 94, 95, 171
Pelletier, Cynthia, 138,
    139, 174
Pelletier, Len, 139, 173
Pelletier, Robert, 33–34
Pendakur, Krishna, 3
Perez-Valdez, Jose Raul, 33
Peterson, Donnie, 161
Phillips, Dain, 228
Pickton, Robert "Willie,"
    158–59, 220–21, 223
Pierini, Alia Brienne, 95
Pires, Francisco "Chico," 84
Plante, Michael, 96–100, 113,
    114, 117, 125, 127
Pooler, Larry, 127
Popovich, John, 86
Porsch, Steven, 122
Porteous, Hal, 169, 231
Potgieter, James, 122
Potts, Randy, 97–98
Prince, Justin, 123
Prince George, British
    Columbia, 93–96, 114,
    141, 153, 154, 162, 171,
    224–25, 228
Prodromidis, Simon, 173
Punko, Johnny, 99, 113, 114,
    125, 126

Q
Quast, Devron, 168, 169

R
Radek, Gladys, 223
Rai, Jaswant "Billy," 106–07

Rankin, Phil, 12
Red Scorpions, 11–12, 66, 67,
    77, 80–82, 83, 90, 122–23,
    124, 128–29, 131, 141, 148,
    159, 170, 178, 180, 183, 184,
    189, 190, 191, 193, 211, 219,
    225, 231, 234
Rehal, Gupreet "Bobby," 81
Renaud, Kerry Ryan, 98–99,
    113–14, 127
Renegades, the, 94, 96, 114, 141,
    142, 150, 171, 219, 228
Riach, James, 231, 234, 239
Richards, Andy, 218
Richards, Ryan "Whitey,"
    190
Rideout, Wayne, 14
Riley Park gang, 26–27
Roming, Donald, 85
Robertson, Gregor, 186
Robin, Serge, 33
Robinson, Dean, 132
Robinson, Lloyd, 32
Robinson, Lonnie, 97
Rogers, Frank T., 111
Rohrer, Yreka, 112
Roueche, Clayton, 54–55, 64,
    125, 127, 148, 155, 168, 186,
    187, 208–09, 212, 241
Roueche, Rupert "Rip," 55
Royal Canadian Mounted
    Police (RCMP), 13, 14, 15,
    28, 29, 34, 39, 41, 87, 94, 96,
    98, 99, 106, 125, 128–29,
    139–40, 151, 155, 157, 183,
    187, 195, 210, 217, 224, 227,
    241, 245

Integrated Homicide
    Investigation Team (IHIT),
    13–14
Outlaw Motorcycle Gang
    Unit, 94
Russell, Dan, 113, 147
Russell, Edward "Skeeter," 81
Russell, Jayme, 95

S
Saed, Karwan, 147
Sahota, Ravi, 109
Salcedo, Teodoro, 44
Samardzich, Mike, 37, 38–39
Sandberg, Eric, 210–11
Sandhu, Rob, 41, 42
Sandu, Balbir Singh, 40
Sangha, David, 40
Sansalone, Vincenzo "Jimmy,"
    126, 127
Satan's Angels, the, 28–30,
    147–48
Satsatin, Michael, 210, 211
Schell, Anson, 228
Schellenberg, Ed, 9–10, 13, 16,
    19, 143, 159
Scholfield, Ronald, 33
Schoutens, Trevor, 110
Scott, Carly, 242
Scott, Wayne, 197, 208,
    241, 242
Sek, Sophon, 209
Shankar, Derek Chand,
    48–49, 50
Shannon, Robert, 168
Sharif, Saff, 88
Shatto, Richard, 63–65

Shinkaruk, Gary, 94
Shoemaker, Shane, 49–50
Simpson, Lyle, 170
Singh, Harpreet "Happy,"
    123, 233
Skreptak, Joseph Bruce, 226–28
Smith, Cedric Michael, 150
Smith, Mickie "Phil," 59
Soluk, Paul Percy, 59
Soomel, Raj, 233–34
Sparks, Ron "The Monster,"
    209
Stadnick, Walter, 201
Stanton, Juel Ross, 12
Stone, Phillip, 168
Sumas Centre, 35, 36, 40, 41
Surrey, British Columbia, 3, 4,
    7, 12, 13, 16, 45, 50, 80, 85,
    86, 97, 108, 114, 117, 128–29,
    141, 156, 182, 183–84, 185,
    191, 193, 195–96, 210
Surrey Six, the, 19, 140, 141,
    142, 143, 178, 179, 191, 194,
    209, 213, 218, 229, 234, 244,
    245, 247,
Sutherland, Fraser, 183, 184, 187
Swanson, Alexander, 110
Sylvestre, Chalsi, 129

T
Terezakis, Anthony "Big Tony,"
    35, 58–59
Thiessen, Peter, 140, 187
Thiphavong, BonLeuth, 81
Thiphavong, James, 81
Thiphavong, Souskavath, 81
Thomas, Robert, 115, 228

Tilli-Choli, Barzan, 147, 187,
    188, 190, 208, 215
Tiojanco, Caesar, 10
Tiojanco, Myrna, 10
Toronto, 2, 22, 91, 126, 127
Trebble, Sarah, 187–88, 238
Turcott, Lou, 29

U
United Nations (UN), 53–71,
    81, 83, 90, 92, 98, 101, 105,
    110, 117, 121, 124
U.S. Immigration and Customs
    Enforcement (ICE), 105,
    109, 110, 111, 112, 113,
    117, 244
Uyeyama, Eugene, 34, 37,
    39, 41
Uyeyama, Michele, 34–35,
    37, 38

V
Vanalstine, Doug, 208–09
Vancouver,
    Chinatown, 21–22, 23, 25
    Downtown Eastside, 3, 59,
        78, 83, 220, 223, 224, 225
    Lower Mainland, 14, 19, 40,
        53, 56, 57, 58, 60, 61, 63,
        66, 68, 79, 85, 87, 88, 89, 90,
        91, 100, 101, 102, 107, 108,
        116, 117, 122, 124, 127, 131,
        133, 137, 140, 141, 144, 151,
        154, 155, 159, 162, 163, 173,
        174, 177, 179, 180, 183, 186,
        187, 190 194, 198, 209, 210,
        211, 220

Varma, Shailen, 111, 112
Vaughan, Thomas, 228
Viet Ching, 21, 22
Vinet, Casey, 190

W
Wafsi, George, 49–50
Walker, Karen, 154
Watts, Diane, 143
West, Eric, 154
Wester, Nicholas, 208–09
White, Mike, 157

Willock, Tyler, 183, 187, 188–89
Woodruff, Jack, 156, 157, 158
Wooley, Greg "Picasso," 57
Wright, Janet, 88

Y
Yaretz, Ken, 195
Yoon, Christina Hyun Oh, 83

Z
Zedong, Mao, 22
Zig Zag Crew, 210, 211

Gangland
by Jerry Langton

A startling look at Mexico's new power elite—their drug cartels

Mexico's war against narcotics and the criminal syndicates that traffic in them not only looks bad on the surface, but compared to Colombia in the '80s and '90s, the situation is even more desperate and terrifying. Since mirroring the policies that Nixon and successive US presidents pioneered, and enacting its own War on Drugs, Mexico's rates of rape, torture, murder and assassination have skyrocketed, as has the business of illegal narcotics. Juárez, what used to be a rollicking party town for Americans and Mexicans alike, now has a murder rate that exceeds both Baghdad and Kandahar—combined.

Gangland is a first-hand examination of the rise of the Mexican drug cartels, and traces their origins, evolution, and how they've grown in lock-step with the failed narcotics policies of North America. Their power has escalated thanks to a police force that's often seen to be corrupt or incompetent, a government barely in control of itself, and military personnel serving within their own borders. Stuck in the center of this maelstrom are the vast majority of Mexican citizens seeking only peace, prosperity and security, and finding little to none in their homeland.

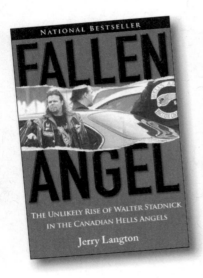

Fallen Angel
by Jerry Langton

The unlikely rise of
Walter Stadnick in the
Canadian Hells Angels

Walter Stadnick is not an imposing man. At five-foot-four, his face and arms scarred by fire in a motorcycle accident, he would not spring to mind as a leader of Canada's most notorious biker gang, the Hells Angels. Yet through sheer guts and determination, intelligence and luck, this Hamilton-born youth rose in the Hells Angels ranks to become national president. Not only did he lead the Angels through the violent war with their rivals, the Rock Machine, in Montreal in the Nineties, Stadnick saw opportunity to grow the Hells Angels into a national criminal gang. He was a visionary—and a highly successful one.

As Stadnick's influence spread, law enforcement took notice of the Angel's growing presence in Ontario, Manitoba and British Columbia. However, Stadnick's success did not come without a price. Arrested and charged with 13 counts of first-degree murder, Stadnick beat the murder charges but was convicted of gangsterism and is currently serving time.

Fallen Angel details one man's improbable rise to power in one of the world's most violent organizations, while shedding light on how this enigmatic and dangerous biker gang operated and why it remains so powerful.

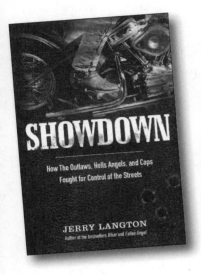

Showdown
by Jerry Langton

Control of Ontario's underworld wasn't decided in a day, a year, or any single event. It was a series of skirmishes, bloodbaths and blunders.

When the old-school Mafia in Hamilton fell apart following the death of Johnny "Pops" Papalia, a frenzy ensued for who would control Ontario's drug and vice traffic. The leader of the Hells Angels, Walter Stadnick, had had his eye on Canada's most lucrative drug market for years but had been kept out largely due to the mafia syndicate that only reluctantly employed bikers of any stripe for their dirty work, and Papalia's refusal to use any Hells Angels.

The war to fill the power vacuum in Ontario would hinge on the broadly supported Stadnick's Hells Angels, a handful of smaller clubs too proud or too useless to join them, and Mario "The Wop" Parente's Outlaws, the top motorcycle club in Ontario since the 70s. Other challengers would emerge from the ever-shifting allegiances of the biker world, including the Bandidos from south of the border, whose presence in the province would end in a bloodbath now known as the Shedden Massacre. Against all of these competing interests stood the various law enforcement agencies responsible for keeping the general peace and shutting down as many operations as they could.